The High Price of Health

The High Price of Health

A PATIENT'S GUIDE TO THE HAZARDS OF MEDICAL POLITICS

GEOFFREY YORK
Introduction by Dr. Philip Berger

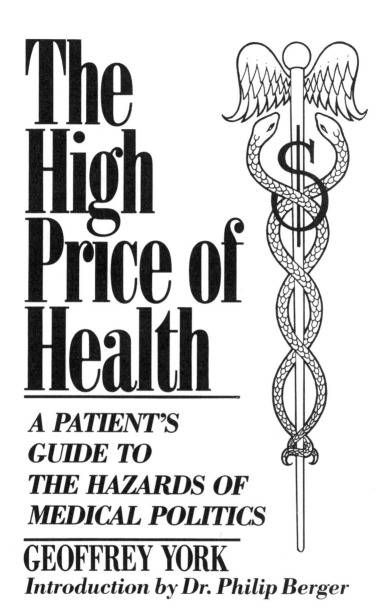

James Lorimer & Company, Publishers
Toronto 1987

Copyright © 1987 by James Lorimer & Company, Publishers.

All rights reserved. No part of this book may be reproduced or transmitted in any form or by any means, electronic or mechanical, including photocopying, or by any information storage or retrieval system, without permission in writing from the publisher.

Cover design: Falcom Design & Communications

Cover illustration: Martin Springett

Canadian Cataloguing in Publication Data

York, Geoffrey, 1960–
  The high price of health

Bibliography

ISBN 1-55028-022-8 (bound). — ISBN 1-55028-020-1 (pbk.)

1. Medical care, Cost of — Canada. 2. Insurance, Health — Canada. 3. Physicians — Canada. 4. Medical ethics — Canada. I. Title.

RA412.5.C3Y67 1987   338.4′33621′0971   C87-094282-4

James Lorimer & Company, Publishers
Egerton Ryerson Memorial Building
35 Britain Street
Toronto, Ontario   M5A 1R7

Printed and bound in Canada

5 4 3 2 1   87 88 89 90 91

CONTENTS

Acknowledgments   vii

Introduction: By Dr. Philip Berger   ix

Chapter 1: Doctor Knows Best: The Politics of Health   *1*

Chapter 2: The Strike Weapon   *15*

Chapter 3: Two Centuries of Activism   *34*

Chapter 4: Your Money or Your Life: How Doctors Control Their Incomes   *55*

Chapter 5: The Fight for Turf   *78*

Chapter 6: Medical Heretics: The Campaign against Salaried Doctors   *99*

Chapter 7: Licence to Practise: The Closed Shop   *118*

Chapter 8: Power Politics: The Medical Associations   *134*

Chapter 9: The Private Policemen   *151*

Chapter 10: Consumerism and the Patients' Rights Movement   *169*

Chapter 11: The Potential for Reform   *187*

Sources   *196*

Acknowledgments

I am grateful to the Canada Council's Explorations Program and the Ontario Arts Council for providing grants to assist in my research expenses.

Many health professionals and health experts were kind enough to allow me to interview them. I thank them all for their patience and cooperation.

I am indebted to the *Globe and Mail* for assigning me to the health-politics beat in 1981 and for allowing me plenty of time to develop stories in this field on many occasions in the past six years.

I would also like to thank Heather Robertson, Philip Berger, Ann Silversides and Maria Bohuslawsky.

Geoffrey York
Winnipeg
May 1987

Introduction

In 1979 a young female patient I had known for about a year was raped. She was still living at home with her unemployed and sick parents, supported by welfare. She was psychologically traumatized by the assault and required expert counselling. I personally requested a consultation for this woman with a female psychiatrist well known for her work with rape victims. The psychiatrist extra-billed. She refused to see my patient because the patient could not pay the extra fees. "All patients should have to pay for medical services," she added.

In early 1980 I visited a man in his 70s at his poorly heated east end Toronto rooming house. He owned few possessions, had little cash, no friends and no family. The patient was weak and sick with terminal cancer. After his discharge from a Toronto acute care hospital, he started receiving bills for medical and other expenses incurred while he was in hospital. He finally began to receive large-print collection agency notices threatening court action and ending with the admonition to "GOVERN YOURSELF ACCORDINGLY." A neighbour eventually brought the notices to me saying that the patient was terrified and did not know what to do. Dying and destitute, he had suffered quietly for two months, consumed with worry about bills and collection notices.

A few months later I related these stories to Mr. Justice Emmett Hall during his review of Canada's health services. Speaking on behalf of the South Riverdale Community Health Centre, I suggested that these situations of hardship should not happen in Canada. Mr. Hall replied that these situations would not happen in the future, as if giving me his personal assurance.

Six years later the Ontario medical profession was plunged into the final fight with government over the Health Care Accessibility Act (Bill 94) — the legislation banning extra-billing in Ontario.

The 1986 Ontario doctors' strike shocked a trusting public. People began to wonder whether doctors practised medicine in the same way they conducted themselves politically. The public had long assumed that doctors who rely on the scientific method would naturally have the tools to assess health care issues rationally, even dispassionately.

When public confidence in the political competence of doctors collapsed during the strike, physicians withdrew under the cloak of special medical knowledge. They stubbornly claimed that their right to set their own fees was best for their patients. The public's overwhelming rejection of this claim should cause the profession to undergo a profound self-examination and to change its ways to adjust to the political and economic realities of the 1980s. A profession lacking in foresight is a profession doomed to losing control and autonomy to a state bureaucracy.

The 1986 Ontario doctors' strike reminded me of an earlier labour dispute in the area of health care. On April 16, 1974, during my final year of medical school at the University of Manitoba, two-thirds of the 1,440-member Canadian Union of Public Employees (CUPE) local 1550 voted 96 per cent in favour of a strike against the Winnipeg Health Sciences Centre. The local represented central supply workers, cooks, housekeeping staff, nursing assistants, orderlies, laundry workers, ward clerks and other employees whose average monthly wage was $430.

The Manitoba Medical Students' Association adopted a policy in support of the CUPE demands. As academic chairperson of the students' association, I, along with other student representatives, initiated an aggressive campaign on behalf of the hospital workers. On April 24, wage negotiations broke down between the union and hospital management and a strike was set for May 9. On April 25, Dr. F. W. Duval, chairman of the medical staff, called for volunteers from the staff and their families to do the workers' jobs in the event of a strike. It was the doctors, said Dr. Duval, "who have an understanding of what the game is all about." The students' association denounced the medical staff and distributed leaflets in support of the union's demands.

This was my introduction to a health care workers' dispute, although the strike itself never materialized. Twelve years later, I found myself in vocal opposition to the strike of Ontario doctors. What were the differences?

The CUPE workers were fighting simply for better wages and benefits. The hospital workers' wages were at that time the lowest in the country except for the wages of Newfoundland hospital workers. In contrast, in 1986 Ontario doctors were among the highest paid doctors in Canada.

The Winnipeg CUPE workers were struggling for fairer wages in a context of absolute domination by hospital and government authorities. The workers had minimal control and power over the health care system which employed them and over the terms and conditions of their work. When the Winnipeg hospital workers threatened to jeopardize medical services, the medical profession denounced them on the high moral ground that the workers were placing their financial interests ahead of patients' well-being.

The Ontario doctors were fighting to maintain control and influence over a medical system in which they were largely self-employed. The doctors did not hesitate to abuse their position of power and to jeopardize patient care all across Ontario in their fight to defend their interests. Doctors' "understanding of what the game is all about" seemed to depend on who the players were.

Finally, the CUPE workers were direct and straightforward in their demands for more money and benefits, demands which posed no threat to the principles of medicare. But the Ontario Medical Association (OMA) placed its struggle above money, insisting that its struggle was for "freedom." The OMA's demands were in direct conflict with medicare, the most popular social service in Canada. Twelve years after supporting the hospital workers, I did not find it difficult to oppose the doctors' strike — a strike against the public's strong interest in a universal medicare plan.

The early 1970s was an unprecedented period of student activism at the University of Manitoba medical school. Learning medicine for the sake of being a competent physician, not for the purpose of attaining high grades, was a constant theme of the educational process. Students in the 1974 graduating class were graded on a pass-fail system (no honours) throughout medical school.

Students were represented on every committee and at every level of faculty decision making — curriculum development, the implementation of the pass-fail system and the faculty council. Students were party to the selection of applicants to medical school, to the interviewing of eminent professors seeking top faculty appointments and to special faculty committees set up to determine the fate of students who had failed examinations or were in trouble.

The new dean of medicine, Dr. Arnold Naimark, and a handful of professors encouraged us to express ourselves freely. They taught us to separate the scholarship of medicine from the politics of those delivering the medical services. Demystification of the medical profession was made possible by unconditionally allowing students to think and act freely.

Medical school had not been my first opportunity to view the profession from an intimate position. I had been born into a family of numerous medical practitioners — all at the specialty level. Not only did this provide a glimpse of the workings of the profession, it also gave me a direct and long-term experience of the economic and social benefits derived from being raised in a physician family. My sense of the security and freedom of my life measured against the lives of others whose parents were far less privileged has stayed with me and has given me a special perspective on a profession which claims to be under attack.

Despite the advantages of their professional status, my physician relatives maintained a far more realistic appraisal of the political realities of the profession than did most of the officials in the medical associations. My family is Jewish. Stories of anti-Semitism at the Manitoba medical school in the 1930s and 1940s were legion and had acquired legendary status. Jewish applicants to medical school were not accepted because of their religion. Jewish graduates could not find internship positions or were refused academic appointments. These were the stories about the profession that took strongest hold in my mind.

A quota (or "numerus clausus") limiting the number of Jewish students in the University of Manitoba medical school had been established in 1932. The quota was finally ended in 1944 after charges of racial discrimination were substantiated by the university's board of governors in a report to the Manitoba legislature. Despite the absence of official and manifest prejudice during my years at medical school, I was still conscious of the ignoble history of the profession.

Though blatant discrimination ultimately failed in Manitoba, the Canadian medical profession has maintained firm hold of its territory. In his thorough analysis, Geoffrey York describes how for two centuries the Canadian medical profession has consolidated its control over the delivery of health care services. Midwives, chiropractors, nurse practitioners and others have fallen victim to the dominance of physicians. Immigrant doctors have been severely restricted from entering the Canadian profession by governments with the support and approval of medical associations. Even salaried physicians at community clinics have come under attack from the medical establishment. The clinic movement in Ontario ground to a halt as a result of the intervention of organized medicine in the mid-1970s.

In 1975 the Ontario government placed a freeze on funding of new community health centres (the freeze was lifted in 1984 with the establishment of Parkdale Community Health Centre in Toronto). The last one promised funding before the 1975 freeze was the South Riverdale Community Health Centre. I started work there in July 1978. Located in a then poor, working-class district just east of downtown Toronto, South Riverdale opened its doors for business in an old police station on November 1, 1976.

The impetus for a community-controlled health centre in South Riverdale came from activists in local community organizations, including the Greater Riverdale Organization, known as GRO and BREMM. BREMM, an acronym for streets surrounding the lead-producing Canada Metal Company plant, was an organization that addressed the concerns about lead pollution in the South Riverdale area. Community residents disappointed with the availability and quality of local medical services were naturally attracted to the concept of a consumer-controlled health centre. The area was ready for a community-run health care service that would truly meet the needs of community residents — the needs being defined by representatives of the community itself.

A major concern of the community then (and now) was the soil pollution by lead from the Canada Metal Company. The Environmental Health Committee of the South Riverdale Community Health Centre has spearheaded efforts to free the area of the lead pollution. The committee has acquired considerable expertise and sophistication, producing major reports, organizing community days for lead testing, and lobbying effectively for a clean-up of the area. The achievements of the Environmental Health Committee illustrate the strengths of community-based political action in effecting changes in the health care status of residents.

From its inception South Riverdale Community Health Centre (known locally as "the Centre") constituted a perceived threat to organized medicine. Some local physicians campaigned vigorously against the funding and opening of the Centre.

The health centre model was and still is anathema to most doctors — salaried physicians whose terms and conditions of work are determined by an annually elected board of community residents, most of whom are patients of the physicians or, more correctly, patients of the Centre. The board controls all matters of finance and hires and fires all staff including physicians. New employees undergo an intensive interview process. My own was conducted by seven people and lasted nearly two hours. The board determines the regular hours of patient service and schedules the hours of the physicians. It requires staff physicians to provide 24-hour call and sets all policy with regard to Centre programs, staffing and activities.

The board, through its committees, holds ultimate authority over areas traditionally within the exclusive control of physicians. Staff doctors require committee and board approval for the timing and duration of their holidays (four weeks per year). They need committee and board approval for attendance at medical conferences — during my employment there had to be some demonstrable benefit to the Centre from the types of conferences attended. In one situation the board requested that a staff doctor improve his orthopaedic skills. The board generously provided two weeks per year of paid professional development time to doctors for continuing medical education.

Medical hegemony was not completely eradicated at the Centre. In one crisis situation, the board expanded the responsibilities of a particular nurse against the advice of the three staff physicians who felt that the nurse did not have the necessary skills to accept greater responsibility. The physicians, relying on their professional obligations to the College of Physicians and Surgeons of Ontario, withdrew all support for the nurse (such as signing prescriptions, reviewing cases and so forth), and the nurse felt unable to remain at the Centre. This was the only instance of physician rebellion against the board from 1978 to 1982.

The board's control of physicians' working conditions never once spilled over to medical decision making. The doctor-patient relationship and its independence (from the board), and the confidentiality of patient information were considered sacrosanct. The board never requested or suggested that the staff doctors use their influence over patients to promote the political interests of the Centre. In all these respects, the board was far more advanced than the leadership of the Ontario Medical Association, which during the 1986 doctors' strike lost no opportunity to propagandize patients and interfere with doctor-patient relationships.

For all its real advantages to consumers, the South Riverdale Community Health Centre has its share of contradictions. With its 1979 renovations, the Centre became one of the few office-based medical buildings physically accessible to the disabled — but it was only accessible for medical services. The disabled are still largely excluded from community and Centre activities which take place on the second floor, reached only by climbing 22 steps. Community control, which should be at least equal in importance to the Centre's health care services, stops at the disabled.

Another paradox at the Centre is the membership of its board of directors. The composition of the board has never truly reflected the population served by the Centre. The elected board members have usually been middle-class, educated, employed homeowners. Despite sincere and largely successful board policies in favour of serving the needs of particular disadvantaged groups, community control has been elusive for these same groups. In this regard the Centre differs little from many other community-based organizations.

The South Riverdale Centre physicians were largely spared the assaults by fee-for-service physicians that clinic doctors elsewhere have experienced. Geoffrey York catalogues the personal and professional ostracism experienced by doctors at similar clinics in Canada and the United States. These clinic doctors, politically isolated, did not have the benefit of an organization of like-minded doctors. During my stay at South Riverdale Community Health Centre, all the doctors were active members of the Medical Reform Group (MRG) of Ontario — a small, politically independent and progressive doctors' group constituted in the fall of 1979.

The members of the Medical Reform Group came together primarily on account of an unwavering commitment to the principle that health care is a right, that it is not a privilege for those able to pay nor a commodity to be subjected to free market forces. The founding group of 60 physicians and medical students (by 1986 membership totalled about 160) was opposed to the OMA notion that an individual financial contract was essential to the doctor-patient relationship.

The MRG formed at a time when almost 20 per cent of Ontario doctors had opted out of the Ontario Health Insurance Plan. Most of the doctors in the MRG had personal knowledge of the effects of extra charges on their patients, and it was this knowledge that led to the MRG's uncompromising opposition to charging patients any out-of-pocket fees, including monthly medicare premiums.

In the six months leading up to the Ontario doctors' strike, the MRG was the only organized group of physicians opposed to the OMA. The MRG provided an informed and alternative analysis of the proposed ban on extra-billing. It rebuked the OMA leadership for misleading the public and debunked the OMA argument that professional independence and freedom were vitiated by Bill 94, the legislation banning extra-billing.

The battle over Bill 94 revealed how anxious most physicians really were and how deeply they distrusted any government that brought forth legislation to control them. While Bill 94 only marginally reduced physicians' incomes and contained no provisions affecting their clinical independence, many Ontario doctors still feel that their autonomy is threatened. To the extent that the legislation did weaken the resistance of the profession to future government attempts to contain costs, Ontario physicians might be right. But Bill 94 was the wrong battle at the wrong time for the profession to protect its independence.

A popular misconception among Canadian doctors is the notion of physician freedom in the United States. Practice in the American free market system has long been held out as an escape route for anxiety-ridden Canadian physicians nervous about the prospect of state control. Yet the facts speak otherwise. In the first issue of the 1987 *Canadian Medical Association Journal* there appeared an article entitled "U.S. Doctors Flock to Salaried Employment."

Estimates of the percentage of American doctors salaried to some degree range from 40 to 58 per cent. Physician employees are found in preferred provider organizations (PPOs) and in many private, profit-making hospitals and health care facilities. Large private health care corporations are moving rapidly into the "free" health care market. Physicians are remunerated according to economically based performance criteria and in some cases are expected to meet quotas for investigations ordered and procedures performed. American physicians are sacrificing their clinical independence to the economic needs of the employers and bureaucrats they serve. And physicians caught in the free market system of the U.S.A. are concomitantly experiencing a shrinking of their incomes.

American private enterprise has launched a major assault on the medical sector in order to increase corporate profits. The crucial point of control is the freedom of physicians to make independent clinical judgments. Clinical autonomy is being limited in order to control the costs of such non-physician items as high-technology equipment, laboratory and radiological investigations, hospital supplies, drugs and salaries for non-medical staff. Loss of physician sovereignty is essential if the American private sector is to contain costs and improve profits. It is widespread and increasing in the United States.

Because of government-controlled medicare, the Canadian corporate sector so far has been unable to profit directly from the labour of physicians. However, provincial governments are anxiously searching for ways to contain costs and impose financial restraint. Governments are alarmed that health care is already the single largest budget item and costs are escalating with no end in sight. If health care costs were voluntarily controlled by a cooperative medical profession, there would be no need for governments to challenge the autonomy of physicians.

Canadian doctors have always held that clinical autonomy is founded on the fee-for-service system of payment. The onus is now on the doctors to demonstrate that a fee-for-service system can provide both high-quality and efficient health care. Medical associations should begin to explore means to control costs generated by physicians' services. One mechanism might be a system of incentives to encourage doctors to lower costs. Bold and creative action by physicians would necessarily require a breakaway from the private medical industry in Canada — medical equipment firms, private laboratories and the pharmaceutical industry — whose profits are dependent on doctors' practice styles. Physicians would have to be guided by the mounting evidence of useless or questionable practices that create an enormous human and financial burden.

If physicians cannot find ways to control costs governments rightfully must, and the medical independence of physicians may be compromised. The only strategy left to Canadian doctors is to use their clout to contain the expansion of provincial health expenditures. Fee-for-service medicine and the independence of medical practice will only be maintained to the extent that governments find it affordable. No mechanism can assure — nor should it — that physicians will continue to influence general health care policy to the degree that they currently do.

Somehow, the medical profession has never demonstrated the commitment required to meet its end of the social contract. Physicians have failed to promote a cooperative, high-quality, universal health care system in which the economic and professional interests of doctors can be preserved.

Geoffrey York's research should alert the public to the power and the politics of an entrenched profession. There may yet be rougher times ahead for doctors and patients across Canada.

Dr. Philip Berger
May 1987

CHAPTER 1

DOCTOR KNOWS BEST: THE POLITICS OF HEALTH

Medicare is less than 20 years old, and already it is the most popular government program in Canada. It is widely recognized as the jewel in the Canadian social system. Many would argue that medicare is the greatest achievement of the federal and provincial governments since the Second World War. Opinion polls consistently show that four-fifths of all Canadians are happy with the national health-insurance program. In the second half of the 1980s, the final steps were taken to guarantee the survival of medicare: doctors were prohibited from extra-billing their patients. Any province daring to jeopardize medicare in the future will be faced with severe financial penalties. For the first time in Canadian history, medicare is now solidly entrenched across the country. No person can be deprived of medical treatment in Canada, regardless of the distinctions of class or income.

Yet medicare has always been a tremendous act of faith. In essence, the citizens of Canada gave a blank cheque to the medical profession. In return for an almost unlimited source of funds, the doctors and hospitals were asked to take care of us. Society has trusted the physicians to decide what is best for our health — and how many of our tax dollars should be devoted to the health sector.

Of course, there are politicians and bureaucrats who influence the health budgets of each province, but the system is driven by the doctors, who decide whether to admit a patient to hospital, to prescribe a drug, to request a follow-up visit and to perform a surgical operation. The doctors are the gatekeepers to the health system. It has been estimated that 75 to 80 per cent of all health expenditures in Canada are effectively determined by the medical profession.

Medicare was founded on a simple premise: there is one single, ideal treatment for every illness and every medical condition. Once the doctor had discovered this ideal treatment, it must be provided, regardless of the cost. Thus, the solution seemed to be equally simple: use government funds to pay for the ideal treatment for each patient. A medicare system would ensure that every Canadian had access to the best medical treatment.

But again this was an enormous act of faith. What if the ideal treatment was uncertain? What about cases where nobody knows whether a surgical operation would be better than ordinary home therapy? What if there are many different ways of providing medical care? What about cases where doctors disagree with each other? What if another kind of health professional could provide the same high-quality care as the doctor?

The Canadian medicare system is based on the assumption that the medical profession should settle these questions. Yet the doctors are not a neutral judiciary. Like any group in society, they are frequently influenced by the financial incentives and vested interests that surround their everyday existence. When the best treatment is uncertain, financial incentives tend to encourage doctors to provide more services, more tests and more operations. Because medicare budgets are open-ended, the system continues to expand rapidly.

Canadians are largely unaware of the incentives and interests that can affect a doctor's decisions. The patient sees the doctor as a guru who can discover the single best treatment. And the taxpayer sees the doctor as an objective judge who can determine the best distribution of medicare funds.

In fact, there are serious disagreements within the health sector. Many experts believe the health system should be arranged differently. There are strong arguments for altering the doctor's financial incentives and increasing the use of non-physicians in the health-care system. The leaders of organized medicine, by contrast, tend to prefer the status quo. By giving power to the medical profession, Canadian society has permitted the physician to make most of the key decisions about the health system. And the vast majority of physicians have a fixed political viewpoint on the crucial questions that are debated by the experts today. By default, it is the beliefs of organized medicine that dominate the health system.

Medicare has entrenched the physician as the primary decision maker in the entire health field. It has reinforced the old assumption that a person's health is best protected by medical intervention and medical cures, rather than by a broader combination of health care and self-help and prevention. In this sense, medicare has hindered some important reforms.

The Evolution of Power

Throughout most of the 20th century, society has been transferring tremendous power to the medical profession. Doctors climbed to a position of extraordinary influence in the early years of the century when science completed its alliance with medicine. The development of antibiotic drugs and new diagnostic techniques led to a golden age of medicine. Society bowed to the healing powers of the medical gods. The doctor stood at the top of the hospital hierarchy — a hierarchy that was replicated throughout the health sector. Doctors were granted a monopoly over the provision of primary health care. Other health workers were as subservient as the patients in their relationship with the medical profession.

Meanwhile, society permitted the doctor's authority to be extended into the field of public policy. The health departments of the provincial and federal governments have traditionally been dominated by physicians. Organized medicine was consulted extensively by politicians and bureaucrats whenever a health reform was considered. The politics of health became, in essence, the politics of organized medicine. In 1960 political scientist Malcolm Taylor concluded that "no other private group is as deeply involved in public administration" as the medical profession. He described the astonishing success of the doctors in obtaining "public and governmental acceptance of organized medicine's views." In the political arena — just as in their private practices — doctors learned to expect deference from the public.

Beginning in the early 1960s, there were drastic changes in the Canadian health system. Saskatchewan introduced the first provincial medicare system in 1962. Two years later a royal commission recommended a national medicare program. Federal legislation was introduced in 1966 to establish the rules for medicare. The legislation came into effect in 1968, and every Canadian province had established a medicare plan by 1971.

The original medicare plans had permitted doctors to ask their patients to pay more than the amount covered by medicare. However, the federal Liberal government, under the leadership of Health Minister Monique Bégin, passed legislation in 1984 to penalize provinces that permitted extra-billing. By early 1987 the practice of extra-billing had effectively ended in every province, and medicare was protected from the threat of gradual erosion.

Medicare was originally perceived as a defeat for the medical profession. After all, the physicians of Saskatchewan had waged a bitter war against medicare in 1962. But by the early 1970s it became clear that medicare was a boon to the doctors. It pumped up their income, eliminated their debt-collection problems and gave them an almost unlimited market for their medical services. And medicare gave the doctors a crucial new power: effective control over a large percentage of the budgets of the provincial governments. Health care now represents one-quarter to one-third of the total spending of provincial governments.

After the patient visits the doctor, his or her path through the health system is guided by physicians. They control the patient's referral to specialists, follow-up visits, admission to hospital, surgery received, and tests and examinations undergone. Since their daily medical decisions are almost completely immune to outside scrutiny, doctors are effectively determining the allocation of a large portion of government spending.

Since the 1970s, bureaucrats and academics have begun to grasp the full implications of the medical profession's new power. Most doctors operate under a fee-for-service system, which encourages them to provide as many medical services as possible. Politicians and public servants cannot veto these services, yet each service is ultimately an additional cost to taxpayers. No provincial government has ever attempted to put a ceiling on total health expenditures. It is a completely open-ended system.

In the period since the late 1960s, the supply of doctors has expanded three times as fast as the rate of population growth in Canada. At the same time, many doctors are encouraging patients to expand their consumption of medical services. The consumption of medical services has increased several times faster than the rate of population growth in recent years. The total cost of health care in Canada has already climbed to $40 billion a year — compared to $22 billion in 1980 and a mere $2.4 billion in 1961. In some provinces the cost of medicare is increasing at twice the rate of inflation.

The consumption of medical services shows no sign of stabilizing. Indeed, it is potentially limitless. However, there is no evidence that the expanding consumption of medical services has provided any significant improvement to the health of the average Canadian in recent years. Much of the increase can be attributed to extra tests and examinations that provide little tangible benefit. Yet every dollar spent on a doctor's services is a dollar that could have been spent on health education, preventive health measures or other social priorities such as job creation or housing.

Canadian taxpayers are spending about $6 billion annually on direct payments to physicians. But this is only part of the story. Hospitals cost about $17 billion annually, and prescription drugs cost a further $2 billion. Physicians are the prime controllers of Canada's expenditures on hospitals and drugs. A patient cannot be admitted to hospital, gain medical treatment or get a drug prescription without a doctor's approval.

As patients and as taxpayers, Canadians should be concerned about the soaring cost of health. Most of the provincial governments are already struggling with huge deficits. Some government services are being reduced, while the health budget continues to devour as much as one-third of provincial resources. The rapidly rising cost of health care has severely limited the spending options of the provincial governments.

Moreover, the inexorable rise of health spending is a symbol of our personal dependence on the medical system. Medicine is becoming a larger and larger element in the daily lives of North Americans. People are turning to the medical profession for a quick cure for a host of non-medical problems. For example, research suggests that mental disorders, such as anxiety, are a factor in 50 per cent of the patients who visit a general practitioner. People see doctors for emotional problems, psychosomatic disorders, nervous tension and even marital conflicts. Physicians have assumed the roles that were once filled by the clergy or family members, but the tools of the physician can be risky. Drugs, tests and operations can have side effects and complications. Even worse, a dependence on physicians can prevent people from learning to take charge of their own lives.

The Resistance Movement

In the 1980s it is the bureaucrats and politicians who are expressing the most concern about the rising cost of health. The provinces, for example, have been forced to consider measures to regulate the supply of doctors. Quebec and British Columbia have already taken steps in this area. Other provinces are wondering whether they can restrict the number of unnecessary medical services.

But the government is not the only threat to the tremendous power of the medical profession. Across modern society there are new challenges to the physician's authority. An increasing number of patients are launching malpractice lawsuits or filing official complaints with regulatory bodies. Nurses, midwives, chiropractors, optometrists and other paramedical groups are encroaching on the vast territory that doctors traditionally dominated. Community health centres are challenging the fee-for-service system. Health economists are questioning the doctor's market power. The media are increasingly critical of organized medicine.

None of these social forces have succeeded in undermining the power and wealth of the medical profession, but they are irritants and the doctors are keenly aware of their existence. Indeed, public resistance shocks the medical profession. And so doctors in the 1980s are fighting back. They have become militant. To battle the politicians, they have organized strikes and slowdowns and protest rallies. At the same time, their public-relations strategies have become more sophisticated and their political intelligence has improved. But they are not simply opposing the governments. The agitation in the medical profession in the past decade can be interpreted as a response to the gradual erosion of society's reverence for doctors.

Medical militance and medical activism will continue to be prominent in the 1990s. Doctors realize that the provinces cannot afford to keep paying their skyrocketing medicare bills without some greater scrutiny of the medical profession. For the doctors, Ontario's decision to eliminate extra-billing was a hint of things to come. By fighting the ban on extra-billing, the doctors signalled their willingness to battle any further action by the provincial governments.

The Ideology of the Medical Profession

The recent conflicts between society and doctors have been heightened by the traditional ideology and professional attitude of doctors. In their private practices, physicians cultivate an attitude of supreme self-confidence and authority. Medical schools train their students to adopt the "cloak of competence" because the patient might otherwise ignore the doctor's advice. Thus, the patient is encouraged to be blindly obedient to the doctor, and the doctor comes to expect this obedience. "Physicians are paternalistic, a fact that is part of caring for patients, and which is an approach that is expected by most patients," the Ontario Medical Association stated in a 1981 report.

A paternalistic attitude might have therapeutic value, but doctors extend the same attitude to the arena of politics and public policy. They assume that the taxpayer and the voter can be guided as easily as the patient. Organized medicine has taken a paternalistic attitude towards Canadian public policy for more than 50 years. In 1934, for example, the Canadian Medical Association argued that it was natural for doctors to control health policy. "This is not a selfish motive because what is best for the medical profession must be best for the public," the CMA said.

The 1981-82 president of the CMA, Dr. Leon Richard, made a similar argument in his inaugural address. There is nothing worse for the public than an unhappy medical profession, Dr. Richard declared. Doctors must have "a climate of security" for the benefit of their patients, he said.

Other leaders of the CMA have displayed an equally paternalistic attitude towards society. For example, consider Dr. R. K. C. Thompson, the 1966-67 president of the CMA. A former chairman of the Eugenics Board of Alberta, he advocated the mandatory sterilization of people with "genetic defects" such as mental illnesses. "I believe sterilization is often very helpful and a very necessary part of living in today's society," Thomson told an interviewer. "We should not be too swayed by pleas for the human rights of someone without the wits to know right from wrong. I feel strongly on this point."

Or consider Dr. Frank Turnbull, the 1964-65 president of the CMA. Here are his views on euthanasia: "Euthanasia is something best left to the doctor. In my day it was never a problem and the patients and their family had so much respect for the doctor that he was allowed to make the decision sometimes. I have had the supporting machines disconnected from a patient and I have never had any remorse. Nor have I ever had any suggestion of criticism from any relative who knew we had permitted the death of a most unfortunate creature."

This attitude is still widespread today among many Canadian doctors, according to some recent studies. A study in 1985, based on extensive interviews with physicians and other professionals, found that many doctors, without consulting the parents, allow severely handicapped infants to die. In some cases, doctors refused to provide treatment to defective newborn babies even when the parents wanted the infants to be treated. In effect, the doctors were deciding whether or not the newborn babies should be subjected to passive euthanasia. They were judging the value of an infant's life.

A survey of 97 Canadian doctors, published in 1983, revealed that more than 80 per cent believed they had the right to interfere in a patient's life if there was a medical problem involved. Almost three-quarters of the doctors felt they should coerce patients into entering hospital if it was considered necessary, and two-thirds believed that patients should be forced into medical tests if the doctor thought it was important. Almost one-third of the doctors felt they had the right to pressure patients who were deciding whether to have an abortion, and one-quarter said they had the right to interfere in sterilization decisions.

Medical paternalism is particularly visible in the treatment of psychiatric patients. Many doctors, including some officials of the Ontario Medical Association, were angry when the Ontario legislature passed an amendment giving psychiatric patients the right to refuse medical treatment. The OMA argued that a physician must have the power to order a psychiatric patient to be treated with drugs or electroshock therapy, even if the patient does not want the treatment.

When medical leaders begin with the assumption that they are the best judges of complex social issues, it is inevitable that they will eventually come into conflict with politicians, who are elected to make the final decisions on social policy. And it is inevitable that they will come into conflict with the consumers of health services, who are beginning to assert their rights. The conflicts of the 1980s would not be nearly so bitter had the medical leaders not been inculcated with the belief that the doctor knows best.

The inculcation begins with the selection of applicants to medical school. Medical students tend to come from privileged backgrounds. One study found that 73 per cent of all Canadian physicians had fathers whose occupational class was among the top 17 per cent in the country, according to a basic index of occupations. A study of Ontario medical students found that 40.4 per cent came from families in the highest of five income categories. Another study, which examined the personality characteristics of first-year male students in the health professions at the University of British Columbia, concluded that these students had higher income expectations than other students, attached more importance to working independently and had less community volunteer experience.

After entering medical school, the prospective doctor quickly learns to adopt his or her professional identity. Dr. Martin Shapiro, who graduated from McGill University's Faculty of Medicine, wrote a memoir called *Getting Doctored* that describes this educational process: "Quite early in the course of their training, medical students observe many examples of doctor-patient interaction, most of them dominated by the doctors. Beginning with their first experience at dissecting cadavers, they are taught to view patients as passive recipients of their professional activity."

In the classroom and in the teaching hospital, medical students learn to exercise authority. "Most members of the class had learned well by fourth year how to play the part fearlessly and with many of its subtleties: paternalism, aloofness, omnipotence." Some of this authority is necessary, Dr. Shapiro noted. "But if the allocation of authority in the physician-patient encounter were entirely rational, the power relation would dissolve as the patient's health improved and he or she became better able to participate in decisions about care. Because it is irrational, however, the physician's authority does not evaporate. It stems not from any therapeutic necessity, but from the desire of the physician to hold power over others, and from the willingness of the patient to submit."

Dr Douglas Waugh, former dean of medicine at Queen's University, has noted that the physician's traditional paternalism is reflected in phrases such as "doctor's orders" and "doctor knows best." He added: "These expressions cast the doctor in the role of an omnipotent and infallible deity."

Doctors often call their patients by their first names, while the patient is expected to address the doctor by his or her title. This adds to the imbalance in the relationship. Moreover, even the most articulate and intelligent patient can succumb to the doctor's authority. Subconsciously we all have a strong fear of death, and the hospital environment can be tremendously intimidating. "You can be a forceful individual in the outside world, but when you're in one of those incredible gowns they give you in hospital you feel very ordinary," said Monique Bégin, the former federal health minister. Studies have found that 50 per cent of patients are unaware of their right to refuse a medical treatment.

In recent years some doctors have moved away from a paternalistic relationship with their patients, but in most cases the authoritarian attitude is still strong. A former president of the OMA reflected this attitude in a speech to a group of medical students: "Because you are a carefully selected group with IQs and memory capacity in the top one per cent of the population, you will spend your days not with your peers, but with patients who are your intellectual subordinates."

When doctors enter the arena of politics or finance or the law, they may have no more expertise than other citizens, yet they often adopt the guise of scientific authority. This phenomenon has been described by Dr. H. E. Emson in his textbook on doctors and the law: "The assumption of unwarranted expertise is often an extension of one of the facets of the total doctor-patient relationship — the desire of the patient for a parent-figure, and the willingness of the physician to assume this role." He continued: "The doctor is conditioned from the first days of training to assume this position of omnipotence and omniscience, and it is remarkable how many intelligent and independent people, finding themselves in the position of a patient, will rapidly revert to a state of dependency." He warned doctors: "Do not pretend to be an expert when you are not."

Eliot Freidson, a prominent U.S. sociologist, has noted the important distinction between an issue of professional expertise and an issue of public policy: "For example, we can all agree that how a road is to be built is a technical question best handled by engineers and other experts. But whether a road should be built at all, and where it should be located, are not wholly esoteric technical questions. There are certainly technical considerations which must be taken into account in evaluating whether and where a road should be built, but engineering science contains no special expertise to allow it to decide whether a road is 'necessary' and what route 'must' be taken. Expertise properly plays a major role in suggesting that already available roads are crowded and determining which routes for a new road would be the easiest and cheapest to construct, but it is social, political and economic evaluations, not the science of engineering, which, in the light of knowledge, determines whether and where to build a road."

There is also a distinction between skills and knowledge. For example, surgeons in Britain were traditionally called "Mister" rather than "Doctor" because a surgeon was believed to possess technical skills rather than broad knowledge. By the same token, a doctor who possesses medical skills and medical expertise is not necessarily knowledgeable about the entire health field.

Canada's medical leaders have failed to grasp these distinctions. They have insisted on the right to govern the field of health policy in Canada. Health policies are based on questions of manpower, economics, government finance and politics. But doctors have maintained that they are specially qualified to decide these questions. Indeed, they have argued that these questions fall within the parameters of the doctor's professional autonomy. Their definition of their professional rights and freedoms is broad enough to encompass a host of crucial issues of public interest in the health field.

The extra-billing debate is a classic example of this syndrome. Extra-billing is clearly a political and financial issue — it involves the question of whether doctors should charge their patients an extra fee, beyond the amount covered by medicare — yet doctors have included it in their definition of their professional expertise and their professional autonomy. They have argued that they are qualified to tell whether an extra charge would be good or bad for an individual. A survey of more than 2,000 Canadian doctors found that almost 70 per cent believed the physician was best able to determine whether extra-billing imposed a hardship on his or her patients. One surgeon, Dr. Gary Willard, told a public audience in 1986 that a doctor can tell by the way his patients walk and talk whether they can afford to be extra-billed.

Many doctors have decided that extra-billing is good for their patients — and for society as a whole. "Paying the doctor directly, the way you would pay any professional for services, clarifies the doctor-patient role," one senior CMA official said in 1979. "Patients are happier this way," he added. "It is not a question of money." In 1986 a Toronto psychiatrist told an Ontario legislative committee that extra-billing "is often an extremely useful and meaningful process within the therapy itself." Another doctor, unable to distinguish between a political issue and a medical issue, wrote comments on a medical chart to indicate his patient's opinions on extra-billing. Above a diagnosis of an ear infection, the doctor wrote that the patient had spoken in "antagonistic tones" about the extra-billing issue.

This blurring of public policy and private medicine was very evident in the 1986 dispute over extra-billing in Ontario. When patients arrived at their doctor's office to be treated for an ailment, the doctor lectured them on the need to oppose the government and preserve extra-billing. When a reporter from the *Globe and Mail* published information undermining the arguments of the Ontario Medical Association, a doctor threatened to prevent the reporter from gaining medical treatment. Another doctor made a similar threat to a *Toronto Star* reporter. In each case, the doctors were trying to extend their private power into the public arena.

In 1979 the Canadian Medical Association created its own list of the "professional rights" of doctors. Once again the definition of "professional rights" was broad enough to include several major questions of public policy. For example, the CMA maintained that doctors had an inherent right to practise where they wish and to decide how they will be paid. Both these "rights" would severely restrict the policy options of Canada's elected governments. Moreover, the CMA asserted that doctors had a right "to be free of bureaucratic harassment." The medical association said that physicians "should be free from complicated or obtuse rules and regulations designed more to show authority than to expedite the administrative process."

The CMA also listed a series of "reasonable expectations" held by doctors, including the expectation that the government would introduce legislation to control "the cost implications of undue legal harassment of health professionals." In other words, the doctors believed they had a right to be protected from expensive malpractice lawsuits.

Medical Self-government

The rhetoric about professional rights and freedoms has obscured the fact that doctors are private businessmen who hold a monopoly over the provision of medical services in Canada. They wield extraordinary powers over the market for their services — and enjoy the right to utilize a multi-billion-dollar hospital system developed at public expense. Other monopolies, such as Bell Canada or Ontario Hydro, are carefully regulated by governments to ensure that the public is protected. The medical profession, which provides an essential public service and is funded almost entirely by the taxpayer, cannot expect to be free from public regulation.

Indeed, it is remarkable that the medical profession has escaped without public regulation for so long. Medicine has traditionally been a self-governing profession, and doctors have assumed that this gives them an inherent right to be exempted from outside regulation. But in fact the power of self-government was delegated to the medical profession from the provincial governments. It is a delegated privilege, not a divine right.

Self-government was given to Canada's doctors in the 19th century for two major reasons. First, there was strong political pressure from the medical profession, which wanted the power of self-government as a means of restricting competition. Second, it was simply more convenient for the governments to allow doctors to regulate themselves. Politicians and bureaucrats tend to have difficulty understanding the complex technical questions of medicine. It is easier for them to allow the profession to govern itself.

For the same reasons, the federal and provincial governments traditionally permitted doctors to make the key decisions about health policy in Canada. H. L. Laframboise, a former assistant deputy minister in the federal Health and Welfare Department, has explained this phenomenon: "Figuratively speaking, each expert group has a mysterious 'black bag' in which it carries the body of knowledge peculiar to it. Society does not have access to the esoteric knowledge and language in that black bag and relies on the elite experts to tell them, in words they can understand, what its contents mean. What they are told, of course, is that things are just dandy the way they are, and that reform will only work to society's disadvantage."

Today governments have recognized that the important questions of health policy cannot be left to the medical profession. There are three major reasons for this change of attitude. First, health care has been accepted as an essential public service. Second, there are billions of dollars of public money in the health sector. Private professionals cannot be permitted to make every decision about such a large public investment. And third, the medical profession has a conflict of interest when it governs itself. Some policy decisions could benefit society but might hurt the medical profession. For example, society could benefit from policies to control the fees of doctors or to permit doctors to advertise their services. These policies might never be introduced if the medical profession were completely self-governing.

Some form of public regulation of the medical profession was inevitable. It finally arrived, in a moderate dose, when medicare was introduced in the 1960s. It continued, in a slightly stronger dose, when extra-billing was banned in the 1970s and 1980s. However, the concept of public regulation was totally foreign to the doctors. They were born and bred in an era of medical domination of the health field. Consequently, they have rebelled against the government actions of the past two decades. Even though these government actions have not seriously threatened the basic powers of the medical profession, doctors were alarmed at the first tentative steps towards public regulation. As a result, the conflicts between governments and doctors have been intense.

The conflicts have frequently resulted in walkouts or strikes by doctors. The obvious examples are the 1962 strike in Saskatchewan and the 1986 strike in Ontario. But there have been brief walkouts by doctors in Quebec (1970 and 1982), Manitoba (1981 and 1982), Alberta (1981) and British Columbia (1981). There were also walkouts by doctors in Ontario in 1982 and by doctors in Saskatchewan in 1985 and 1986.

The conflicts over extra-billing have ended. By 1987, the last province had officially prohibited the practice. But larger battles are looming. Health costs are rising dramatically. The surplus of doctors is worsening every year. Governments cannot afford to keep increasing their payments to doctors and hospitals when other social needs are urgent. There is a strong possibility of further government action to reform the health sector.

The politicians are aware of the strength of the medical profession. They were willing to challenge the doctors on the extra-billing question because opinion polls showed that the voters were strongly in favour of a ban on extra-billing. But the voters are generally unaware of the manpower issue and the cost issue, and without public sentiment behind them, politicians will be reluctant to tangle with the doctors over these issues. Even though there are significant pressures for reform, the medical profession could still succeed in escaping further regulation.

The medical profession is articulate and wealthy. Doctors often have extensive social connections with senior politicians and decision makers. The medical profession enjoys solid support from the average citizen — opinion polls show that the public has more respect for doctors than for any other group in society. Doctors have a strong strategic position within the health sector — they dominate the hierarchy of health occupations and occupy many key posts in the administration of health care. The opponents of organized medicine tend to be fragmented and disorganized. And finally, there is overwhelming internal cohesion and solidarity within the medical profession. Doctors are almost unanimous in their views on most government policies. Medical associations can usually count on the strong backing of their membership on most policy questions. Surveys have found a tremendous homogeneity of opinion among doctors on key issues in the health sector.

These are the sources of medical power. But they are also the explanation for the occasional tactical blunders of the medical leaders. Some of Canada's medical associations have been politically naive precisely because of their traditional strength. They have never been required to organize their weapons carefully. Compared to business associations or industry groups, doctors are often unsophisticated in the political arena. Some medical associations have never needed to hire outside experts to help them lobby the government. After decades of influence in the health sector, medical leaders have assumed that they understand the subtleties of the political process. Often they don't. When doctors finally find themselves in conflict with government, they are unprepared. The conflicts are intensified because they attempt to use brute strength in their battles with government.

This book is about the overt conflicts between doctors and governments, and between doctors and patients. It is also about the conflicts that have been successfully suppressed by the doctors — the conflicts that were limited to the backrooms of government. The medical profession has managed to block the rise of community health centres, for example. It has succeeded in limiting the growth of health occupations that threatened to compete with doctors. It has preserved its power to control doctors' annual income. And it has ensured that the profession is virtually immune to the anxieties of a strong disciplinary system or quality-control mechanism.

The success of the medical profession in these little-known issues has a major impact on Canadian patients. Professional power has distorted the health-care system. This book is an attempt to explore the exercise of power by Canada's doctors and the resulting distortions in the kind of health care we receive.

CHAPTER 2

THE STRIKE WEAPON

Four-year-old Dino Cormio was bleeding from a gash on his forehead when he arrived at the emergency ward of North York's Northwestern General Hospital on June 13, 1986. Dino had injured himself in a fall, and his father had rushed him to the emergency ward. But as blood dripped over his eyes, the boy was turned away from the hospital. The doctors at Northwestern were on strike. They had closed the emergency ward. The boy's father, Johnny Cormio, was angry. "I've never seen anything like this in Canada," he told reporters. Johnny Cormio had immigrated to this country from Italy seven years earlier. "I'm a hard-working man without much money and my son is bleeding," he said. "Don't those doctors have enough?"

Dino Cormio was eventually treated at another hospital. But his father remained angry. The doctors wanted him to blame the Ontario government for Dino's plight; the doctors were striking to protest the government's ban on extra-billing and they were banking on their patients' traditional reverence and respect for the physician. They were mistaken. In 1986 the patients were not afraid to question the politics of their doctors. The spell was broken.

The Ontario Medical Association, the organizers of the 1986 strike, had chosen a powerful bargaining weapon. Strikes by doctors had succeeded in extracting concessions from governments in 1933 in Winnipeg and in 1962 in Saskatchewan. During these strikes, patients had rallied to support their doctors. Forced to choose between the government and the medical profession, the patients of Winnipeg and Saskatchewan were governed by their respect for their doctors and their fear of losing them.

Today the climate has changed. Most people do not blindly accept the political pronouncements of the medical profession. Throughout the Ontario dispute, polls showed that a clear majority (from 54 to 77 per cent) of the province's residents supported the government's decision to ban extra-billing. The doctors were unable to sway the politicians or the public. The government remained firm, and the doctors found themselves in deep trouble.

After decades of influence over the Conservatives, who had ruled Ontario since the Second World War, the OMA was unprepared for an aggressive Liberal government. The medical association was overconfident. Its leaders had never suffered a serious defeat. Indeed, a former OMA president — Dr. Bette Stephenson — was a key member of Ontario's Tory cabinet in the 1970s and early 1980s. When the Liberals finally took office under the leadership of David Peterson in 1985, the OMA had become complacent and arrogant.

In the past the Ontario Liberals had always supported the concept of extra-billing by doctors. The party was rooted in the conservative farmland of southwestern Ontario. Now, under Peterson's leadership, the Liberals realized that they had to adopt a more progressive platform if they wanted to appeal to urban voters. The party's 1985 election platform thus included, for the first time, a promise to ban extra-billing.

The Liberals formed a minority government in 1985 after signing a written agreement with the Ontario NDP. The agreement included a clause requiring the Liberals to proceed with their promised ban on extra-billing. But even if there had been no commitment to the NDP, the Liberals would probably have fulfilled their election promise. The demise of extra-billing was inevitable. By 1985 most Canadian provinces had banned the practice. Those provinces that refused to ban extra-billing were facing the threat of severe financial penalties from the federal government. Moreover, the public was strongly opposed to extra-billing. The Liberals were assured of widespread support for their action.

The OMA, meanwhile, was paying no attention to the gathering storm clouds. The medical association was blithely confident. The OMA leaders assumed they could duplicate their smashing victory of 1982, when a series of rotating strikes by OMA members had convinced the Conservative government to provide a generous fee increase to doctors. The Tories had given the physicians a five-year agreement that increased their fees by 47.75 per cent. Compounded, this amounted to a fee increase of 59 per cent — far more than the inflation rate in the period from 1982 to 1987. As the opposition politicians noted, the Tories had wrestled the doctors to the ceiling.

The doctors argued that the hefty fee increase was necessary because their incomes in the 1970s had failed to rise as fast as other groups in society. The gap between doctors and other groups had narrowed after 1971, and the OMA wanted a return to the 1971 differential. The OMA ignored evidence suggesting that the relatively high incomes of doctors in 1971 were actually a historical anomaly — an unusual peak, resulting from the introduction of medicare in the late 1960s. Indeed, an independent fact-finder had recommended a smaller fee increase for Ontario doctors. But when the rotating walkouts were over, the OMA emerged victorious. The gap between doctors and the average wage earner was restored to its 1971 level. By 1984 the average Ontario doctor was earning a net income of $103,400 after expenses, according to Revenue Canada. Medical incomes in Ontario were the third highest in the country.

Before the introduction of medicare, the average Ontario doctor earned about four times as much as the average industrial wage earner. By 1971 the ratio had climbed to 6 to 1. The ratio declined somewhat in the mid-1970s, when the doctors volunteered to restrain their incomes as part of the anti-inflation battle. But by 1986 the income of the average Ontario physician was almost six times the level of the average industrial wage.

The OMA's consistent success with the Tory government had lulled the doctors into a sense of security. "Our strategy for pursuing political objectives was developed over 42 years of Tory government," said Dr. Ed Moran, general secretary of the OMA. "We enjoyed historically a very strongly elitist relationship with the government. The government just didn't make moves on health care policy without consulting us. We developed the necessary checks and balances over the bureaucracy by virtue of the trust and respect we enjoyed with the elected government. Fee disputes aside, our relationship with the Tory government was very strongly a consultative relationship. So we didn't have to get into 'issues management' or a sophisticated professional approach to the managing of the public forum debates because we managed quite nicely without it."

Moreover, the OMA in the mid-1980s had become almost contemptuous of the political process. Its leaders simply did not believe the election promises of the Liberals. The doctors were convinced that the politicians were unprincipled cynics who would say anything to get elected. They failed to see the connection between the politicians and the public. They did not understand that the public wanted a ban on extra-billing and that the politicians were simply the agents of the public.

"I don't think the Liberal government had a commitment to end extra-billing," Dr. Moran said. "Peterson had a macho need to be a man of his word. He made the pre-election commitment, not having even the faintest thought that he might have to deliver on it. We tried to convince him that it wouldn't be a world-shaking event if a politician didn't keep an election promise — it was kind of expected now and then. But he had political needs, and the political needs won out. That's why I have difficulty talking about a 'commitment' in the sense that a 'commitment' has a noble ring to it. I don't think that was there. I'm sure the political needs over-rode the intellectual force of our arguments."

Introduction of the Legislation

The Liberals introduced Bill 94 in December 1985. The proposed legislation, which would effectively ban extra-billing in Ontario, sparked an immediate uproar in the medical profession. Dr. Earl Myers, OMA president, called it "an act of violence against the medical profession." Dr. Bette Stephenson, former OMA president, described the bill as "a blatant act of terrorism" and "sheer vindictiveness." Three days after the bill was introduced, the OMA began talking about the possibility of strikes and walkouts.

The inflamed rhetoric of the doctors was a reflection of their uncontrolled fury. Like a wounded elephant, the OMA was lashing out wildly. Never before had an Ontario government defied the wishes of the medical association on such a major issue. The doctors were astonished and outraged. They spurred themselves into an instantaneous militancy. Indeed, they completely lost any sense of perspective. One doctor compared the Liberals to Hitler's Nazi party. Another doctor described the Liberals as "communistic." The OMA's president, Dr. Myers, drew parallels between Ontario and countries behind the Iron Curtain.

Very quickly, the doctors realized that one of their biggest political advantages was their relationship with their patients. In a doctor's office, the patient is vulnerable and often frightened. The doctor, after establishing a position of authority on medical matters, can choose to extend this authority to political matters. Unless patients can escape the normal feeling of intimidation, they are apt to believe that doctors have a special expertise on political questions. Many patients accept a doctor's political prescriptions as blindly as they accept a medical prescription.

By early February 1986, the doctors were distributing hundreds of thousands of pro-extra-billing postcards in their waiting rooms for patients to send to the premier. In Cornwall, physicians prepared a stack of form letters for their patients to sign. Some doctors were lecturing their patients on the need to oppose Bill 94. Others were silently suggesting the same thing by wearing anti-government buttons while they treated their patients. Posters proclaiming "Patients back doctors" (printed by the OMA) were displayed in the waiting rooms. The pressure was difficult for patients to resist. "I don't agree with extra-billing, but I didn't want to argue about the issue because he was in the middle of filling out my chart and a prescription, and I didn't want him to get excited and make a mistake," said one patient whose doctor raised the issue of Bill 94.

Medical ethicists pointed out the implications of the OMA's strategy. "I would say this is a conflict of interest," said Professor Abbyann Lynch of the University of Western Ontario medical school. "The patient is coming to receive help with a problem. The physician's problem is not the patient's problem — but the physician has a captive audience."

The doctors enjoyed another significant advantage: their wealth and financial strength. Within a few weeks of the introduction of Bill 94, the OMA was beginning to build a war chest. The medical association asked its members to contribute $200 each to help fight the legislation. The contributions paid for advertisements, special mailings, legal fees and other expenses. Later in the dispute, other provincial medical associations sent money to the OMA, and a further levy of $200 was requested from Ontario's doctors. In the end, the OMA raised more than $1 million from its members. The money allowed the association to launch an expensive advertising campaign. Indeed, the OMA was swimming in so much cash that it was unable to spend all its funds before the dispute ended.

The militancy of the doctors took an ominous turn in early February. A surgeon in Cornwall, angered by Bill 94, refused to treat a man who had suffered a severed tendon in his thumb. The local hospital was forced to send the victim to Ottawa, an hour away, for the necessary surgery. The Cornwall surgeon, Dr. Robert Harris, made no secret of the reasons for his refusal to perform the surgery. The hospital had called him at home at 2 a.m. after the victim had arrived at the emergency department. Dr. Harris, a specialist in hand surgery, would normally have gone to the hospital to perform the operation. But he refused. "I was overcome with the thoughts that have been uppermost in our minds latterly: government interference into our affairs," Dr. Harris explained in a letter. "I called the hospital back and suggested that the casualty officer do the best he could with the case." He added: "Don't forget that I have the last say in who I treat and who I do not. . . . And if we are all going to be conscripted, this is how it will be."

The doctors made their first major blunder in late February, when they disbanded an abortion committee in Sarnia. It was essentially a wildcat strike — an unofficial action by some of the most militant members of the medical association. For the first time, the doctors were endangering the health of patients. Without the abortion committee at Sarnia General Hospital, it became impossible to obtain a legal abortion in the Sarnia region. Pregnant women were faced with hazardous delays, as well as a trip to another region of Ontario or the United States.

Resistance from the Public

The doctors were seriously hurt by the Sarnia episode. At a time when the OMA was still hoping to negotiate a peaceful solution to the dispute, the Sarnia doctors were antagonizing many people who might have otherwise remained neutral. Women's groups, in particular, were alienated by the Sarnia incident. "We are appalled that doctors have chosen to use the misery and the relative weakness of women to try to illustrate a point they are making about money," said Doris Anderson of the National Action Committee on the Status of Women. The abortion committee was eventually revived by other doctors in Sarnia, but by then the damage was done.

Other organizations were also challenging the OMA. A group of about 130 doctors, known as the Medical Reform Group, spoke out strongly against the policies of the medical association. Since its formation in 1979, the MRG had been the OMA's most consistent opponent. The reform doctors had always believed in the need to prohibit extra-billing. They pointed to studies which demonstrated that extra-billing tended to hurt the poor, who could not afford the extra medical fees. The MRG was the first medical group to provide organized opposition to a medical association in Canada's history.

Spokespersons for the MRG were widely quoted in the media during the 1986 dispute in Ontario. As doctors, the members of the reform group had a credibility that other critics sometimes lacked. The public-relations success of the MRG could be measured by the fact that the OMA refused to debate the reform doctors. The medical association bitterly attacked the reformers, complaining that they were "an insignificant rump group" which represented nobody.

A committee of the Ontario legislature held public hearings on Bill 94 in March and April of 1986. The hearings became a forum for the enraged rhetoric of the OMA and its members. One physician predicted that the proposed legislation might lead to "state doctors like the notorious Mengele of the Nazi concentration camps and like the state psychiatrists in Russian political prisons." Another doctor said the government was behaving like a person who threatened to "break your arm above or below your wrist." The OMA, in its official submission, described Bill 94 as "this mortal attack on our professional freedom." It accused the Liberals of "wielding its power ruthlessly to bring an honorable profession to its knees." The medical association said Bill 94 would result in the "enslavement" of the doctors. The profession would be "shackled . . . a captive group."

Outside the hearings, the hyperbole was equally astounding. Medical students carried protest signs reading "Bill 94 — from Russia with love." Dr. Moran, the OMA's general secretary, suggested that the government was approaching fascism. He told the *Canadian Medical Association Journal* that "if you look at the natural extension of liberalism you're looking at fascism, which is the controlled approach that requires the greatest good for the greatest number. At some point liberalism, which is designed to free the individual, becomes oppressive because, to free the larger group, we enslave the smaller." Later in the dispute, Dr. Moran compared the doctors to Gandhi and Martin Luther King.

The OMA offered to refrain from extra-billing all senior citizens, welfare recipients and emergency patients. But the medical association refused to go further. Dr. Myers told the legislative committee that there were no conditions under which the doctors would accept a complete ban on extra-billing.

The doctors were frustrated by their inability to control the publicity surrounding the dispute. Doctors, after all, are not accustomed to negative publicity. In their private careers, doctors are praised and revered. But in the public arena, they were taking a battering for the tactics they had adopted against the Liberals. Some of the criticism was difficult to dismiss. The United Senior Citizens of Ontario, representing about 300,000 people, appeared before the legislative committee to complain about the "confrontational approach" of the OMA. A spokesperson for the coalition said the rhetoric of the doctors was causing "consternation" among seniors. The organization called for a total ban on extra-billing. One survey by a group of Canadian pensioners found that 62 per cent of seniors had been extra-billed by doctors and, in many cases, the extra-billing caused hardship.

The doctors knew they could not win a public-relations battle against senior citizens. The public was more likely to sympathize with elderly people on fixed incomes than with younger, well-paid professionals. Leaders of the OMA called in the seniors for a private meeting to try to convince them of the merits of the medical association's position, but the seniors refused to endorse the doctors.

The Negotiations

Throughout the spring, cabinet ministers met with OMA officials for negotiating sessions at posh restaurants and hotels in downtown Toronto. Some major concessions were offered to the OMA. At a negotiating session on April 17, the government submitted a 10-point offer. Among the proposed concessions: the OMA would get a $100-million "excellence fund" to provide bonus pay for superior doctors; the doctors would get a "bill of rights" that included a guarantee that they could locate their medical practices wherever they chose; the generous 1982 fee agreement would be extended for a further two years; the government would help improve the financial position of general practitioners; a fund for medical research would be established; the OMA would be recognized as the only negotiating body for doctors in Ontario; a task force would be commissioned to study health-care problems; and the penalties for violations of the proposed legislation would be reduced.

If the OMA had accepted the 10-point offer, it would have severely restricted the government's power to control health costs in Ontario. For example, the bill of rights would have prevented the Ontario government from following the example of Quebec and British Columbia, which have made it difficult for new medical graduates to practise in regions that have a surplus of doctors. Moreover, the 10-point offer was an expensive proposal. Under the Canada Health Act, the province was losing more than $50 million annually as a federal penalty for allowing extra-billing. Ottawa would refund the money if Bill 94 was approved, and it could be used to build hospitals and improve health services in Ontario. But the 10-point offer proposed to give this money to the OMA to be distributed as merit pay.

However, the doctors rejected the offer. They continued to demand the complete withdrawal of Bill 94. At a meeting on April 19, the OMA's 250-member governing council voted to authorize a province-wide strike to protest the proposed legislation.

Before launching the first walkouts, the OMA organized a mass protest rally at the Ontario legislature. About 3,000 doctors and their supporters travelled by bus and chartered airplane to attend. (The attendance was lower than the OMA's prediction of 5,000.) Non-emergency surgery was cancelled, as the doctors closed their offices for the day. Many physicians brought their spouses, children, office staff and friends — all wearing white medical smocks to resemble the doctors. While the doctors waved protest placards, two airplanes circled overhead, towing banners proclaiming: "Bill 94 may be hazardous to your health." It was the first province-wide rally by doctors in Ontario's history.

Meanwhile, the OMA was setting the machinery in motion for a mass walkout. On May 22, two weeks after the rally at Queen's Park, the OMA announced plans for a two-day withdrawal of all non-emergency services. Doctors in Cornwall went a step further. They threatened to launch a complete strike, including a refusal to provide emergency treatment.

Three days later the OMA unveiled another twist in their protest strategy. The medical association urged its members to delay the discharge of patients from Ontario hospitals. The OMA predicted that this would clog up the hospital wards and eventually result in long delays for patients seeking non-emergency services. Premier Peterson criticized the tactic, calling it an attempt to "punish" patients.

Negotiations between the OMA and the Liberals continued until May 20. This was not the standard labour-relations bargaining between blue-collar union leaders and prosperous management lawyers. The doctors and the cabinet ministers shared the same tastes and the same social circles. Dr. Moran was a personal friend of several Liberal cabinet ministers — including one who had shared a fishing trip with him. The government's chief negotiator, Attorney General Ian Scott, had previously done legal work for the Canadian Medical Association. He was a long-time friend of several leaders of organized medicine.

A total of 11 bargaining sessions were held, but the negotiations were fruitless. The government delayed its legislation for 10 months before the talks finally broke off. At one point, the government offered to modify the legislation to establish the "Quebec model." Under this system, doctors would be free to extra-bill their patients, but the patients would not be reimbursed by medicare. The doctors rejected the offer.

The Two-Day Walkout

The doctors began their two-day province-wide strike on May 29. They locked their offices, cancelled hundreds of non-emergency operations and refused to renew prescriptions by phone. The OMA claimed that 75 per cent of Ontario's 17,000 physicians took part in the strike. However, independent surveys by major newspapers put the actual figure at about 60 per cent.

The leaders of the OMA insisted that the doctors would not jeopardize the health of their patients. But the walkouts were a traumatic event for some. Joyce Louise Save, a 59-year-old victim of lung cancer, was scheduled to undergo surgery to remove a lung on May 30. The operation was cancelled because of the two-day strike. The woman said she felt like a scapegoat. "I guess I'm classed as elective surgery," she said, "but how do I know that the delay won't make a difference? Is the cancer spreading outside the lung meanwhile? Will they catch it in time?"

According to Dr. Moran, each doctor decided whether an operation could be postponed. "You can't draw a sharp line between inconveniencing patients and hurting them," he acknowledged.

In early June the OMA escalated its advertising campaign. The medical association spent $50,000 to produce a 30-second television commercial describing Bill 94 as "hazardous to your health" and "a lethal dose of politics." The OMA spent a further $100,000 to purchase air time on television stations across the province. The commercials featured a crowd advancing on Queen's Park, singing: "They want the whole world in their hands." For many patients the commercials were frightening. The doctors seemed to be suggesting that the Liberals were a deadly threat. Several television stations refused to run the commercials.

On June 2 the Liberals announced that Bill 94 would be amended. The maximum fines for violations of the legislation were reduced from $10,000 to $250 for a first offence. The OMA was not appeased. Within a week the OMA's governing council voted to begin an indefinite strike.

The medical association urged its members to refrain from bolstering the emergency departments of their local hospitals during the strike. OMA leaders predicted that the emergency departments would begin to clog up with patients. "Our intent is to back up the emergency departments," said Dr. Tom Dickson, a director of the OMA. The association's 1986–87 president, Dr. Richard Railton, said the indefinite strike would "really turn the heat up on the government." The OMA also asked its members to resign from their positions as chiefs of staff or chiefs of medical services in hospitals. This tactic was designed to cripple the administration of the hospitals.

The Strike Begins

The strike began on June 12. In its early stages, about 50 per cent of the province's doctors locked their offices and refused to provide any non-emergency medical services. The provincial Ministry of Health and the College of Physicians and Surgeons of Ontario were flooded with hundreds of calls from worried patients who had problems finding a doctor. The college tried to patch up the problems by contacting some doctors and hospitals and persuading them to provide medical services. "We've got a major crisis on our hands," said Dr. Michael Dixon, registrar of the Ontario college.

It quickly became clear that the strike would have a serious effect on some patients. At some emergency departments, patients had to wait as long as five hours for treatment. One woman, 11 weeks pregnant as a result of a sexual assault, was told that her abortion would be cancelled because her doctor was on strike. The procedure was finally performed after the college intervened. Another woman, 21-year-old Bonnie Habib, was forced to wait three hours in pain at Mississauga General Hospital after she suffered severe chest pains and almost fainted at a nearby shopping mall. She was finally given an electrocardiogram test and a prescription for a painkiller. Despite these cases, the OMA refused to reconsider the strike. "A little pain now will save the people of Ontario a lot of pain later," Dr. Railton told a reporter.

The college, the self-governing body for Ontario's medical profession, had the power to discipline any doctor who failed to provide medical services. But in the early days of the strike, the college preferred to adopt a gentle approach. The college is guided by a council of 21 doctors and six lay people. At least six of the 21 physicians were active in the OMA before joining the college council. The striking doctors openly defied the college. At Northwestern General Hospital in North York, for example, more than half of the 150 doctors voted to resign from the hospital if the college disciplined any doctor at Northwestern.

On June 13 Northwestern became the first hospital to close its emergency department as part of the strike. No patients were admitted to emergency unless their cases were considered to be life threatening. Two days later the doctors announced that a dozen emergency departments would be closed under the same conditions. "It's going to put unbelievable pressure on the people in Peel County," said Dr. Tom Dickson, describing the shutdown at Peel Memorial Hospital. OMA leaders began threatening to close hospitals completely.

Patients continued to bear the brunt of the strike activities. Two-year-old Tiffany Rutherford, her face swollen from an ear infection, waited in a hospital emergency department for five hours without being treated. As the swelling continued, her mother came close to hysteria. She was told to expect a further two-hour wait. She telephoned her husband, and they decided to take their daughter to another hospital, where Tiffany was finally examined. She was diagnosed as having a temporary facial paralysis. Doctors at the second hospital told the Rutherfords that the damage could have been permanent if their daughter had gone untreated much longer.

The strike intensified on June 16 when about 700 angry doctors marched to the Ontario legislature. They screamed, they chanted, they banged their picket signs like clubs on the steel barricades, then they clambered over the barricades and pushed security guards who wouldn't allow them to enter the building. The raucous demonstration was a morale booster for the most militant of the doctors, but it was a monumental public-relations fiasco. "That did us more harm than anything else in the whole strike," Dr. Myers admitted later.

Dr. Irvin Wolkoff, one of the doctors who marched to Queen's Park that day, said the demonstration was completely disorganized. "It was an example of something that went very wrong," he said. The public, watching the incident on television, saw the doctors as a mob of aggressive bullies. Criticism of the doctors became even more widespread. On June 17 a group of about 20 people held a demonstration outside York-Finch General Hospital to protest the closure of the emergency department. A few days later another group of 80 protesters urged the college to force the doctors back to work. Some members of the Medical Reform Group were receiving 100 to 200 calls a day from people who opposed the strike. The medical profession was rapidly losing the trust of the public. "The behavior of many doctors during this strike terrifies me," one woman wrote in a letter to a newspaper. "Are these shouting and yelling people our supposedly revered doctors?"

Many doctors were putting strong pressure on colleagues who refused to strike. Three doctors in Etobicoke went door-to-door in their medical building, demanding that the physicians close their offices. One doctor, who ignored the demand, found his door glued shut with Krazy glue. Another doctor, who also refused to join the strike, had to fix the lock on his door after a militant doctor slammed the door hard enough to loosen the screws. Dr. Ross Sullovey of Etobicoke said he would stop referring patients to specialists who continued to work during the strike. And a medical clinic in Mississauga closed its doors after local doctors threatened to stop referring patients to the clinic.

The public image of doctors suffered another blow on June 18 when a hemorrhaging pregnant woman was turned away from the emergency department at Ajax-Pickering Hospital. The woman, 35-year-old Theresa Black, was two months pregnant. She had spent two days trying to reach her family doctor after she first started bleeding. Her doctor was on strike. Bleeding heavily and feverish, she was finally taken to the emergency department. A doctor in emergency refused to treat her, saying that a few minutes would make no difference to the case. The woman's sister had to drive her to another hospital, 15 minutes away, where she was admitted. She lost the baby. The doctors argued that the miscarriage could not have been prevented, but their assurances were little comfort to Theresa Black. She said she felt deserted by the medical system.

Undeterred, the medical leaders maintained their militant stand. Two dozen doctors confronted Premier Peterson in Trenton. One of them, shouting at the premier, called him a "Hitler." About 100 doctors taunted Peterson at a hospital sod-turning ceremony in Ottawa. Some of them got into screaming matches with patients who supported the premier. Meanwhile, the Durham Medical Society vowed to launch a complete withdrawal of all medical services if Bill 94 was approved by the legislature. The society's president, Dr. Joan Atkinson, said a complete withdrawal would mean "sitting on the curb and watching the ambulances pulling in to the front door and watching the funeral directors pulling out the back door."

The college of physicians and surgeons sent a warning letter to the province's doctors on June 20. "We think there is increasing risk to the public," the college's registrar told reporters.

Passage of the Legislation

After 272 hours of public debate on Bill 94, the provincial Conservatives were continuing to stall the approval of the legislation. In desperation the Liberals invoked a time limit. The bill was passed on June 20, after a final all-night debate. A Tory backbencher talked from midnight to 6 a.m., but the vote was finally held after a marathon 24-hour session of the legislature. About 50 doctors marched outside the legislature, shouting "Liberalism is communism" and waving placards.

The OMA vowed to escalate its strike actions "dramatically and decisively." Several hospitals stopped performing abortions. Doctors at five hospitals refused to admit new patients except in emergencies. Ten internists at York County Hospital refused to handle any cases — even emergencies. Medical specialists at Etobicoke General Hospital were considering similar action. "We want to force the closure of the hospital," said one of the internists at York County Hospital. A single internist remained on duty to handle emergencies at York County Hospital. "He probably won't hold out more than another 48 hours," said Dr. Murray Weingarten, one of the striking internists. "After then, who knows what will happen. But I don't think anyone will die as a result of this. At least, I hope not."

The college of physicians and surgeons quickly intervened in the York County and Etobicoke hospitals. It threatened to lay charges of professional misconduct against the specialists. "We pointed out to the doctors at York County that their move in essence made the emergency department nothing more than a first-aid station," said the college's registrar, Dr. Michael Dixon. The specialists reconsidered their stand and agreed to maintain emergency services.

For the first time, the college was voicing serious concerns about the rotating closure of emergency departments. "There is a real risk that misjudgments will be made in the heat of the moment," Dr. Dixon said. "The increasing concern that we have is that a real tragedy will occur. I think that, realistically, it's just a matter of time. I think we've been lucky to date, but that luck just might run out if the protest continues."

By June 27 there were signs that the strike was crumbling. Most of the striking doctors were beginning to return to work. The Ontario Hospital Association reported that many hospitals were almost back to normal. "The public is upset, the public doesn't like the strike and the public wants it to be over," Dr. Moran said. "Frankly, that's the way the profession feels too."

If the Liberals had introduced back-to-work legislation, the doctors could have ended their strike with a sense of pride. But the Liberal strategists knew that back-to-work legislation would have been a mistake. It would have extended the dispute, allowing a few militant doctors to become martyrs in jail. The Liberals knew that the doctors would eventually return to their offices voluntarily.

Even in the waning days of the strike, patients shouldered the burden of the OMA's crusade. In Ottawa an 80-year-old woman who had suffered a broken ankle was forced to wait in an emergency department for more than four hours without being treated. As part of the strike, the doctors at the emergency department were restricting their services. The elderly woman was finally transferred by ambulance to another hospital, but by then she was experiencing an irregular heartbeat and she had to have a pacemaker implanted to stabilize her condition.

On July 2 about 700 doctors held a pep rally in downtown Toronto to boost their spirits. "We will not give in to these bastards," Dr. Brian Backman told the rally. About half of the doctors marched to Queen's Park for another demonstration. But once again there was evidence that the doctors had lost the sympathy of the public. Dozens of bystanders, who supported the ban on extra-billing, ended up in arguments with the doctors at the demonstration.

Two days later the OMA held a meeting to discuss further strategy. "I think the doctors will want to continue the strike," Dr. Myers told reporters before the meeting. "We're doing a great job putting pressure on the government." However, it was becoming obvious that the strike was collapsing. At the July 4 meeting, the OMA decided to end the strike.

It was the longest full-scale strike in the history of the Canadian medical profession. When it officially ended on July 7, the Ontario strike had lasted two days longer than the legendary 23-day Saskatchewan strike of 1962.

Although an estimated 50 per cent of Ontario's doctors took part in the strike, very few of them actually sacrificed their incomes during the dispute. A large number of the striking doctors were returning to their offices in the evenings or weekends to treat their patients. Medicare billings declined only 8 to 9 per cent in June.

The Aftermath

The strike of 1986 was not really about extra-billing. Only 12 per cent of Ontario's doctors — those who were opted out of medicare — were directly affected by Bill 94. At its core, the Ontario strike was a backlash against several decades of social change. Patients and governments had once been subservient to the medical profession. Today they are challenging the doctors on several fronts. Malpractice suits are increasing. Patients are joining the consumer movement. Midwives and nurses are becoming more assertive. Governments are realizing that the cost of health care must be controlled. Bureaucrats have a major role in decisions about the supply of hospital beds and medical equipment. In some provinces, doctors no longer enjoy automatic access to medicare payments if they locate in regions with a surplus of doctors. For the Ontario physicians, Bill 94 was just a symbol of these new challenges. It was the final insult to the ego of the profession. The doctors struck back blindly. The strike was a chance to vent their frustration. It was a futile attempt to return to the golden age of medicine, when doctors had complete control of their working conditions.

To a large extent, the failure of the Ontario strike was due to the OMA's lack of expertise in public relations. After decades of success with the provincial Conservative government, the medical association had lost the ability to read the public mood. The doctors simply assumed that the public would rally to their side. They did not even bother to leave themselves a fall-back position in case the strike failed.

Jurij Bilyk, a Toronto public-relations consultant, has noted that doctors are unaccustomed to compromise in their daily routines. They prescribe a treatment and the patient complies. They transferred this attitude to the political arena, with disastrous results. The patients rebelled. An opinion poll by Goldfarb Consultants found that 55 per cent of Ontario residents believed that the doctors were more concerned with how Bill 94 would affect their incomes than with its impact on health care. About 70 per cent blamed the doctors, not the government, for the strike. "Up until the time they started closing things down, they had a lot of public sympathy," Bilyk said. "As soon as they started closing things down, they were dead meat."

To make matters worse, the OMA could not control the most militant elements of its membership. The medical association knew that the wild-eyed lunatic fringe of the profession was damaging the OMA's public image by making outrageous statements to the media, but the leaders could not prevent it. "I couldn't shut anybody up," Dr. Myers said later. He recalled one doctor who was particularly volatile: "I begged him not to say anything. But he thought he was doing great. He was on an ego trip." Dr. Irvin Wolkoff said the OMA failed to train its membership properly: "The doctors weren't prepared, so doctors popped off, saying stupid things."

With a sense of horror, the doctors eventually realized their blunder. Dr. Jim Rodgerson said the strike "makes us look like evil monsters." Dr. Kenneth Axmith said the strike allowed doctors to be portrayed "like a bunch of animals." This realization was crippling to doctors. They enjoy the prestige of their profession. Public esteem and high social status are crucial to their reward system. "Doctors, probably more than most other groups, have a need for approval," Dr. Moran acknowledged after the strike. Unable to tolerate any further decline in their public image, the doctors lost their will to continue the strike.

There were other reasons for the failure of the strike. The firm stand of the Liberals was a major factor. The strong warnings from the Ontario College of Physicians and Surgeons were another. The Medical Reform Group helped to stiffen resistance to the striking doctors. The MRG argued that the leadership of the medical association was out of touch with its membership. The reform group called for a strike vote to see whether Ontario's doctors really supported the OMA leaders. The medical association wanted the media to ignore the dissident doctors, but the media consistently presented both sides of the debate. Eventually the striking doctors became so frustrated they urged their colleagues to boycott the *Toronto Star* and the *Globe and Mail*.

The strike probably had a built-in deadline. Doctors could postpone their patients' appointments for two or three weeks, but eventually the patients had to be seen — if their health was to be preserved. If the strike continued past the three-week point, patients — out of anger or frustration — might abandon their doctors permanently. Since the incomes of the doctors depended on their regular patients, they were reluctant to lose these regular clients. For this reason, it was inevitable that the strike would collapse after a few weeks.

Some of the OMA leaders speculated privately about a different action: a short, sharp and complete withdrawal of services. This was the so-called Japan option. Doctors in Japan had once gone on a complete strike — refusing to provide even emergency services. The strike lasted only a few hours before the government surrendered. But this could not have succeeded in Ontario. Only a few hard-core extremists in the medical profession would have supported a complete withdrawal.

The Ontario strike was doomed to failure. But in a deeper sense, the doctors did not suffer a significant loss. Their defeat was merely symbolic. Despite their loud complaints, the Ontario doctors were able to maintain their incomes and virtually all their traditional powers. Bill 94 was an irritation for the doctors, but it did not alter the fundamental powers of the medical profession.

First, let us consider the incomes of Ontario doctors. The ban on extra-billing was, in effect, a theoretical ban. It could not be enforced unless a patient complained to the province. Doctors were free to continue extra-billing if their patients agreed to pay the extra charge. Many prosperous patients enjoy the feeling of paying extra for certain medical services — it convinces them that they are obtaining better medical care. Traditionally, wealthy patients represented a large portion of the extra-billed patients (although low-income patients were also frequently extra-billed). By increasing their extra charges to wealthy patients who accepted the practice, doctors could avoid any significant loss of income after Bill 94 was approved.

In addition, a host of medical services fall outside the medicare plan, and doctors are free to charge whatever they want for these. After the passage of Bill 94, many patients faced the sudden introduction of "administration fees" at their doctor's office. Some general practitioners, for example, announced a new annual fee of $50 or $100 per patient. They argued that it was a "retainer" to help pay for expensive operating costs. Other doctors charged $10 or $25 for writing a referral letter or for completing medicare forms. Others charged a "booking fee" for making an appointment for a patient. Obstetricians charged a "stand-by fee" for making themselves available to pregnant women outside office hours. In some cases, the stand-by fees were as much as $500 per patient. Women who needed abortions were occasionally asked to pay as much as $200 to doctors who applied to a hospital abortion committee on their behalf.

As a result of the administration fees, some patients ended up paying more extra charges after Bill 94 was approved than they had paid before the legislation. For other patients, the extra charges were equal to the amount they used to be extra-billed. This was particularly true in specialties such as psychiatry and obstetrics, where patients are often vulnerable. Some psychiatrists began to charge 35 per cent extra for each session. Different psychiatrists found different ways to justify the extra charges. "In psychiatry, nothing much has changed," a Toronto psychiatrist said in a newspaper interview. "Most patients who paid extra before are paying the same amount now, only it is not called extra-billing. It is called an administrative fee."

What about the power of doctors? Did it suffer any significant decline as a result of the strike's failure? The strike itself was strong evidence of the clout of the medical profession. No other occupational group could have commanded as much publicity as the doctors did in their 25-day walkout. No other occupational group could have seized the front-page headlines for several weeks, while insisting on lengthy meetings with the premier and his top cabinet ministers. Indeed, no other occupational group has the legal right to strike in Ontario's hospitals. Other hospital employees have been jailed, suspended and fined for striking in Ontario.

More important, the strike helped the doctors win a guarantee of their freedom from future government action. As mentioned earlier, at several points during the dispute the Liberal government offered to give the doctors a bill of rights to guarantee their freedom to locate wherever they want and to provide as many medical services as they want. In the heat of the dispute, the OMA refused to discuss these issues, but the Liberals cannot pretend the offer wasn't made. Politically, it will be almost impossible for the Liberals to restrict the freedoms they had offered to guarantee. In effect, the Liberals have ruled out the kinds of government actions essential for controlling health costs in Ontario. The governments of Quebec and British Columbia have begun to regulate the supply of doctors in their provinces because doctor surpluses are contributing to the growing number of unnecessary medical services and are thus driving up the cost of health care. The surplus of physicians is just as serious a problem in Ontario, yet the strike of 1986 has forced the Liberals to agree to surrender most of their strongest weapons for controlling the surplus.

Finally, the Ontario doctors still enjoy the ability to socialize with the most senior members of the provincial government. In early 1987, just as the OMA was beginning its negotiations with the government for a new agreement on medical fees, Premier David Peterson and his wife attended a gala ballet performance as the guests of Dr. Hugh Scully, the OMA's chief negotiator. It was the kind of cozy cronyism that marked the traditional relationship between the OMA and the provincial Conservatives. It was almost as if the strike had never taken place.

CHAPTER 3

TWO CENTURIES OF ACTIVISM

In the late 1770s and early 1780s, the young colony of Quebec was gripped by an epidemic of syphilis. An estimated 3,000 to 4,000 people (about 3 per cent of the population) were suffering from the incurable disease. But as they rushed from victim to victim, the physicians of Quebec had something else on their minds. They were engaged in a lobbying campaign. The physicians were putting pressure on the colonial government to introduce legislation to ensure that every medical practitioner was licensed and certified. The public, they said, needed protection from unqualified practitioners: the horrors of syphilis would only be worsened by the dangerous practices of poorly trained men.

Meanwhile, the physicians were faithfully applying their orthodox treatment for syphilis. This consisted chiefly of massive doses of corrosive sublimate (mercuric chloride), washed down by an infusion of mallow, barley or rice. There was one problem with this treatment: there was a strong probability that it would cause mercury poisoning and death.

Not surprisingly, the mortality rate from syphilis remained high in Quebec. The physicians pointed with alarm to the high death rate. It was proof, they argued, of the need for better regulations to suppress the quacks and illiterates who attempted to practise medicine. And so, in 1788, the colonial government approved legislation to prohibit anyone from practising medicine without a licence from the governor. Physicians would only be granted licences if they passed examinations testing their knowledge of medicine — including, presumably, their knowledge of the orthodox treatment for syphilis. Violations of this legislation were punishable by fines or prison sentences.

The British colonial rulers, who had conquered Canada in 1759, had never previously attempted to restrict the supply of medical practitioners in their northern colony. But the legislation of 1788 would soon be followed by a long series of restrictive measures in the 18th and 19th centuries. Licensing boards were established, governing bodies were created, and the medical trade was transformed into a self-regulating profession. In every case, the physicians justified the strict regulations by arguing that the public needed protection from quacks and charlatans. This indeed sounded like a noble goal. Yet in the late 18th century (and for much of the 19th century) there was very little difference between quacks and regular physicians. Both were capable of jeopardizing the health of their patients. The syphilis treatment was merely one example of the hazards of falling into the hands of an orthodox physician. Another example: physicians often prescribed large doses of calomel as a treatment for sick children. In many cases, the children died of overdoses of this toxic substance. A third example: physicians routinely administered a variety of mineral poisons to "cleanse" the patient's stomach and bowels. They also gave arsenical compounds to their patients, and they frequently used lancets to perform blood-letting treatments. Clearly, the public interest did not require these early physicians to be given a monopoly over medical services. There was no evidence that they were markedly superior to their unlicensed rivals. The restrictive legislation simply protected physicians from competition and increased their incomes.

Ronald Hamowy, a historian at the University of Alberta, has documented the lengthy list of barriers erected to prevent outsiders from competing with physicians. From 1832 to 1837, for example, 14 people who applied for medical licences were rejected by the Medical Board of Upper Canada because they were judged to have an insufficient knowledge of Latin — a language unnecessary for medical practices in this period.

Canada's physicians also succeeded in restricting the number of students who were permitted to study medicine. In the mid-19th century, Canadian medical schools were much stricter than American medical schools. The Canadian schools required a more extensive period of preliminary education before an applicant was permitted to enter medical studies. On top of that, a longer course of study was required before a student could graduate. As a result, only students from wealthy families could afford to enter a Canadian medical school.

In the period after Confederation, medical organizations fought to limit the number of medical schools and medical students in Canada.

"It would be a great boon to the country if not another student passed for ten years to come," a representative of the Ontario Medical Council remarked in 1869. The Canadian Medical Association's president, Dr. Michael Sullivan, argued in 1884 that Canada was burdened with "four times too many" medical schools.

The physicians were remarkably effective in their campaign to limit the supply of new entrants to the medical profession. In Ontario no new medical schools were established during the entire period from 1881 to 1945. There were far fewer medical schools per capita in Canada than there were in the United States in the 19th and early 20th centuries. In 1870 Canada had only six medical schools, while the United States had more than 400 in the same year. By 1888 there were 13 medical schools in Canada — but the number dropped to eight in 1909. As late as 1950, there were just nine medical schools in the country.

In their petitions for legislation to restrict unlicensed competitors, the physicians often acknowledged that their goal was to increase their personal status and income. This target was explicitly stated in 1846, for example, when the Toronto Medico-Chirurgical Society petitioned for legislation that would establish a new governing body to license doctors. (The governing body was eventually created in 1865.) The physicians complained that their incomes were weakened by competition from unlicensed practitioners. In their petition the physicians argued that "no sufficient inducement is held out to young men of talent to adopt a profession in which there is so slight a prospect of obtaining an adequate return for the necessary, laborious, and expensive study required."

In 1893 a Canadian medical journal, the *Canada Medical Record*, openly admitted the connection between medical incomes and the profession's efforts to raise educational standards: "As we have often said, each Province or State should see that its own professional men are not subjected by overcrowding to too keen a struggle for existence." The journal advised the Quebec Medical Board to "limit the number of practitioners by raising the standard of candidates who are about to begin the study of Medicine."

Meanwhile, the Ontario Medical Council obtained a regulation in 1891 to toughen the requirements for candidates who wanted to enter medical school. "It may be urged against the new Ontario regulation that it will make it increasingly difficult for the poor man or the poor man's son to become a doctor, but we are not aware that poor men or poor men's sons make better doctors than the rich men or the rich men's sons," the *Maritime Medical News* wrote in defence of the regulation.

Despite the loud complaints from the physicians, there was no evidence of overcrowding in Canada's medical profession in this period. Indeed, the restrictions on the supply of competitors had allowed the income of the average physician to reach a comfortable level by the second half of the 19th century. In 1885, for example, the physicians of Toronto enjoyed a median income of between $1,200 and $1,600 per year. Their income was two and a half to three times as high as the average carpenter or plumber in Ontario. Economist Malcolm Brown of the University of Calgary has found some evidence that the average Canadian doctor was earning considerably more than the average American doctor in the 19th century. Since there were many more medical schools per capita in the United States, the supply of doctors was greater and the competition among them sufficient to keep their incomes below the level of Canadian medical incomes.

Yet the Canadian physicians continued to put pressure on medical schools in the 1890s. Again the physicians called for stricter standards — and again their public statements made it clear that their primary motive was to protect their incomes, not to protect the public. The *Canada Medical Record* argued that "it is the first duty of the profession to protect itself against the disastrous competition which the schools would inflict upon it if the latter were not under state control; the only machinery the profession has at present for this purpose is the Provincial Medical Boards, which have the power of saying how crowded they will allow its ranks to become." In another article, the *Medical Record* urged the provincial medical councils to "either raise the license fees or raise the standard of the entrance examinations in order to keep down the number of practitioners to 1 per 1,000 of inhabitants."

Dr. Alexander Sangster, a member of the Ontario Medical Council, echoed this opinion in 1895: "The profession is overcrowded in Ontario, and unless drastic measures are taken immediately the profession will be brought into disrepute, and will soon be ruined. The greater majority of members of the profession in Ontario are not more than making a bare living at the present time, while year after year hundreds of young men are being turned loose as full fledged medical men. Something has to be done." Dr. Sangster persuaded the Ontario Medical Council to raise its education requirements once again. As a result, the number of medical graduates in Ontario actually decreased from 1888 to 1910, even though the province's population grew by almost 500,000 people in this period. Similar requirements were adopted in Quebec, and the number of medical graduates there declined steadily from 1901 to 1916.

Even in the sparsely populated Prairie territories, where only a handful of doctors were working, the medical profession strove to limit the supply of competitors. In the North-West Territories (part of which were to be divided into present-day Alberta and Saskatchewan), the registrar of the college of physicians and surgeons complained that the marking of licensing examinations was not strict enough. The registrar, Dr. J. D. Lafferty, clearly believed that the strictness of the examinations should depend on the economics of the profession. In his report of 1903, Dr. Lafferty said: "Reverting again to the supply of medical men being greatly in excess of the demand, I would ask the opinion of the (Medical) Council if it would not be wise to issue a circular to examiners to be careful in the preparation of their papers and to exercise their best judgment in marking them." He added: "I think the marking has been too generous in many instances."

Restrictions on Female Doctors

The medical profession was particularly alarmed at the prospect of competition from women doctors. Female students had begun to gain entry to Canadian universities by the 1850s, and soon the medical schools were receiving applications from women. Clearly, the entry of a significant number of women would inflate the supply of doctors and jeopardize medical incomes. Moreover, most physicians simply did not believe women could cope with the demands of medicine. For all these reasons, the profession fought strongly to prevent the emergence of women doctors.

From 1870 to the end of the 19th century, medical journals in Canada argued that women should not enter the medical profession. The journals urged female students to "devote their energies to that to which they are so much suited . . . bearing children and nursing children."

Dr. Francis Wayland Campbell, dean of medicine at the University of Bishop's College in Quebec, made this comment about female doctors in 1889: "They may be useful in some departments of medicine, but in difficult work, in surgery, for instance, they would not have the nerve. And can you think of a patient in a critical case, waiting for half an hour while the medical lady fixes her bonnet or adjusts her bustle?"

From the 1860s until the 1880s, Canadian women were generally required to travel to the United States if they wanted to enter a medical school. Canadian medical colleges simply refused to admit them. When a half-dozen women were finally admitted to the medical school at Queen's University in 1880, the male students threatened to transfer immediately to another university. The faculty agreed to establish a completely separate medical school for the women. (This school closed in 1894.) Special medical schools for Canadian women were created at several other universities from 1883 to 1893, deliberately kept separate from the traditional medical school at each university.

Even after graduating, the women found that many hospitals refused to allow them to serve internships or residencies. In some cases, male doctors refused to consult with female physicians. Licensing bodies often made it difficult for qualified women graduates to obtain medical licences. In the early 20th century, several Canadian medical schools continued to reject all female applicants. Queen's University, for example, would not allow any women to enter its medical school from 1894 to 1943. Other medical schools set quotas to limit the number of female students.

Because of widespread discrimination, women had to endure great hardships in order to enter the medical profession. Canada's first woman doctor was forced to pose as a man for 46 years. Her true name is unknown, but she called herself James Barry. She rose to become the chief military doctor in Canada in the 1850s. She was also the supervisor of hospitals in Kingston, Montreal, Quebec and Toronto. Her secret was not discovered until her death in 1865. Nobody is certain of the details of her early life, but historians believe that she had to pose as a man to enter medical school in Edinburgh in the early years of the 19th century. "It was the only way she could become a doctor," one historian concluded.

Another early pioneer was Dr. Emily Stowe, who was born in 1831 in a small town in Upper Canada. The University of Toronto refused to let her study medicine, so she entered a medical college in New York. She graduated and returned to Canada in 1867, but the provincial licensing body would not give her a licence. The licensing agency insisted that Dr. Stowe had to attend a session of lectures at a medical school in Ontario — but women were not permitted to enter medical schools in Ontario. She was thwarted by a classic Catch-22. Nevertheless, for nearly five years she persistently applied to medical schools in Ontario. She was finally accepted by the Toronto School of Medicine in the mid-1870s. Although harassed by faculty and students, she completed the required session of lectures. Even then, the licensing body refused to issue a licence to Dr. Stowe. She was eventually given one in 1880 — fully 13 years after she graduated from medical school.

As late as 1941 only 3.7 per cent of Canada's doctors were women. However, it is estimated that by the late 1980s and early 1990s, 43 per cent of Canadian medical school graduates will be women.

Price Fixing

By the early 20th century, Canada's physicians had erected an effective series of barriers to deter potential competitors from entering the medical profession. After decades of lobbying and agitating, a complicated process of medical licensing had been established and strict educational requirements were enforced. Largely because of these barriers, medical services were more difficult to obtain in Canada than in the United States. In 1891 there was one doctor for every 1,087 Canadians, while in the United States the ratio was one doctor for every 629 Americans. In other words, the average Canadian doctor enjoyed almost twice as many potential patients as the average American doctor. The supply of doctors increased only slightly in Canada in the first half of the 20th century. By 1951 there was one doctor for every 977 Canadians, compared to a ratio of one doctor for every 751 people in the United States.

At the same time, the Canadian medical profession was successful in reducing the amount of price competition among physicians. This was accomplished largely by setting a fixed fee schedule and by prohibiting doctors from advertising. The code of ethics of the Canadian Medical Association, as approved in 1868, required all physicians to follow their local fee schedule and to refrain from advertising.

In addition, the medical profession put a damper on price competition by discouraging hospitals from providing free care to charity cases. "Whether for clinical material or for any other reason, no hospital has the right to do anything that would cheat a member of the profession out of a fee," the *Canada Lancet* editorialized in 1905. The medical profession also campaigned to restrict the activities of provincial public health clinics, which competed with private doctors. In Alberta, for instance, physicians put up a strong resistance to the travelling government clinics that provided medical care in rural regions of the province.

In another move to reduce the amount of price competition in Canada, the medical profession discouraged its members from accepting contracts with groups of patients who offered lump-sum payments in return for guaranteed medical services. These contracts, known as "lodge" or "club" practices, were an early form of private insurance for patients. For example, a group of 200 patients (probably belonging to a fraternal order or a benevolent society) might each pay $1.25 to a doctor who agreed to cover their medical needs. The doctor would therefore receive an annual payment of $250 from this group of patients, regardless of the amount of services provided. When the lodge contracts became widespread in the 1890s, physicians did their utmost to dissuade their colleagues from joining a lodge practice. Medical journals said the lodge doctors were accepting "cut-rate" fees for their services. "In this class of practice . . . fees are cut down to the merest pittance," the *Canada Lancet* complained in 1891. The *Montreal Medical Journal* said the lodge contracts were "degrading both to the medical man and to his profession." The *Canadian Medical Review* alleged that the lodge doctor "gives away his independence, and has to hob-nob with those who are his inferiors in every way in order to retain his hold on the lodge." One physician maintained that "a vampire never bled its prey more effectively than do the lodgers their medical attendants."

In 1894 the Ontario Medical Association condemned the lodge contracts as a violation of the medical profession's code of ethics. It urged the Ontario Medical Council to discipline any doctor who engaged in lodge practices. The OMA's president in 1898, Dr. William Britton, described the lodge contracts as "a rotten plank in the platform of gentlemanly dignity and independence." In some Ontario towns the local doctors collectively decided to refuse to work for the lodges. Similarly, the members of the Vancouver Medical Association signed an agreement in 1895 in which they vowed to abstain from lodge practices. Five years later the Victoria Medical Society decided to prohibit its members from participating in contracts with lodges. (One member of the medical society wanted the Victoria doctors to refuse to provide any medical services to lodge members.) Two physicians were expelled from the Victoria Medical Society in 1900 because they participated in lodge contracts.

The campaign was effective. The lodge contracts reached their peak in the 1890s and declined in the following decades. By the First World War, lodge contracts had essentially disappeared in Canada, largely because physicians were worried about the threat of disciplinary action.

After the war, some doctors accepted contracts with communities of miners and lumbermen in remote areas of Canada. The contracts specified that the doctors would work on salary. The leaders of organized medicine disliked the contracts and were alarmed at the notion of doctors working for a salary. In 1922 the Alberta College of Physicians and Surgeons added a new clause to its code of ethics to discourage these contracts. Two years later the college sent a letter to all of its members urging them to reject any offer of contract practice.

Throughout the late 19th and early 20th centuries, physicians were expanding the definition of medicine to squeeze out their competitors. They were particularly keen to suppress the osteopaths and chiropractors, who were constant challengers to the medical monopoly. The code of ethics of the Canadian Medical Association, adopted in 1868, prohibited doctors from participating in any consultations with these rival practitioners. In the 1890s, chiropractors were prosecuted and convicted by the provincial colleges of physicians and surgeons.

In 1925 physicians persuaded the Ontario government to approve the Drugless Practitioners Act, prohibiting osteopaths and chiropractors from issuing prescriptions, treating patients in public hospitals or gaining access to provincial laboratories. At the same time the Manitoba medical profession maintained a lobbying committee to oppose the legalization of chiropractors and osteopaths on the grounds that they were "cults" and "irregular practices." This lobbying process has been candidly described by Dr. Gordon S. Fahrni, an eminent surgeon who practised in Manitoba in the early and middle decades of this century: "Each year some group of irregular practitioners would sponsor a bill for legal recognition and bring it up before the provincial legislature. It was the committee's job to see that the MLAs [the members of the legislature] were informed on the subject. Year after year the bill or bills were defeated and it was not until World War Two that the committee ceased to function."

Interestingly, while the Manitoba doctors denounced their competitors as cultists, their belief in science was apparently suspended when they learned that the president of the Manitoba Medical Association, Dr. T. G. Hamilton, was engaging in psychic research and seances at his home in Winnipeg. According to the official history of the Manitoba medical profession, Dr. Hamilton "carried on experiments with mediums" and provided demonstrations of "levitation, trance manifestations, teleplasm and telekinesis." These experiments continued for 13 years, from 1922 to 1935. Rather than accusing Dr. Hamilton of cultism, the physicians elected him to the executive of the Canadian Medical Association.

The Beginnings of the Golden Age

By the early 1920s, Canada's doctors had emerged victorious in most of their major political and economic battles. The period from the early 1920s to the late 1960s has been described as "the golden age of medicine" in Canada. Malcolm Brown explains the reasons for this: "Medical technology had improved to the extent that medical practitioners really could alleviate many health care problems. The general public was aware of this and bestowed on the physician a social status which he had never had before. Economically, the profession was not only able to limit entry into its ranks, but it was able to press for social capital, like hospitals, which would increase medical incomes, without appearing greedy and in opposition to the public interest."

The income of the average Canadian physician in the 1920s was considerable. A survey of 500 Ontario physicians in the last half of the 1920s found that their average gross income was $6,262. General practitioners in Winnipeg had an average gross income of $6,523, while that of specialists in the same city was $11,368. A survey of doctors in British Columbia in 1923 showed an average gross income of $6,575. About 30 per cent of these incomes had to be deducted to pay for overhead expenses, but even after deductions the average Canadian doctor had an income four times as high as the average industrial wage earner, whose average income in 1928 was $1,024.

In the Great Depression of the 1930s, the incomes of doctors fell sharply. Many of their patients were simply unable to pay their bills. According to one estimate, medical incomes dropped by 40 to 60 per cent from 1929 to 1932. This still left doctors with above-average incomes, but they began to lobby for government aid. They wanted the local governments to pay the medical bills of unemployed patients who could not afford the cost. In Vancouver the city's medical association recommended the closure of the out-patient department of Vancouver's general hospital because the association felt too many patients were seeking free medical care in the department. On August 1, 1933, every doctor in Vancouver signed an agreement to refuse to work in the out-patient department unless the patient needed emergency treatment or had been referred to a specialist for treatment. The doctors also threatened to launch a full-scale strike against relief recipients. In December 1933 the city finally caved in and accepted the medical profession's demands for a medical relief plan that would provide payment to doctors who treated the unemployed.

Doctors in Winnipeg demanded the same kind of medical relief plan in 1933. When the city was slow to introduce a plan, the dispute turned into the first doctors' strike in Canadian history.

The Winnipeg doctors took the first step towards a strike in March 1933 when the medical staff at every civic hospital in Winnipeg authorized their leaders to organize a boycott of all patients on unemployment relief except in cases of emergency or where the patient had been referred by another doctor. All but three of the 132 hospital staff doctors in Winnipeg signed a document to confirm that they would participate in this boycott when it was called.

After fruitless negotiations with the city, the doctors proceeded with their preparations for a full-scale strike. The Manitoba Medical Association warned its members that the municipality might attempt to hire physicians to provide medical care for relief recipients. Any physician who agreed to work for the municipality was liable to receive an "unfortunate repercussion in his relations with his professional colleagues in later years," the medical association said in a bulletin to its members. Essentially, this meant that a doctor who broke the boycott could expect to receive no referrals from other doctors after the strike had ended.

The strike began in July 1933. For eight months, the Winnipeg doctors refused to provide any medical services to the recipients of unemployment relief unless it was an emergency or unless the patient had previously belonged to the doctor's paying practice. The withdrawal of services affected more than 50,000 relief recipients in the city. The doctors ignored the code of ethics of the Canadian Medical Association, which required them to provide medical care "cheerfully and freely" to any indigent patient. (The CMA revised its code of ethics in 1936–37 to lessen the obligations of doctors towards low-income patients.) Five of the city's six hospitals cooperated with the striking doctors. In these hospitals, relief recipients were turned away unless they needed emergency care. In some cases, relief recipients spent all day searching for a doctor or a hospital to treat them.

Unlike the situation in Ontario in 1986, the general public tended to sympathize with the Winnipeg doctors and there was no organized opposition to their strike. The doctors cultivated a good relationship with the unions and associations representing the unemployed. The relief recipients tended to blame the city for failing to bow to the demands of the doctors. Some of the unemployed workers held parades to demonstrate support for a medical relief plan. In one case, the Winnipeg police resorted to tear gas to disperse the demonstrators.

In late July the doctors escalated their strike by deciding that sexually transmitted diseases would not be classified as emergency cases. In October the doctors began to put pressure on Victoria Hospital, the only hospital providing medical care to relief recipients. Eleven of the hospital's 15 medical consultants threatened to quit, and in early November they carried through their threat and resigned.

Late in the autumn of 1933, the Winnipeg doctors were convinced that the city would soon be forced to capitulate. "It is probable that the normal increase of illnesses during the winter will force the issue," said Dr. Ernest Moorhead, chairman of the strike committee. In January 1934 the strike action was escalated again. About 150 doctors pledged to refuse to provide free medical service for any patient unless the patient's life was in "imminent danger." Even a woman in labour would only be considered an emergency case if there was an immediate risk of death.

Within five days of this threat, the city surrendered. City council agreed to provide exactly the kind of medical relief plan the doctors were demanding. Some suburban municipalities did not approve a medical relief plan immediately, and there the doctors went ahead with their threat to withdraw all free medical care except for life-threatening cases. More than 10,000 relief recipients in the outlying municipalities were affected. Within two weeks of this action, the suburbs agreed to provide a medical relief plan.

Health Insurance

In British Columbia the severe effects of the Depression prompted the B.C. Medical Association to endorse the idea of a provincial health-insurance plan. The BCMA came out in support of health insurance in the early 1930s, and in 1932 a provincial royal commission made the same recommendation. By 1933 the Vancouver Medical Association was strongly urging the province to introduce a system of public health insurance. And in 1934 the Canadian Medical Association added its voice to the chorus of medical organizations seeking a public health insurance system. Accordingly, B.C.'s Liberal government introduced a bill in the provincial legislature in 1935 to establish a health-insurance plan. If adopted, it would have been the first provincial health-insurance plan in Canada.

But suddenly the doctors began to have second thoughts. Even though the government's proposal was almost identical to the plan recommended by the CMA, the doctors in B.C. decided that the proposed legislation failed to give them enough economic protection. The British Columbia College of Physicians and Surgeons, negotiating on behalf of the province's medical profession, demanded that the legislation be amended to reduce the number of people covered by health insurance. The college did not want the higher-earning patients to be covered by health insurance, since the doctors wanted to bill these patients directly. The college also insisted that the government should establish a reserve fund to guarantee all payments to doctors. In addition, the college opposed a provision that would give doctors only half-payment for medical services to the indigent. (The Winnipeg doctors, by contrast, had settled for half-payment from the municipality for relief recipients.) And finally, the college wanted the legislation to guarantee that doctors could send the insurance plan a separate bill for every medical service they provided.

Early in 1936 the Liberal government revised the health-insurance legislation. The government made two major concessions to the doctors: it reduced the number of high-income people to be covered by the insurance plan, and it increased the maximum level of payments to physicians for each patient in the plan. Because of the government's concerns about the cost of the health-insurance plan, the legislation was further amended to eliminate any coverage of indigent patients.

The college of physicians and surgeons remained unhappy with the legislation. It contacted every doctor in the province, urging each one to send telegrams of protest to the premier. The college recruited the assistance of the CMA, which held a meeting with the provincial cabinet to argue against the legislation. The CMA was also reported to have established a $10,000 lobbying fund to help the B.C. doctors. Two members of the Liberal caucus were physicians; both of them defied their premier and joined the medical profession's battle against the legislation.

The government amended the legislation again to sweeten the payments for doctors, and it was finally approved. The doctors, however, continued to fight the plan. An official of the BCMA toured the province to rally doctors against the government. The Vancouver Medical Association distributed a bulletin that included a letter from the college of physicians and surgeons urging its members to maintain a united front against the insurance plan. Early in 1937, more than 10 months after the provincial legislature had approved it, the plan was still not in operation.

In its opposition to the insurance plan, the doctors frequently cited the lack of coverage for indigents. But in January 1937, when the doctors met the government to discuss the plan, they emphasized their demands for improvements in the level of payments for doctors. Shortly after this meeting, an overwhelming majority of the doctors in Vancouver and Victoria voted to refuse to participate in the insurance plan. In effect, they were threatening to launch a strike if the plan was introduced.

Meanwhile, the BCMA recruited the support of several hundred businessmen and professionals. The Vancouver Board of Trade joined the doctors in a protest meeting. In an effort to unite the profession, the college of physicians and surgeons organized a plebiscite among the province's doctors. Every doctor received a ballot, along with a letter from the college stating that "our struggle is not yet over, and will only be settled satisfactorily by the absolute solidarity of the profession." When the ballots were counted, the doctors had rejected the insurance plan by a vote of 622 to 13.

In June 1937 a provincial election was held. The election included a referendum on health insurance. The Liberals were re-elected, and health insurance was supported by 59 per cent of the voters. But the battle was over. The government made no attempt to introduce another health-insurance proposal.

While the opposition from the business community was a factor in the government's decision to abandon the insurance plan, "the pivotal factor was organized medicine's rejection of the government plan," medical historian C. D. Naylor has concluded. "The pressure-group strategies used by the B.C. profession were numerous and surprisingly successful."

According to Naylor's analysis, the government's proposal was unacceptable to the doctors because it failed to provide "income maximization" for the medical profession. The doctors wanted to receive insured payments for low-income patients, but they also wanted to be free to charge higher fees to wealthier patients. Moreover, they wanted a guaranteed fee-for-service system so that their incomes would rise as the demand for medical services increased. Because the government did not accept these demands, the doctors defeated the proposed system.

At the national level there was close cooperation between the federal government and the medical profession for most of the 20th century. Physicians dominated the federal health department, which was established in 1919. The key officials of this department were members of the medical profession, and the department consulted Canada's physicians on every major decision. Under the constitution of the Canadian Medical Association, the deputy minister of health was automatically a member of the CMA General Council. This ensured a close link between the CMA and the health department. "It is obvious from studying the records of this department that privately or publicly employed members of the medical profession were in charge of deciding what was best for the health of Canadians," historian Janice McGinnis has written.

Federal politicians believed that the medical profession had a special status in Canada. In the 1920s and 1930s, for example, a number of members of Parliament argued that physicians should not be prosecuted for narcotics offences. From 1929 to 1941 the federal Narcotics Division agreed to withdraw narcotics charges against an estimated 120 doctors after the doctors promised to "take a cure." This option was not available to ordinary Canadians.

Given the medical profession's special status, it is not surprising that the CMA was intimately involved with the federal government's first major study of health insurance in the early 1940s. The drafting of federal legislation is usually a confidential process, but a committee of the CMA was permitted to participate in the drafting of the first proposed health-insurance legislation. In 1941 the federal director of public health acknowledged that the legislation was "revised to meet the views of the Canadian Medical Association." Federal officials regarded the CMA committee as "the parent committee."

By 1944 the draft legislation was still under study in Ottawa. The CMA was gradually becoming ambivalent about public health insurance. Its earlier strong support had primarily been a result of the Depression. By the mid-1940s, when medical incomes were returning to their previous high levels, physicians became less enthusiastic about health insurance.

The *CMA Journal* began to publish commentaries critical of the idea of public health insurance. One letter to the journal in 1944, from Dr. M. G. Burris, stated: "The philosophy of the proposal is as plain an example of National Socialism and State Control as one could imagine or desire."

Dr. Harris McPhedran, president of the CMA in 1944, criticized the "Utopians" and "blueprinters" who were pushing for a medicare program. "We do not want the practice of medicine to be completely state-controlled," he said.

Meanwhile, the federal government was unable to obtain a health-insurance agreement with the provinces. Health insurance was quietly shelved.

Canada's physicians soon realized that they preferred a system of voluntary health insurance directly controlled by medical associations. Voluntary plans, under the sponsorship of the medical profession, sprung up in several provinces. Medical leaders openly acknowledged that these voluntary plans were designed to reduce the pressure for a public system of health insurance. By the late 1940s and early 1950s, the medical associations were campaigning fiercely against the idea of public health insurance. They called it "socialized medicine" and warned that it would mean "a crushing burden on the taxpayer" and "inferior medical service." They described it as "enforced subservience to either the false god of paternalism or to the equally dangerous one of bureaucratic power." The new stance of the medical profession was a remarkable turnaround from the CMA position of 1934.

Despite strong opposition from doctors, the vast majority of Canadians favoured a system of public health insurance. Opinion polls from the 1940s to the 1960s consistently showed that 60 to 80 per cent of Canadians wanted a comprehensive health-insurance plan. It was inevitable, then, that some government would eventually respond to the voters. Yet it was personal experience, as well as the opinion polls, that motivated the pioneer of the first provincial medicare plan in Canada.

In the early years of this century, a young Scottish boy named Tommy Douglas had fallen and injured his knee. He developed a bone disease which lingered for several years. After his family immigrated to Canada, the disease became worse. Tommy's father was an iron moulder, and his family could not afford a doctor. The boy was placed in the public ward of a Winnipeg hospital, where he was treated as a charity patient. The house doctor said that Tommy's leg would have to be amputated. But an orthopedic surgeon happened to be looking for patients for a teaching demonstration for medical students. Tommy was chosen, and the surgery prevented him from becoming a cripple.

"Had I been a rich man's son, the services of the finest surgeons would have been available," Douglas said later. "As an iron moulder's boy, I almost had my leg amputated before chance intervened and a specialist cured me without thought of a fee. All my adult life I have dreamed of the day when an experience like mine would be impossible and we would have in Canada a program of complete medical care without a price tag."

Tommy Douglas became the premier of Saskatchewan in 1944. His CCF (Co-operative Commonwealth Federation) government promised to introduce a system of comprehensive health insurance financed by taxes. Hospital insurance was established first, and then the CCF and its leader turned their attention to medicare. "I made a pledge with myself long before I ever sat in this house, in the years when I knew something about what it meant to get health services when you didn't have the money to pay for it," Douglas said in the Saskatchewan legislature in 1954. "I made a pledge with myself that some day if I ever had anything to do with it, people would be able to get health services just as they are able to get educational services, as an inalienable right of being a citizen of a Christian country."

The Saskatchewan Strike

In 1959 Tommy Douglas announced that his government was ready to introduce a medicare program that would cover the entire province. This set the stage for a bitter confrontation between the Saskatchewan doctors and the provincial government. It became the testing ground for the medical profession's resistance to comprehensive public health insurance. The doctors knew that medicare would spread across the country if it succeeded in Saskatchewan. They were determined to stop it.

The Saskatchewan College of Physicians and Surgeons, the official negotiating body for the province's doctors, began by refusing to participate in an advisory committee established in December 1959 to study medicare. Three months later, however, the college finally agreed to participate. Meanwhile, a provincial election was called for June 1960. Aware that medicare would be the major election issue, the college decided to organize its own campaign against medicare to coincide with the provincial election campaign.

The doctors gained the support of the Saskatchewan Chamber of Commerce and the Saskatchewan Liberal Party, both of which were fighting the CCF government. They also received $35,000 from the CMA, and the Ontario Medical Association contributed a public-relations expert who lobbied the politicians, spoke at meetings and talked to the news media on behalf of the Saskatchewan medical profession.

To raise funds for the battle, the college asked every doctor to pay a special levy of $100. At first the college denied that this was a compulsory levy, but within a few weeks the college's president, Dr. A. J. M. Davies, sent the doctors another bulletin, making it clear that the $100 levy was "not a voluntary assessment." The college received money from 600 of the province's 900 physicians. Combined with the contribution from the CMA, this gave the college a total fund of $95,000.

The doctors sent a summary of their position to every household in Saskatchewan. This summary included a dire warning from a prominent physician: if medicare was introduced, doctors would abandon the province and the government would "have to fill up the profession with the garbage of Europe." The college also sent publicity kits to most of its members. The publicity kits accused the government of following the precepts of Karl Marx. The college suggested that compulsory health insurance would be reminiscent of a time "when a minority group dictated its will upon the masses and used every means of cruelty known to men — the whip and the rod

— to make sure slaves toed the line." The college also warned that medicare was a threat to "certain dogmas and views of the Catholic Church relating to maternity, birth control, and the state."

Finally, the college gave its members a document entitled "Women and Their Personal Doctor" that was designed as a speech for doctors to deliver to female audiences. This speech was clearly intended to frighten women, stating, for example: "Many times we have sat down in our office with a woman and discussed emotional situations which crop up during pregnancy or other critical periods in a woman's life. We know that under Government administration we would be prevented from rendering these vital services. . . . During a woman's life, she is subjected to many disturbances which she does not understand. . . . It could very easily be that this type of condition under state medicine must be referred to a psychiatric clinic or a mental hospital, a situation which we, as your personal physician, would deplore." The speech concluded by warning that medicare "could mean the end of your personal Doctor."

Four days before the provincial election, 243 doctors placed an advertisement in the Saskatchewan daily newspapers arguing that medicare "would be a tragic mistake" for the province. "Compulsory state medicine has led to mediocrity and a poorer quality of care everywhere it has been put into practice," the advertisement said. The doctors vowed that they would refuse to work under any system that would "lead to a poorer type of medical care." However, the doctors also promised to "always attend the sick." This was a promise they would eventually break.

Tommy Douglas and the CCF were re-elected with an increased majority, and the physicians prepared for a continuation of the battle. The CMA sent another $44,000 to the Saskatchewan doctors and also added $2,000 to the budget of its economics department to help produce "information briefs" for the Saskatchewan dispute.

The provincial legislature approved the medicare legislation in November 1961. The medicare plan was scheduled to begin operating in April 1962. The government tried to meet the doctors to discuss the implementation of the plan, but the doctors refused to talk. The plan was postponed, and the government offered several concessions to the medical profession. These concessions were rejected, and the doctors organized an emergency meeting in Regina. Two-thirds of the province's doctors closed their offices for two days to attend the meeting. Premier Woodrow Lloyd (Tommy Douglas had resigned to enter federal politics) addressed the meeting, but he was jeered and booed. It became clear that a doctors' strike was a distinct possibility.

The depth of the medical profession's anger and hostility was manifested in letters to the provincial Medical Care Insurance Commission in early 1962. One doctor signed his letter: "Yours in bitter hatred." Another doctor said the Saskatchewan physicians were witnessing "the rape of their profession by politicians." A third said the medicare bill was "much in keeping with Russia or Cuba."

Meanwhile, the public was alarmed by the prospect of a strike. Many patients supported their doctors. With the assistance of the medical profession and the Liberal party, the patients formed "Keep Our Doctors" committees. The KOD committees held a rally at the provincial legislature and claimed to have 46,000 signatures on their petitions. The doctors told the local media that many physicians were leaving the province and relocating as far away as Texas. Another doctor asked the Saskatoon Board of Trade to warn tourists that it would be dangerous to come to Saskatchewan.

The strike began at 12:01 a.m. on July 1 when the medicare legislation officially came into effect. The doctors maintained emergency services at 34 of the province's 148 hospitals. Only about 35 of Saskatchewan's 900 doctors willingly worked under the medicare plan. On the first day of the strike, a nine-month-old infant died in his parents' car while the parents searched desperately for a doctor. The parents drove 85 miles in a futile search for a physician in three different towns. A coroner's jury later ruled that the baby's death could not have been prevented, but the death became a symbol of the strike.

In the second week of July, the KOD committees organized a huge rally at the provincial legislature. However, they were unable to gain as much support as they had hoped. They had predicted a crowd of 40,000, but only about 4,000 showed up. The strike began to lose momentum, and by July 10 some doctors were returning to work. To ensure that patients would receive medical care, the government recruited a total of 110 doctors from Britain, the United States and elsewhere in Canada.

The strike ended after 23 days. A British mediator helped the doctors reach an agreement with the government. The doctors agreed to work under medicare, but they obtained several concessions from the government. The biggest concession was a clause allowing extra-billing. Under this clause, the doctors were free to charge their patients more than the amount covered by medicare. The patients would then send a claim to the province, receive the amount covered by medicare and pay the balance themselves.

Though the doctors were unable to block the medicare plan, they inflicted serious damage on the CCF politicians. Tommy Douglas was defeated in the 1962 federal election, and the CCF lost the 1964 provincial election. Many historians believe that both defeats were partly the result of the uproar sparked by the medical profession's opposition to the medicare program.

As for the bleak prophecies of the Saskatchewan physicians, the passage of time quickly proved them wrong. The province lost 260 doctors by the end of 1963, but they were soon replaced by an influx of new physicians. By June 1964 the number of doctors in Saskatchewan had reached an all-time peak. The new Liberal government did not attempt to dismantle medicare, and the medical profession rapidly learned the advantages of the new insurance system. Doctors were now guaranteed payment for the medical services they provided to low-income patients. Because the financial barriers had been removed, more patients flocked to the waiting rooms of Saskatchewan doctors. The income of the average Saskatchewan doctor rose by 35 per cent in three years. In 1965 a survey found that 72 per cent of Saskatchewan's physicians were in favour of the medicare system.

In the other provinces, the medical profession continued to promote its voluntary insurance plans as an alternative to medicare. By the early 1960s one-quarter of the Canadian population were enrolled in voluntary plans sponsored or approved by medical organizations. A further one-quarter were enrolled in private insurance plans. Nevertheless, the federal government could sense a mounting pressure from voters for a comprehensive national system. In an effort to postpone the inevitable, the CMA in 1960 had convinced the federal government to establish a royal commission to study every aspect of medicare. The commission, finally delivering its report in 1964, recommended the creation of a national medicare program. In July 1966 a medicare bill was introduced in the House of Commons. Despite heavy lobbying and delaying tactics by doctors, the medicare bill was approved by the House of Commons in December 1966. The physicians did obtain one major concession: the right to extra-bill was enshrined in the federal legislation.

By the start of 1971 every province in Canada had adopted medicare. Just as in Saskatchewan, the medicare system has been a gold mine for the medical profession. In most regions of Canada the average doctor's income rose by 20 to 40 per cent within one year of the introduction of medicare. Under the new system, doctors became free to determine their own incomes by controlling the number of services provided to their patients. Unlike physicians of the 18th and 19th centuries, modern-day medicare doctors are not directly affected by the supply of physicians. A hundred years ago, each new physician was seen as a competitor by established physicians, and the medical profession had to limit the supply of doctors to avoid the practice of price-cutting among doctors. Today medicare has guaranteed the medical profession's fee schedule. Physicians can protect their incomes regardless of the supply of doctors. These issues will be explored further in the next chapter.

CHAPTER 4

YOUR MONEY OR YOUR LIFE: HOW DOCTORS CONTROL THEIR INCOMES

Robert Evans is a rumpled, mild-mannered professor who toils in a cluttered office at the University of British Columbia. His eyesight, severely damaged by a childhood bout of glaucoma, was partially repaired by a series of complex operations, but he still has to use a huge magnifying glass to peer at the fine print of a telephone book. Despite his early dependence on doctors, Robert Evans is now a nemesis to the official voices of organized medicine. He is the ringleader of a small band of health economists who have demolished the myth of the free-market doctor.

For many decades, Canadian physicians have successfully portrayed themselves as rugged individualists — independent businessmen who negotiate contracts with their patients. They expanded the concept of "professional freedom" to shelter themselves from any hint of government interference in their trade. They resisted the introduction of medicare because it undermined their business relationship with their patients. Implicitly, doctors were asking society to have faith in the invisible hand of the marketplace to ensure that the suppliers of health services were perfectly matched with the consumers. They wanted their patients to trust the law of supply and demand.

By the mid-1970s these traditional notions still prevailed in Canada — and the cost of health care was soaring out of sight. Canada's rate of surgery was mysteriously much higher than the rate in Britain, and patients were being wheeled through the health system at a faster and faster pace. The provincial governments discovered that one-third of their budgets was essentially controlled by 45,000 doctors. In desperation, the provinces began to listen to a new social force — the health economists.

There are barely a dozen of them in Canadian universities: one or two in each of the western provinces, a handful in Ontario and Quebec. Yet the impact of these dozen academics in the past decade has been tremendous. Their research has been quoted extensively by several provincial health ministers who have retained the health economists as special consultants. And the implications of their research, for taxpayers and for patients, are shocking. Their studies suggest that Canadian doctors may be performing thousands of unnecessary medical services and unjustified surgical operations every year. The potential cost to provincial treasuries — and to the health of patients — is too serious to ignore.

As a graduate student at Harvard University in the 1960s, Robert Evans became curious about the economics of the medical profession. His wife was a nurse who worked at a local hospital. "We used to sit around and compare notes," he recalls. He noticed that the cost of medical services was consistently rising faster than the rate of inflation. Evans was perplexed by this. "There was nothing in any of the theories of economics to provide a rationale or explanation."

Evans and his fellow health economists began by dissecting the claim of professional independence. Are doctors merely responding to the demands of consumers, like any other group of small businessmen?

The first step was a close examination of the market power of doctors. The market for medical care is unlike any other market. Consumers do not have enough expertise to challenge the advice of their doctor — and they cannot afford to ignore the doctor's recommendations. They are purchasing services from a seller who insists that the service is essential for their health. " 'Your money or your life' is not a normal market offer," Evans says wryly.

In a traditional market, suppliers have no significant control over the demand for their products. In the health system, doctors can control the demand for their services — an incredible advantage for any businessman. It means that doctors can maintain their income at almost any level they want — with virtually no constraints on their activities. Richard Plain, a health economist at the University of Alberta, makes an analogy to show how bizarre this would be in a traditional market: "It's as if you or I would walk into our friendly neighbourhood supermarket and go to the meat market manager and say to him, 'Would you please accompany me and tell me what type of meat products I should be buying this week to take home for my family to use.' And as we went by, he would pick the various products off his counter and put them into the cart, and I would pay for them and take them home and faithfully eat them."

This phenomenon, known as "supplier-induced demand," allows doctors to defy the law of supply and demand. Instead of being controlled by the invisible hand of the marketplace, doctors are controlled only by their conscience and integrity. Most doctors, of course, are conscientious and honest. But those who want to improve their incomes can easily do so — with no restrictions imposed by their customers. There are many medical services or operations whose benefits are uncertain. In such cases, any doctor can recommend the service or operation without fear of losing his or her customers.

The problem is particularly acute in a health system such as Canada's, where the government pays the full cost of the patient's consumption. And it is worsened by this country's traditional fee-for-service system, which gives doctors a financial incentive to provide as many services as possible to their patients. Doctors are paid for each service they persuade their patients to accept, instead of simply receiving a weekly salary or lump-sum payment for every patient in their care.

More than 75 years ago, George Bernard Shaw ridiculed the monetary incentives inherent in a fee-for-service system. "That any sane nation, having observed that you could provide for the supply of bread by giving bakers a pecuniary interest in baking for you, should go on to give a surgeon a pecuniary interest in cutting off your leg, is enough to make one despair of political humanity," Shaw wrote. "Scandalised voices murmur that these operations are necessary. They may be. It may also be necessary to hang a man or pull down a house. But we take care not to make the hangman and the house-breaker the judges of that. If we did, no man's neck would be safe and no man's house stable."

Thirty-five years after Shaw's critique, Britain terminated the fee-for-service system for most of its doctors. Canada and the United States, however, continue to trust the system.

Medical associations have argued that the fee-for-service system is the best method of paying doctors. They maintain that fee-for-service ensures a fair payment for each hour a doctor works. However, there is strong evidence to suggest that Bernard Shaw was correct — the fee system has an effect on the behaviour of doctors. As early as 1970, researchers in Nova Scotia found that doctors were increasing the frequency of a service whenever its fee went up. A 65 per cent increase in the fee for Sunday house calls, for example, produced a 121 per cent increase in the number of Sunday calls. (In the same period there was an 8 per cent decline in the number of weekday house calls.) A federal inquiry concluded that there was a "direct relationship" between the fee level and the behaviour of physicians.

Having established the potential for overservicing in Canada's health system, Robert Evans and his colleagues began to study the national data. Poring over computer printouts of medicare payments, the health economists discovered some remarkable coincidences. They found that the number of physicians in Canada has been growing two or three times as fast as the number of patients — yet the doctors have succeeded in maintaining their incomes at a consistent level. In classical economics, increasing competition is supposed to force the producers to slash their prices. Instead, each doctor was doing more business, and the incomes of the doctors were rising as fast as the inflation rate. The supply was creating its own demand.

In the 1970s provincial governments tried to control their health budgets by restricting doctors' fees. In response, doctors maintained their incomes by pushing more patients through their offices. Robert Evans examined the period from 1972 to 1984, when the fees of Canadian doctors declined by 18.2 per cent (after inflation is taken into account). Evans discovered that the average Canadian physician had increased his or her level of billings by 17.1 per cent in the same 12-year period. The drop in fees was almost exactly equalled by the extra volume of billings. The doctors were doing enough new business to neutralize the declining fees. Their incomes were protected.

The Quebec government was proud of its success in freezing doctors' fees in the early 1970s. After inflation, the fees of physicians dropped by 9 per cent from 1972 to 1976. But by an amazing coincidence, the doctors increased their billing claims by almost exactly the same amount — 8.3 per cent. The cost of medical services in Quebec remained at the same level, and the doctors maintained their incomes.

Similarly, the Alberta government imposed a freeze on medical fees in 1983–84. However, by seeing more patients and providing more services, the Alberta doctors — despite the freeze — succeeded in increasing their gross incomes by 12.37 per cent during that year.

Consider a fourth example. The number of general practitioners in solo practice in Winnipeg doubled from 1971 to 1982. Although the general population remained roughly constant, the average doctor managed to increase his or her patient load by 6.5 per cent, with only a slight drop in income. A study by Evans and his colleagues suggested that the doctors were informally referring patients to each other so that each patient could be shared by a larger and larger number of doctors. The rising supply of doctors failed to create any real competition. Each doctor found plenty of business, and incomes were protected.

The Target Income

After studying these examples, many experts have concluded that doctors have a "target income" that they insist on maintaining. No matter what happens in the external world — a large increase in the supply of doctors, a freeze on fees — each doctor has enough freedom and power to protect this target income.

Indeed, doctors openly acknowledge the importance of maintaining their incomes. A survey by three York University researchers in 1983 found that general practitioners admitted increasing the number of patients they saw in the previous year by 9.2 per cent "specifically because of the need to maintain an adequate income." In the same period, specialists increased their patient loads by 8.1 per cent for the same reason.

"The Canadian fee-for-service system is really a fee-for-income system," Dr. J. M. Forster wrote in the *Canadian Medical Association Journal* in 1985. "The physician is challenged to augment his or her income by increasing the volume rather than the quality of services, and decisions on the type of service given are often made more on the basis of income generation than on the needs of the patient." This observation does not come from a casual observer; Dr. Forster is the chairman of the family practice department at Memorial University's medical school in St. John's.

As long ago as 1945, a former president of the CMA openly acknowledged that doctors often consider their incomes when they are deciding whether a medical service is necessary. "As long as practitioners are forced to resort to surgical procedures to make the difference between a bare living and a decent income, just so long will the scales be weighted against any patient who presents himself for examination," the CMA president remarked.

Contemporary physicians make the same point. "All the doctors want to earn more money, so there's a tendency to ensure this through excessive testing and treatment," Dr. Douglas Waugh told a Toronto newspaper. "The temptation to over-service patients increases dramatically as the number of patients per physician continually goes down." Dr. Waugh is a former executive director of the Association of Canadian Medical Colleges and a former dean of medicine at Queen's University.

Most doctors are convinced that they have an inherent right to maintain their incomes. Dr. Duncan Kippen, a former president of the CMA, provided an articulate summary of this belief in an article in the *CMA Journal*. He lectured his fellow physicians on the importance of "the individual doctor's right to control his income in relation to his workload to maintain his standard of living."

As the supply of physicians continues to grow much faster than the supply of patients, the CMA is helping its members learn the craft of "patient recruitment." The association's subsidiary, MD Management Ltd., organizes seminars to teach doctors how to build their practices. Among its tips: send flowers to a deceased patient's family; send thank-you notes to patients who refer new patients to the doctor; send birthday cards to all patients; and telephone patients at home after surgery.

Provincial governments are becoming frightened by the rapid rise in the volume of billing claims by doctors. The number of billing claims is increasing much faster than the population growth in each province, and the average doctor is providing more services to the average patient. In Ontario, for example, physicians increased their billings by 20 per cent from 1975 to 1979, even though the population grew by only 5 per cent in that period. The average Ontario physician increased his or her volume of services to the average patient by 2 per cent annually from 1974 to 1982. This added $270 million to the cost of health insurance in Ontario. A provincial fact-finder, Paul Weiler, said he could find no evidence to suggest that the annual increase was merely due to an increase in the number of hours worked by the average physician. Instead, doctors were seeing patients more frequently, and their incomes were rising faster than their workload. Weiler called for a "sustained study" of this phenomenon — but the Ontario Medical Association refused to cooperate with the government during the lengthy period of conflict over the extra-billing issue. By 1986 physicians were receiving 24.8 per cent of the Ontario health budget. A decade earlier they were receiving only 20.3 per cent of the budget.

Most other provinces are running into the same expensive problem. Almost everywhere the supply of doctors is rising much faster than the supply of patients — and coincidentally the number of medical services is rising at the same rapid rate. In British Columbia the number of billing claims jumped by 5.6 per cent from 1983 to 1984, even though the province's population grew by only 1.3 per cent in that period. In Alberta the number of billing claims by doctors has been increasing by 8 per cent annually, even though the population has remained roughly the same.

After studying this data, the health economists issued a warning: the volume of medical services will continue to increase as long as the supply of doctors continues to rise. "What we believe, collectively, is that there aren't any medical limits to what can be done," Evans says. "You can always find more work to do on the patients. Where's the saturation point? There isn't one. At least, if there is one, we haven't seen it yet. There doesn't seem to be any tendency for the workloads of doctors to fall when there are more of them around. We keep putting more docs in there, and the average level of activity per doctor just doesn't seem to change. It drifts up. It certainly doesn't seem to come down."

Medical associations have consistently argued that doctors are simply responding to the mounting demands of their patients. "And yet they're perfectly comfortable with the notion that, as professionals, they have the superior expertise and control and judgment and so on," Evans points out.

Whenever the medical associations blame their patients for the rising number of medical services, the health economists question how the demands of patients could be increasing at exactly the rate necessary for doctors to maintain their incomes. "It's remarkable that it happens to be changing at just this rate," Evans observes.

Needless to say, the medical associations become agitated when reminded of Evans and his research. "They do seem to get a little excited," Evans admits. Privately, however, some doctors agree with his conclusions. These doctors are among his best sources. "I get a lot of information from them — in plain brown wrappers."

Clinical Uncertainty

To understand how doctors can control their incomes, one must appreciate the uncertainty that surrounds most clinical treatments. It's easy for a doctor to justify an extra test or an extra visit by the patient. "You can spin out the amount of time that goes into an episode of care," Robert Evans says. "And you don't have to do that with one eye on the bank account. You can probably do that with the best will in the world — simply saying, 'Look, if I've got the time, I just want to make sure that the patient is getting better and everything's going well.' "

Some medical services are so vague that they can be justified in almost any circumstance. For example, a doctor can argue that a patient needs counselling to help cope with an illness. The doctor can then bill the provincial health-insurance plan for the counselling session. In British Columbia the number of counselling sessions by doctors jumped from 125,000 to 565,433 in the decade from 1974–75 to 1983–84, and the cost of the sessions increased from $1.6 million to $19 million. This phenomenon finally set off alarm bells in the provincial health ministry, prompting a review and forcing the B.C. Medical Association to send a warning letter to its members.

Even in their treatment of conventional illnesses and diseases, doctors enjoy a great deal of flexibility. In many cases, they are free to choose an aggressive attack or a moderate treatment. For each patient, several different kinds of treatment could be medically justifiable; a doctor's decision can thus be determined by his or her financial incentives. "People do not understand the great uncertainties that pervade medical care and the variety of acceptable treatments," American health economist Alain Enthoven has written. "Caring for a patient can be open-ended, especially if he or she has a chronic disease. In most cases there is not one correct or standard treatment. There may be several accepted therapies."

For the provincial governments of Canada, this is a radical notion. The provinces have rarely expressed any understanding of the implications of medical uncertainty. Yet in the United States this theory has become widely accepted. Dr. John Wennberg, a professor at Dartmouth Medical School, has investigated the sharp differences in surgery rates in different regions of the U.S. He concluded that these variations reveal "the intellectual confusion and chaos that sit at the root of much medical practice."

The same conclusion was reached by Joseph Califano, the former U.S. secretary of health, education and welfare: "In many communities the standard is: when unsure about treatment, put the patient in the hospital and when you can, cut. When there is doubt about diagnosis or a more complex ailment is found, the uncertainty increases, and so does the incentive to do more tests, prescribe more pills, perform more surgery. However well motivated the physician's urge to do something to help the patient, it costs billions of dollars in unnecessary procedures."

The U.S. experts are convinced that a doctor's financial incentives are a crucial factor in determining the number of medical services that are provided. They point out that patients are hospitalized much less frequently in prepaid health plans, where the doctors are not paid on a fee-for-service basis. In a prepaid scheme, the government or a private organization gives the doctor a lump-sum payment for every patient under his or her care. The doctor's income does not depend on the number of services provided to each patient. These plans have been tremendously popular in the United States — about 24 million Americans are enrolled in them. (Doctors have succeeded in resisting these plans in most Canadian provinces — as we shall see in chapter 6.) Dozens of American studies have shown that the prepaid schemes cut the cost of health care by 10 to 40 per cent — without affecting the health of their members. At the same time, the prepaid plans have reduced the rate of hospitalization by 30 to 45 per cent, again without hurting the health of the patients. Similar results have been found in a handful of Canadian studies. In other words, your chances of encountering a doctor's office or a hospital ward are significantly reduced when your doctor's financial incentives are altered — and your health will remain the same.

What are the costs of the oversupply of medical services in Canada? There have been several attempts to calculate the cost to the taxpayers. Each excess doctor costs the provincial treasuries an estimated $500,000. This includes the doctor's income, office staff and overhead expenses, and the hospital costs the doctor generates. When this figure is multiplied by the number of excess doctors in Canada, the total is staggering. One study suggested that Canada will have a surplus of 6,000 doctors by the end of the century. These excess doctors could cost the taxpayers about $3 billion a year.

Indeed, this might be an underestimate of the financial cost. Another study concluded that there is already a surplus of 1,000 physicians (at an annual cost of $500 million) in British Columbia alone. The doctor surplus in B.C. will rise to 1,430 by the year 2000, the study said. The study, conducted by Peat Marwick and Partners, was commissioned by the governments of the four western provinces.

The financial expense is just a small part of the total cost to Canadians. Unnecessary services can be damaging to your health. Drugs prescribed by doctors can have serious side effects, X-rays can cause harm, and there is a risk of death in every surgical operation. There is a vast medical literature on "iatrogenesis" — the clinical name for illnesses and injuries caused by doctors. In one 30-month period, there were almost 200 articles on iatrogenesis in medical journals. According to one estimate, the number of deaths and hospitalizations directly caused by medical intervention is greater than the total number of casualties from the Vietnam or Korean wars.

It is worth exploring some of this literature to illustrate the potential hazards of unnecessary medical services. Consider, first, the effects of prescription drugs. U.S. studies have concluded that adverse reactions to prescribed drugs are one of the top 10 causes of hospitalization. American patients spend an estimated 50 million days in hospital every year as a result of adverse drug reactions. Almost one-third of hospital patients suffer at least one adverse drug reaction during their time in hospital, the studies suggest. About 4 per cent of all hospital admissions are due to adverse drug reactions. And of course this does not include the widespread effects of addiction to tranquillizers and other prescription drugs.

Consider the dangers of the hospital environment itself. Of every 100 patients who enter hospital, seven will catch an infection from the hospital staff or equipment. These infections cause an estimated 15,000 deaths annually in the United States, at a cost of more than $1 billion a year.

Finally, consider the risks of surgery. Complications are experienced by 14 per cent of all patients who undergo a surgical procedure, a recent U.S. study found. In the United States, about 250,000 patients die during surgery or shortly after surgery every year. A congressional subcommittee estimated that 12,000 of these deaths were caused by unnecessary surgery. The death rate for routine elective surgery is five in 1,000. The death rate for coronary bypass operations can be as high as 15 in 100. The death rate for hysterectomies is 16 in 1,000 — and roughly one-third of these deaths result from unnecessary surgery. When the doctors of Los Angeles County went on strike in 1976 to protest the rising cost of malpractice premiums, there was a 50 per cent decline in the number of operations — and an 18 per cent drop in the county's death rate.

The overall level of iatrogenic disease is astonishingly high. A study in a teaching hospital in Boston found that 36 per cent of the hospital's patients had illnesses caused by the medical system and 9 per cent of the patients had an iatrogenic disease that prolonged their disability or threatened their lives. In 2 per cent of the cases, the iatrogenic disease was believed to have contributed to the patient's death.

There is nothing to indicate that Canada is immune to these risks. It is reasonable to assume that medical services are as hazardous in Canada as they are in other countries.

Iatrogenesis in Canada

In fact, iatrogenesis is rarely studied in Canada — itself an interesting comment on our deference to the power of doctors in this country.

Medical associations have made several attempts to suppress doctors who openly discuss the harmful consequences of unnecessary medical services. In 1983, for example, the Lincoln County Academy of Medicine sought the dismissal of Dr. David Lorenzen, a coroner in St. Catharines, who told a local newspaper that orthopedic surgeons sometimes perform unnecessary and painful surgery on elderly patients. In some cases, the unnecessary surgery had hastened the death of the patients, he said. The Academy of Medicine complained that Dr. Lorenzen was undermining public trust in the medical profession, and it succeeded in obtaining an official inquiry into his conduct. At the inquiry a regional coroner testified that Dr. Lorenzen had informed him of 32 patients who had died on the operating table or within a few days of the surgery. Dr. Lorenzen believed that the operations had hastened the death of the patients and that the surgery should not have been performed. The regional coroner testified that he agreed with Dr. Lorenzen in some of these cases. The inquiry was eventually stalled by legal wrangling. A final decision has yet to be rendered.

Despite the lack of encouragement by the medical associations, a few Canadian investigators have studied the negative effects of surgery. One of the most interesting of these studies was an examination of gallbladder operations in Manitoba. The researchers looked at every case of gallbladder surgery in the province in 1974. They found that seven deaths occurred within six weeks of elective surgery for gallbladder removal. (Remember that elective surgery is an optional procedure, intended to prevent gallstone disease. It is not an emergency operation.) The researchers found that 82 years of life were lost because of the seven deaths from elective surgery. Ironically, only 52 years of life were lost from deaths caused by gallstone disease itself. In other words, the "cure" was worse than the disease. In addition, Manitoba residents spent more time in hospital for elective gallbladder surgery than they spent for gallstone disease. The researchers said their findings provided some support for the hypothesized link between high rates of elective surgery and unnecessary surgical deaths. They concluded that the effects of the elective surgery seem to be "at least as bad, it not worse, than the effects of the acute disease the prevention is designed to avoid."

Another investigation found clear evidence of iatrogenesis in Saskatchewan. The investigation concluded that 17 operating-room fatalities in 1985 could have been prevented by the surgeon, the cardiologist, the anesthetist or a combination of the three.

Since surgery can be dangerous, physicians should be making every effort to minimize the number of unnecessary operations. Yet the evidence suggests that there is a tremendous amount of unnecessary surgery in Canada. For example, a team of researchers examined every tonsillectomy performed in a single year in Manitoba (a total of about 4,600). Based on the recommended standards for tonsillectomies, at least 82 per cent of these operations were unnecessary. The researchers did not attempt to calculate the death rate, but earlier studies have suggested that the death rate for tonsillectomy is between one in 1,000 and one in 5,000. It is thus quite possible that three or four children died from unnecessary tonsillectomies in Manitoba in a single year.

Many studies have confirmed that the rate of elective surgery in Canada is much higher than in European countries. One study showed that tonsillectomies were performed on 107 of every 10,000 children in British Columbia and 200 of every 10,000 children in Ontario. (Similarly, the Manitoba researchers found that tonsillectomies were performed on 107 of every 10,000 children in Manitoba.) By comparison, the rate was only 26 of every 10,000 children in Liverpool, England, and just 17 of every 10,000 children in Uppsala, Sweden. Coincidentally, there are no financial incentives for surgery in England and Sweden, since both countries abandoned the fee-for-service system many years ago.

A landmark study in 1973 showed that the rate of elective surgery in Canada is almost twice as high as the rate in England. Have the English suffered from their lack of surgery? Apparently not. For example, the death rate from gallstone disease in England is only half of the Canadian death rate for the same disease, even though gallbladder surgery is five times more common in Canada. The death rates for cervical cancer, uterine cancer and breast cancer are essentially the same in England and Canada, even though in Canada hysterectomies are twice as common and radical mastectomies are three times more frequent.

In a commentary in the *New England Journal of Medicine*, two professors looked at the Canadian research and suggested that the high rate of elective surgery in North America might help to explain why the overall death rate (up to the age of 65) is higher in North America than in other industrial countries such as Britain and Sweden. Obviously the large number of murders and automobile accidents in the United States is part of the reason for the higher death rates in North America, but the professors estimated that the deaths caused by elective operations could account for half of the difference between North American countries and other industrialized countries.

As technology improves, the number of unnecessary operations doesn't seem to decline. One study revealed that the number of pacemakers implanted in Canadian patients as a cure for the so-called sick sinus syndrome is almost triple the number of implants for the same syndrome in Britain. An article in the *New England Journal of Medicine* in 1985 suggested that a significant proportion of pacemaker implants for this syndrome are unjustifiable by any reasonable medical standard.

Other medical services also seem to be provided in abnormally high numbers in Canada. A study of several teaching hospitals in Canada and Britain showed that the Canadian hospitals are conducting up to eight times as many biochemical tests per patient as the British hospitals. Some radiologists in Canada have suggested that X-rays are taken 30 per cent more often than necessary. And a Manitoba study found that some doctors are "hospital-prone." Elderly patients of hospital-prone physicians spent an average of 21 days in hospital between 1972 and 1974, compared to an average of only 6.1 days in hospital for the elderly patients of other doctors. The Manitoba study said there was no evidence that the additional time in hospital was helping the elderly patients.

Canada's fee-for-service system is clearly one key reason for the high rates of surgery here. Another major reason is the huge number of doctors in Canada. After decades of growth at a much faster rate than the general population, the supply of physicians per capita is much larger in Canada than in Britain. By the 1970s Canada had 164 doctors per 100,000 people, compared to 105 doctors per 100,000 people in Britain. At the same time, the average Canadian patient saw a physician 4.6 times a year, compared to just 3.5 annual encounters by the average British patient. And to complete the picture, there is definitely a connection between the supply of doctors and the number of surgical operations performed in a country. Newfoundland, which has the lowest number of physicians per capita in Canada, enjoys the country's lowest surgical rates. An analysis of 28 surgical procedures in Canada revealed that 23 of them became more common per 100,000 people when the supply of physicians increased. Another wide-ranging study of Canadian surgery in the 1960s and 1970s found similar results.

One of the best examples of unnecessary surgery in Canada is the fascinating case of the Saskatchewan hysterectomies. The number of hysterectomies in Saskatchewan mysteriously jumped by 72 per cent from 1964 to 1971. Then the operation suddenly became less popular, and the number of hysterectomies dropped by 33 per cent in the following four years. What caused the drop? Was there an abrupt change in the demands of Saskatchewan patients? In fact, the explanation had nothing to do with the patients. In 1972 the provincial government had launched a major review of hysterectomies in Saskatchewan hospitals, because of widespread alarm over the high rate of surgery. An expert committee was established, and it drafted a careful list of the justifiable medical reasons for a hysterectomy. The committee reviewed every hysterectomy in several Saskatchewan hospitals in 1970, 1973 and 1974. After this review, the committee met the hospital officials and medical staff to discuss the findings and to recommend a reduction in the number of unnecessary operations. As the province's doctors gradually realized that their actions were being scrutinized, the number of unjustified hysterectomies began to decline.

Amazingly, the committee found that as many as 59 per cent of the hysterectomies in some hospitals in 1970 had been unjustified; in the other hospitals, 17 to 45 per cent of the hysterectomies had been unjustified in the same year. Two years after the committee launched its review, the number of hysterectomies in Saskatchewan had dropped sharply — and the proportion of unjustified operations had also declined, to a new level of 2 to 16 per cent of the total. The results of this research were published in the *New England Journal of Medicine*. The authors concluded that the high rate of hysterectomies before 1972 was definitely the result of "a breakdown of adequate review and control at the hospital level." In recent years, U.S. experts have frequently cited the Saskatchewan case as a classic example of unnecessary surgery by doctors.

Variations in Rates of Surgery

When a medical detective is searching for unnecessary surgery, there is one good clue to look for: an extreme variation in the rate of surgery from one region to another. If surgery is far more popular in one region than in another, this could be a tip-off that unnecessary surgery is taking place. In the Saskatchewan case, for example, the hysterectomy rate in one city in 1970 was almost triple the rate in another city. (The rate was 1,258 per 100,000 women in the first city and only 499 per 100,000 women in the second.) After the review was launched and after the number of unnecessary operations declined, the disparity between the two cities narrowed considerably.

Bearing this in mind, we can look at the variations in surgical rates in other parts of Canada. Extreme variations were discovered as early as 1972 in Manitoba. Some communities in Manitoba had astonishingly high rates of hysterectomies and tonsillectomies, compared to Winnipeg. Similarly, a study in Ontario found some tremendous differences in the rates of surgery in different counties of the province. For example, the rate of tonsillectomies and adenoidectomies was eight times higher in one county than in another. The rate of removal of the colon was up to seven times higher, and the rate of hysterectomies, appendectomies and gallbladder removal was up to five times higher. A second Ontario study found that some kinds of surgery were up to 15 times more common in some counties of Ontario than in others. This study concluded that the variations were probably not caused by any difference in the rate of disease or illness.

The second Ontario study made another fascinating discovery: the rates of surgery for most types of operations were consistently lower in counties that had teaching hospitals. Teaching hospitals are much more likely to have a well-organized system of peer review. Under a peer-review system, a decision to perform an operation is liable to be carefully scrutinized by a committee of medical experts in the hospital. This usually means that the standards are higher and the number of unnecessary operations is reduced. The Ontario researchers concluded that the lack of peer review could be a "key factor" in explaining the high rates of surgery in some counties.

A similar conclusion was reached by yet another study, this time in Alberta in 1983. This study examined the rates of surgery for seven of the most common kinds of elective (optional) surgery. It concluded that the presence of a teaching hospital was "a very important variable" in determining whether a region of Alberta had a high rate of surgery. For almost all of the different types of elective surgery, very few operations were performed in teaching hospitals in the regions that had the highest rates of surgery.

The Alberta study began with the reasonable assumption that the surgical practices in Edmonton had the highest standards in the province, since the city's medical school is the oldest and best established in Alberta. The researchers then looked at the regions where surgery was more frequent than Edmonton in a single year, 1978. For most of the elective procedures, more than half the regions in Alberta had higher surgery rates than Edmonton. The study concluded that there were 1,375 excess tonsillectomies and adenoidectomies in Alberta in 1978. In addition, there were 399 excess appendectomies, 202 excess gallbladder operations, 294 excess hysterectomies and 734 excess Caesarian sections. The total cost of these excess operations was almost $3 million. "This is quite separate from the effect on the patient," the researchers added dryly.

There were other disturbing findings in the Alberta study. The researchers found that the fee-for-service method of payment was more common in the regions with high rates of surgery for most of the elective procedures. "This would seem to indicate that fee-for-service might influence the surgeon's decision-making for elective surgical procedures," the study said. The researchers also discovered that there were "significantly more" non-qualified surgical specialists in the regions with high rates of surgery. (Non-qualified specialists are doctors who lack a specialized qualification in the particular surgery that was performed.) This was the "almost universal finding" for the elective operations, the study said. In other words, there were regions of Alberta where a patient had a high risk of receiving unnecessary surgery from a non-qualified specialist.

The 1983 study was commissioned by the Alberta College of Physicians and Surgeons after a previous study had revealed that the province had the highest rate of surgery in Canada. The 1983 study called for a detailed examination of death rates in the areas where surgery was frequent. It also recommended a system of peer review to improve the standards in the non-teaching hospitals. Further, it urged the college to establish a watchdog committee for each of the elective procedures where excess surgery was common. It recommended that these review committees be based on the Saskatchewan hysterectomy committee that had been so effective in reducing the number of unnecessary operations. But the college refused to establish any review committees, declaring that they would be useless. Essentially, the college ignored the entire study.

All these studies simply confirm U.S. research that has found wide variations in the rates of surgery from region to region. And the U.S. studies have failed to find any evidence that the health of a region's residents is improved when surgery is more common.

Moreover, several U.S. experiments found that the number of operations declined sharply (by as much as 34 per cent) when a second opinion was sought from another doctor. As a result, the U.S. government produced television commercials to encourage patients to get a second opinion before agreeing to surgery. Despite opposition from the American Medical Association, the idea caught on. By 1984 three-quarters of the largest private health-insurance companies in the U.S. had established programs to pay for a second opinion when a doctor recommended non-emergency surgery. The insurers required the second opinion to be given by an independent physician who had no financial interest in the surgery. These programs reduced the rate of surgery by 20 per cent. Thousands of unnecessary operations were prevented. In Canada, however, no provincial government has ever dared to experiment with a second-opinion program.

Caesarian Sections

Until recently, the debate over unnecessary surgery has been hidden behind the walls of Canada's universities and hospitals. The average patient has been kept in the dark. But there are signs that the debate is finally on the verge of going public. One surgical procedure in particular has sparked a major controversy: the Caesarian section.

The number of Caesarian sections has skyrocketed in Canada in the past 20 years. In 1968 less than 5 per cent of hospital deliveries were C-sections. By 1977 doctors were using a C-section for more than 12 per cent of all hospital deliveries. Today the rate has been estimated at 18 per cent of all deliveries. In some cities in Ontario, the rate is 30 per cent.

Many experts believe that a large proportion of Caesarian sections in Canada are unnecessary. After all, Canada's rate of C-section deliveries is at least twice as high as the rate in European countries. Moreover, a study in Ontario found a wide variation in the rate of C-sections in different regions of the province. The study discovered that some teaching hospitals were diagnosing "fetal distress" more than twice as often as other hospitals. The variations could not be explained by any differences in the characteristics of patients in different hospitals. Instead, the study concluded, the variations seemed to be the result of decisions made by doctors. And these decisions often contradicted the recommendations of medical experts who have studied the question of Caesarian-section deliveries. For example, a major U.S. task force recommended in 1981 that vaginal delivery be considered for term infants in the breech position, yet in Ontario the rate of C-sections for breech presentation actually increased from 1979 to 1982.

Unlike other operations, the C-section has become a matter of public controversy. This is largely because of the rise of the women's movement and the emergence of self-help groups. Women have begun to assert control over the birthing process. They have become aware of the risks of C-section deliveries. (A Caesarian patient is 10 times more likely to die in childbirth than a patient who delivers vaginally, and Caesarian sections can cause infection and bowel problems.) Increasingly, women are challenging the conventional policies for Caesarian sections. For example, they have pointed to recent medical evidence disputing the traditional notion that a Caesarian patient should have all future children delivered by C-section.

In 1985 the high rate of Caesarian sections led to a national investigation in Canada. A large group of medical experts held a national conference to establish stricter guidelines for C-sections. The experts are currently trying to convince hospitals and doctors to follow these guidelines so that the number of Caesarian sections can be reduced.

The rise of a consumer movement helped to undermine the power of the doctor in the case of Caesarian sections. However, most operations are too complex for patients to challenge. Most patients are completely unaware of the debate over the costs and benefits of elective surgery. In the medical community the non-emergency gallbladder operation (for example) is almost as controversial as the Caesarian section, but very few patients realize the extent of the uncertainty — and of course their doctors rarely tell them. Patients who face a gallbladder operation are usually not aware that this procedure is associated with death more frequently than any other operation in North America. Nor are they aware of the extensive medical debate over the question of whether surgery is needed for routine gallstone problems. (Indeed, an estimated 80 per cent of all patients with gallstones will never require surgery.) When the consumer is deprived of this kind of crucial information, the market power of the doctor is perpetuated. Without any checks or balances from the consumer, the doctor is free to follow the financial incentives of the fee-for-service system.

Many surgical operations have never been subjected to rigorous scientific trials to see whether their benefits outweigh their risks. Nor have they been subjected to the kind of national conference that led to the establishment of stricter guidelines for Caesarian sections. University of Toronto health administration professor Eugene Vayda, who has worked extensively on the question of Caesarian sections, believes that national conferences could be held to set tighter rules for a long list of surgical procedures, including tonsillectomies, gallbladder surgery and coronary bypass operations.

Similarly, there is a lack of rigorous evaluation of the costs and benefits of new medical technology and laboratory tests. When these evaluations are performed, the results can be startling. For example, the electronic monitoring of the heart rates of unborn babies has become widespread in North America with the introduction of new medical technology. Yet a recent scientific trial showed that the routine monitoring of fetal heart rates did not provide any improvement in the infant mortality rate. Instead, the fetal monitoring simply increased the number of Caesarian sections. This kind of scientific evaluation can provide valuable information, but such evaluations are infrequently performed in Canada.

Even when scientific trials have occurred, it can take many years to convince doctors to change their behaviour. Some surgical procedures continue to be performed regularly in Canada, even though their value has been questioned by a scientific trial. Certain kinds of coronary and cranial operations are still frequently performed despite scientific trials that suggested the surgery is no more effective than ordinary therapy. Doctors can earn as much as $1,000 or $1,500 for the surgical procedures.

We should make it clear, at this point, that nobody is alleging deliberate fraud by the vast majority of doctors. Most physicians are striving to preserve the health of their patients. When they recommend a treatment or an operation, they honestly believe their patient might benefit from it. But the problem is this: the excess supply of doctors has produced a massive expansion in the number of medical services provided to the average patient — and a large proportion of these services are in a twilight zone where the benefits are uncertain. The patient might conceivably benefit from an extra service, but the service has a risk attached to it.

When the doctor is uncertain of the benefits and risks, the financial incentives can spell the difference. And in Canada the financial incentives are pushing the doctor towards a decision to provide the medical service — to order another laboratory test, to conduct another X-ray, to perform an operation. There is nothing in the Canadian marketplace to limit the power of doctors in their private offices. Regardless of their good intentions, most doctors cannot be immune to the incentives of the system — particularly in those thousands of cases in the twilight zone of uncertain benefits. The financial incentives are a crucial component of a system that makes no attempt to restrict the market power of doctors or even to provide some basic scrutiny of their practices.

Billing Fraud

But at the same time, a small minority of doctors are deliberately defrauding the system. Even the leaders of the Canadian Medical Association have acknowledged this. Dr. Peter Banks, the 1972–73 president of the CMA, estimated that 4 or 5 per cent of all Canadian doctors are "outright crooks whose licenses to practice should be taken away, because they will always be crooked." If this estimate is correct, more than 2,000 crooked doctors are practising in Canada. It is an amazing figure. Assuming that these doctors have a typical patient load, it means that at least one million Canadians are being treated by crooked doctors. The potential health risks are enormous.

There is good reason to believe that Dr. Banks is well informed on the subject. He has served as the commissioner of health insurance in British Columbia, and he spent many hours studying the billing profiles of the province's doctors.

Apart from the "outright crooks," Dr. Banks estimated that 16 per cent of all doctors are "easily influenced" by financial temptations. These doctors "have to be watched," he said. However, there are some serious weaknesses in the system for scrutinizing doctors in Canada. In most cases, patients never see the billing claims that are submitted to the government by their doctors. If patients saw their bills, they could spot an exaggerated claim. As it is, the doctors usually have a free hand.

The billing practices of doctors in most provinces are supposed to be monitored by a medical review committee. But these watchdog committees are usually dominated by the medical profession. In some provinces, such as Alberta, the medical review committee is entirely controlled by the medical profession. In other provinces, half the committee members are appointed by the provincial medical association. In every province, the doctors who dominate these watchdog committees are often dependent on their fellow physicians for referrals of new patients. Even when they aren't dependent on referrals, they tend to socialize with other physicians. In either case, the doctors on the watchdog committees tend to be reluctant to antagonize their colleagues. If they are strict in their duties, they run the risk of losing business or losing friends. Clearly, the watchdogs have an incentive to be toothless.

Moreover, the medical review committees do not scrutinize the average physician. They examine only the "deviants" — those doctors whose billing claims are obviously abnormal. Thus, if a large number of doctors are claiming extra fees, they might not be noticed. Dr. Banks has acknowledged this loophole: "There is dependence on the detection of statistical deviations from the pattern of the peer group, but if the whole group is out of line the impropriety is unnoticed."

Another physician, Dr. Arthur Pratt of Burnaby, B.C., has identified the same weakness in the system. "Practitioners in most provinces can put anything on their billing cards and submit them to the anonymous paying agencies, which then pay into effectively anonymous accounts," Dr. Pratt wrote in an article in the *CMA Journal*. "No one scrutinizes each transaction. The only practitioners who are periodically reviewed are those with anomalous billing patterns or very high incomes." The Canadian health system "invites abuse and misuse," Dr. Pratt said. "And one would have to be naive to believe that overservicing never occurs in medical practice."

Only a handful of doctors are caught by the existing watchdog system in Canada. In many cases, there is no significant penalty for these doctors. A few are prosecuted, but many are simply asked to repay their excess billings. In these cases, they face no penalty from the courts or from the college of physicians and surgeons. In British Columbia, for example, 27 doctors were ordered to make repayments to the provincial health-insurance plan from 1982 to 1985, but none of them were ejected from the health-insurance plan, none were successfully prosecuted by the RCMP for fraud or other offences, and none were suspended by the British Columbia College of Physicians and Surgeons.

In Ontario an average of 68 doctors per year are referred to the medical review committee because of overservicing or other billing irregularities, but only four physicians were charged with fraud from 1980 to 1985. Quebec seems to be the only province that takes a strict approach to medical fraud. Its health-insurance plan regulates the medical profession directly, instead of relying on a peer-review system. As a result, there are more prosecutions in Quebec than in all the other provinces combined. It is hard to believe that the number of dishonest doctors in Quebec is greater than the number in the rest of Canada. The reasonable conclusion is that the dishonest doctors in other provinces are getting away without any real penalty. Clearly, there is a strong argument for ending the peer-review system in the English Canadian provinces.

In an article in the *Canadian Journal of Criminology* in 1986, three university experts concluded that white-collar crime by physicians is treated much differently from traditional working-class crime. When the researchers talked to officials from medical associations and medical review committees, they found that the officials preferred to use "gentle persuasion" to modify the level of overservicing by a doctor. "Deviant acts by physicians are seen as 'mistakes' rather than crimes, and 'misunderstandings' rather than irresponsible or criminal behavior," the researchers noted. A health-insurance official in B.C. told them: "The doctor-dominated (medical review) committee treats some of the physicians with kid gloves when they should be treated like criminals."

In addition to the peer-review system, there are several other reasons for the low level of prosecutions against doctors. First, patients are often reluctant to testify against their doctors. Second, because of the medical problems of the patients, it is sometimes difficult to use them as witnesses. In one case, for example, law enforcement authorities were reluctant to traumatize children with psychiatric problems by asking them to testify against their psychiatrist, even though the RCMP had witnessed the psychiatrist playing golf and having dinner when he was claiming to be treating patients.

Third, it is difficult to prove that a doctor had wrongful intent. One member of a medical review committee told the criminology researchers: "All a physician has to do is to say he accidentally completed a form incorrectly or was too busy to record all the details at the time of consultation and you've got problems. Are you going to tell a fellow professional he is a liar?" And finally, doctors are protected by their financial resources and their political and social power. A health official told the researchers: "We have to be very careful with physicians because we are taking on a really potent group of people. They can buy the best lawyers, delay the investigation indefinitely, and then tell us we don't know what we're talking about and to stop interfering in the privacy between doctors and patients."

The criminology researchers listed several types of medical fraud. Among them: "revolving-door consultations," where doctors conduct their services quickly and superficially with a large number of patients in order to maximize their incomes; "double-dipping," where salaried doctors receive a second fee for the same service by billing the health-insurance plan as if they were in private practice; "medical snowballing," where doctors claim payment for a more expensive service than was actually provided; "ping-ponging," where specialists pay kick-backs to doctors in return for referring patients to the specialists; and "phantom treatment," where doctors claim payment for services they simply did not provide. In addition to these categories of fraud, some doctors regularly provide unnecessary services to their patients. This overservicing will sometimes be visible in their billing profiles, but of course it is difficult to detect if a large number of doctors are overservicing.

The criminology researchers concluded that Canadian doctors may be fraudulently claiming as much as $400 million annually from provincial medicare plans. Their estimate is based on detailed studies in Australia, which found that "medi-fraud" amounts to 7 per cent of total medicare payments in that country. Canadian governments have never attempted to study the level of medi-fraud here. Nor have the provinces attempted the kind of crackdown that has been extremely successful in the United States. During the 1970s, the U.S. government programmed its computers to detect obvious abuses by doctors — for example, billing Medicare or Medicaid for more than one appendectomy on the same patient in the same year, for more than one tonsillectomy on the same patient, for more than 10 X-rays on the same patient in one year or for more than 40 office visits by the same patient in a year. It also established limits for pharmacists. The project identified 47,000 physicians and pharmacists who broke the computer limits. Thousands of them were prosecuted, and millions of dollars were recovered.

The power of doctors in their private offices is probably the biggest weapon in the arsenal of the Canadian medical profession. While the politicians and the media were preoccupied with the issue of extra-billing, the true source of physician power was overlooked. Canadian physicians have successfully portrayed their day-to-day practices as a strictly private business. Their medical practices are almost immune to the influence of consumers or bureaucrats. Yet their daily decisions have a tremendous impact on public health and government treasuries.

Unlike any other group of businessmen, doctors can control the demand for their services and can protect their incomes from the effects of increased competition. They have defied the law of supply and demand. Every day, as Canada's supply of doctors continues to soar upwards, the private power of each doctor guarantees that the number of unnecessary medical services and surgical procedures will increase. There is overwhelming evidence that Canada's high rate of elective surgery is encouraged by our fee-for-service payment system and by the absence of any strict system of monitoring most doctors.

Unlike other countries, Canada has shown no interest in even the simplest measures to limit the private power of doctors. Provincial governments do not encourage patients to seek a second opinion before receiving surgery, even though this would prevent some unnecessary operations and save millions of dollars. Most provincial governments do not encourage the development of alternatives to the fee-for-service system. And most provincial governments are content to allow doctors to police themselves, despite the evidence that self-policing has failed to prevent doctors from overservicing. As a consequence, Canadian taxpayers are spending hundreds of millions of dollars on unnecessary medical services. At the same time, thousands of Canadian patients are suffering injuries or death as a result of unnecessary surgery.

CHAPTER 5

THE FIGHT FOR TURF

Vicki Van Wagner is a bright, energetic woman who has been practising her profession since 1979. In any other Western country, she would be a respected member of an honourable profession. But in Canada, she has no legal status. Technically, she could be prosecuted any time she practises her profession. Vicki Van Wagner is a midwife. Despite their proven record and popularity in other countries, midwives are relegated to the fringes of Canadian society. More than a century ago they lost an unofficial battle with Canada's physicians. They could not match the political strength of the medical profession, and they were eventually squeezed out of the system. Today midwives in Ontario are finally regaining their legal status. In other provinces their struggle is continuing.

Midwives are just one of several occupational groups that represent a threat to the power and income of physicians. Nurses, nurse practitioners, chiropractors, optometrists, physiotherapists and naturopaths are among the other professions that are knocking on the door of the medical monopoly. In some cases, the doctors have succeeded in defeating their rivals. In other cases, territorial skirmishes are continuing. In every case, doctors have argued that the public interest is served by their domination of the health-care turf. The evidence, however, suggests that consumers prefer to choose from a variety of health professionals. They want the services of doctors, but they want the freedom to choose other health-care workers as well. Moreover, this freedom of choice can save millions of dollars in taxpayers' money. Doctors are the most expensive of the health professionals, and their expertise is not required for many routine medical services. There is tremendous potential for cost savings if they are replaced by other health-care workers in certain circumstances.

The territorial clashes between physicians and midwives in Canada can be traced back to the 18th century. In 1795 doctors persuaded the legislative assembly of Upper Canada to include midwifery in the official definition of medical acts that could legally be performed only by licensed physicians. Violations of this law were to be punishable by a fine. The assembly adopted this law despite the severe shortage of physicians outside the major towns of Upper Canada.

In the 19th century the laws were revised several times. Midwives were not always illegal, but in 1865 they were again barred from practice in Ontario and in the 1870s the Ontario College of Physicians and Surgeons began prosecuting nurses who had acted as midwives. At the same time, the Quebec college refused to certify any midwife in a parish in which a medical practitioner was already operating. It prosecuted those who were uncertified. Meanwhile, legislation to define midwifery as a medical act was approved in 1885 in the North-West Territories (including modern-day Alberta and Saskatchewan) and in 1899 in Nova Scotia. Again, the definition of a medical act ensured that only physicians were legally permitted to practise midwifery in those provinces. Suppression of midwives continued in the 20th century. The Alberta Nursing Act of 1919, for example, prohibited nurses from practising midwifery unless there was no registered physician in their region.

Midwives never did succeed in establishing themselves in Canada. Their numbers were too small, they were too isolated, and the medical profession was too strong. In Europe, the midwives were well entrenched before the physicians became organized. They could not be driven out of the health field. But in Canada the physicians gained political strength before the midwives could secure a place in the system. As a result, Canada is the sole exception to the universal acceptance of midwives in the Western world. Dr. Marsden Wagner, a pediatrician at the World Health Organization, has described Canada as "an extraordinary enigma" because of its refusal to provide legal recognition of midwives. Among the 210 countries belonging to the World Health Organization, only eight have not legalized the practice of midwifery. Canada is the only major industrialized country on this list; the others are Venezuala, Panama, New Hebrides, El Salvador, Dominican Republic, Colombia and Burundi.

The Canadian Medical Association and its provincial divisions have continued to fight strongly against the legalization of midwives for home births. (By opposing home births, the CMA is effectively opposing midwifery. Women who prefer midwives usually want the delivery to take place outside a hospital.) At its annual meeting in 1985, the CMA again emphasized its opposition to home births. Some doctors at the 1985 meeting alleged that women who insist on home births are "members of a lunatic fringe" who are subjecting their children to unnecessary dangers. The official CMA policy is that a planned home birth is "retrogressive and irresponsible" unless the mother is living in a remote region where a hospital is unavailable.

The Medical Reform Group of Ontario asked the CMA to provide scientific reference to support its opposition to home births. The CMA responded with a list of 19 references. But only eight of these referred to scientific medical journals. Among the eight references, four were actually favourable to planned home births, while two others did not study the issue of home births, one article did not consider the question of safety, and one was basically neutral.

In early 1987 the CMA made another attempt to counteract the midwifery movement. The medical association released a national survey of 2,013 Canadian women indicating that most were satisfied with their obstetrical care. The CMA said the survey proved that midwives aren't needed in Canada. The legalization of midwifery "should not be pursued," the CMA said. The medical association admitted that midwives are strongly supported by many women. But by a strange twist of logic, the CMA's Council on Health Care argued that the popularity of midwives cannot possibly continue: "Much of the infatuation with the services provided by midwives is attributable to their total involvement with the patient during the perinatal period. Council believes that the level of dedication and commitment demonstrated by some midwives working currently in an unregulated fashion would hardly be achievable under more normally regulated circumstances. The behaviour of such modern-day zealots who work for a cause provides an artificial context which is impossible to imagine for normally motivated health workers of whatever profession."

The provincial medical associations have also taken a tough stand against midwives. Dr. Edwin Coffey, secretary of the Quebec Medical Association, has phrased it this way: "Uncontrolled midwifery has no place in modern obstetric care." The Ontario Medical Association has argued that midwives cannot be allowed an independent role in the health-care system. The OMA wants midwives to be kept under the supervision of doctors. "The idea that a 'nurse-midwife' will provide independent health care for both mother and baby throughout pregnancy, labour and birth and the postpartum period is not compatible with today's approach to health care," the OMA has said.

The British Columbia Medical Association has taken perhaps the most aggressive position of any provincial association. "The midwifery movement has played fast and loose with statistics, laying down a smokescreen of misinformation, usually presented in an emotional 'motherhood' style," the BCMA said in a bulletin to its lobbying committee. "The campaign has been clever, and often left unquestioned by the media." The bulletin went on to raise the spectre of "unfortunate, brain-damaged babies born at home."

Most provincial colleges of physicians and surgeons have adopted an equally strong stand against home births. In 1983 the Ontario college declared that home births were unsafe. It strongly discouraged doctors from attending home births. Indeed, most doctors who had been attending home births in Ontario abandoned the practice after the college's 1983 statement.

In 1981 the Alberta college prohibited any doctor from delivering babies at home. Three years later a committee of the Alberta college said the supporters of midwifery were "a small but vociferous group of women." It opposed the legal recognition of lay midwives. In 1984 the B.C. college described home deliveries as "negligence" and "abuse of the newborn."

Clearly, the attacks by the medical profession have helped delay the legalization of midwifery. Ontario is the only province where midwives are winning official recognition. Still, despite the resistance from doctors and their illegal status, midwives have gained the support of thousands of Canadian women. In Ontario alone, more than 1,000 women have joined an association to support midwives, and several thousand have signed petitions. About 50 midwives are delivering approximately 3,000 babies per year in Ontario, and an estimated 5,000 nurses or nursing assistants have some training in midwifery. Vicki Van Wagner is perhaps typical. She is the attending midwife at 50 to 75 home births in Toronto every year. She herself is the mother of a nine-year-old daughter who was born at home. In addition to attending births, she spends four days a week visiting pregnant women and young mothers at their homes and at clinics.

Why have so many Canadian women ignored the dire warnings from doctors? The biggest reason is the mounting dissatisfaction with hospital births. In a brief to the Ontario government by a group of health consumers, one woman explained why she has switched to a midwife: "I was brutalized by my hospital experience. . . . My vagina was treated like a cheap piece of butcher's meat. It was shaved, cut, and stitched. I was thrown on my back with my legs split, sprawled, and suspended in stirrups. The doctors were between my legs, poking, probing, mauling, and manipulating my vagina."

Many women are afraid of the risks of infection in a hospital. They perceive the traditional maternity system as paternalistic and impersonal. And they are worried about the possibility of unnecessary intervention by doctors and hospital staff. Indeed, studies have shown that Caesarean sections, episiotomies (a painful surgical procedure to enlarge the birth canal), anesthesia and the use of forceps are much more common in hospital births than in home births. A survey of Canadian hospitals in 1985 found that the rates of episiotomy were as high as 75 per cent. The survey also found that 30 per cent of the hospitals routinely gave enemas and suppositories to the pregnant women; 84 per cent routinely did perineal shaves; and the doctor chose the delivery position in 46 per cent of the hospitals.

Many women have found that doctors concentrate on the mother's physical health, whereas midwives also pay attention to the emotional and psychological needs of their clients. Moreover, midwives develop a close relationship with their clients, providing a continuity of care that a busy doctor cannot match. A member of the Ontario consumers' group said her midwife "was quicker to answer phone calls than the doctor with his full and busy practice. He's a good doctor, but he is busy. I felt our midwife cared about me and was more willing to slow down to my pace. She knew my concerns and irrationalities because she took the time to talk."

When the medical profession raised the spectre of death and injury in home births, the supporters of midwifery found plenty of evidence to contradict the doctors. They pointed to the Netherlands, where 35 per cent of all babies are delivered by midwives. The infant mortality rate in the Netherlands is 20 per cent lower than the infant mortality rate in Canada. And the Caesarean-section rate in the Netherlands is less than 4 per cent, about one-fifth of the Caesarean rate in Canada.

One of the most scientific studies of the safety of home births was conducted by Dr. Lewis Mehl, a professor at the Stanford University School of Medicine. Dr. Mehl selected a sample of 1,046 women who had given birth at home, and he compared them with a sample of 1,046 women who had given birth in a hospital. The two groups were chosen to be equivalent in average age, education, number of children and likelihood of risk in birth. His study found no statistically significant difference in the mortality rates of the home births and the hospital births. The women who delivered their babies in hospital had almost three times as many hemorrhages as those who gave birth at home. There were no injuries in the children born at home, but 30 of those born in hospital were injured — including one who suffered a fractured skull.

Dr. Mehl conducted another study in which he looked at 421 women whose children were delivered by physicians in hospitals and 421 women who delivered their babies at home with the help of experienced midwives. He concluded that the babies born at home were injured less often and generally fared better than those born in the hospital, primarily because the midwives were less likely to intervene with forceps, scalpels, drugs and needles.

Clearly, the medical profession cannot say it has proven the superiority of physicians over midwives. There is enough evidence on the side of midwifery to raise some serious questions about the motivations of the physicians in their battle against midwifery and home births. As the Canadian birth rate declines and the supply of doctors expands, are the doctors simply trying to protect themselves from the competition of midwives? Why does the medical profession insist that a general practitioner is always more competent than a midwife, even in cases where a young GP has delivered only a dozen babies in medical school and a midwife has delivered several hundred in her career?

Meanwhile, the suppression of midwifery is adding millions of dollars to the cost of health care in Canada. A joint committee of the Canadian Hospital Association, the Canadian Medical Association and the Canadian Nurses Association concluded in 1972 that the use of non-physicians in delivering babies would save at least $8.2 million a year. Today, after a further 15 years of steady increases in the cost of medical care, the potential savings are probably close to $20 million a year.

Nurse Practitioners

This $20 million is merely a small fraction of the cost savings that could be achieved by the greater use of non-physicians. The prime example is the nurse practitioner — nurses who receive extra university training to allow them to handle routine medical work. Their duties can include physical examinations, counselling and patient education, diagnosis of minor ailments such as colds and flus, and the monitoring of patients with chronic conditions such as diabetes and high blood pressure.

Research in Canada and the United States has established that 40 to 90 per cent of primary visits to a family physician could be safely delegated to a nurse practitioner. A study by health economists at McMaster University estimated that Canadian taxpayers could save more than $300 million a year by increasing the use of nurse practitioners. The economists concluded that at least 20 to 30 per cent of Canada's general practitioners could be replaced by nurse practitioners with only minimal changes in the regulations for health insurance.

A review of 21 controlled experiments with nurse practitioners across North America concluded that the quality of care provided by nurse practitioners was "indistinguishable" from the quality of care provided by physicians. In some cases, nurses actually provided better care than doctors. A randomized controlled trial of nurse practitioners in Burlington, Ontario, found that 96 per cent of the patients were satisfied with the services of the nurse practitioners — virtually the same level of satisfaction as reported by patients who received all their care from doctors in the same location. Moreover, the Burlington study discovered that nurse practitioners could function alone (without the supervision of a physician) in 67 per cent of all patient visits. At the end of the 12-month study, the researchers found that the patients who received two-thirds of their care from nurse practitioners were just as healthy as the patients who received all their care from doctors.

Similarly, there is strong evidence to support the increased use of ordinary nurses in medical practices. In the northern regions of Canada, where physicians are normally unavailable, nurses routinely perform many medical tasks without any difficulty. Indeed, nurses often perform medical work in southern hospitals during the night shifts. The Canadian Nurses Association calls this the "reverse Cinderella" syndrome: "At the stroke of the night shift, 'nursella' is deemed capable of performing tasks which she is not allowed to perform with the coming of the day shift and the physicians."

A study in a large Montreal teaching hospital concluded that nurses might be superior to physicians in providing preventive health services. The study was conducted as follows: When an influenza vaccine became available in Quebec in 1980, nurses who worked in the hospital's morning clinics were permitted to vaccinate every eligible patient. For the sake of comparison, nurses in the afternoon clinics were permitted to vaccinate patients only when requested by a physician. The study found that nurses vaccinated 35 per cent of the eligible patients in the morning clinics. But in the afternoon clinics, the doctors requested vaccinations for a mere 2 per cent of their eligible patients. The study noted that the fee-for-service system in Quebec in 1980 provided no incentives for doctors to provide preventive health services such as vaccinations. Without any financial incentives, the doctors provided few vaccinations. The nurses, operating solely on their consciences, provided far more vaccinations than the doctors — even though the vaccinations were an extra burden in the nurses' daily work.

Other studies in Canada and the United States have produced the same kinds of results. A study in Manitoba found that patients attending a hypertension clinic staffed by nurse practitioners were able to lose more weight and reduce their blood pressure further than patients attending a clinic staffed by doctors. A study in rural Newfoundland demonstrated that the rate of hospitalization declined by 5 per cent among patients who received primary care from nurses, while the rate of hospitalization jumped by 39 per cent among patients who received traditional care from physicians. Moreover, the cost of health care was 24 per cent lower for the patients who received their primary care from nurses.

A study in California found that four nurses in collaboration with one physician could deliver as much medical care as four physicians, and at a much lower cost. A study of chronically ill patients found a greater reduction in the level of disability and discomfort among patients who were managed by nurses than among those managed by doctors. The authors of this study noted that the physicians were concentrating on the biological and technical aspects of diagnosing and treating the patients. The authors suggested that this kind of emphasis is less appropriate for the chronically ill. A more appropriate approach, the researchers said, was the nurse's approach: "supporting-role" activities such as psychological counselling and assessing the needs of the patient.

Not surprisingly, dozens of government task forces and commissions of inquiry have been impressed by the overwhelming evidence of the benefits of nurses and nurse practitioners. It was difficult for any government inquiry to ignore a reform that could save millions of dollars without harming health care. In the 1970s and 1980s the increased use of nurses and nurse practitioners was recommended by the Hastings Report on community health centres, by the Boudreau Report on nurse practitioners, by the federal Task Force on the Cost of Health Services, by the Lalonde Report on health care, by the Hall Report on federal-provincial health programs and by major provincial reports in Quebec, Ontario, Manitoba and Nova Scotia. But despite the consensus, the provinces have refused to take any action to implement the recommendations. More than 15 years have passed since the task forces and commissions began to call for the transfer of routine medical procedures to nursing personnel, and almost nothing has been accomplished. Nurse practitioners have been hired by a handful of community health centres and have been as successful as predicted by the studies, but in private practice they are virtually non-existent.

Even when nurse practitioners became widely used in the United States, they remained almost unknown in Canada. The last university program for nurse practitioners in this country was terminated in 1983, when McMaster University discontinued its program. A 1984 article in the *New England Journal of Medicine*, written by Dr. Walter Spitzer of McGill University, concluded that the concept of the nurse practitioner was dead in Canada. "The ideas and concepts may be disinterred from time to time, but they are unlikely to be resuscitated," Dr. Spitzer wrote.

How can we explain this strange phenomenon? Why did the provinces ignore every report in the past two decades? Dr. Spitzer reached this conclusion: "In Canada, the economic imperatives of a physician surplus in the context of universal health insurance, coupled with the inevitable political pressures brought to bear by an older and somewhat threatened medical profession, have killed the nurse-practitioner movement." To understand the death of the nurse-practitioner concept, one has to understand the attitudes and behaviour of physicians.

The voices of organized medicine have consistently opposed any significant expansion in the role of nurses and nurse practitioners. Of course, this is perfectly understandable, since physicians could suffer a decline in their incomes and their autonomy if nurses were allowed to expand their responsibilities. But in its campaign to limit the role of nurses, the medical profession has portrayed itself as the protector of the public interest — despite the overwhelming evidence that the public interest would actually be served by the greater use of nurses and nurse practitioners.

The Canadian Medical Association has spearheaded the battle to restrict the role of nurses. The CMA established a committee to examine the issue of "allied health personnel" — the association's euphemism for nurses and other non-physician health workers. (Note that this phrase implies that nurses are merely personnel, unlike doctors, who are professionals.) The committee's coordinator, Brian Henderson, argued that nurses were just trying to increase their status. His committee insisted there was no need for nurses to provide primary care. "The nurse practitioner was always intended as an exceptional creature for special areas," Henderson said. "They were not intended as a new point of contact with health services across the country. Today we must ask whether nursing education is an appropriate base from which to offer primary care. Frankly, I'm not convinced it is."

Other CMA officials suggested that the introduction of nurse practitioners would increase the cost of health care — despite the dozens of studies concluding the opposite. "It is entirely possible that one result could be an unnecessary new layer in the health care system," an article in the *CMA Journal* warned. The medical association's director of publications, David Woods, accused the nurses of making "territorial forays" in the health field. Woods said the nurses seemed to be trying to become "pseudo-doctors." He wrote: "If nurses want to be doctors, let them train as such. If men or women want to enter the nursing profession, let them do so — and practise nursing."

At its 1983 annual meeting, the CMA's general council argued that the cost-effectiveness of nurse practitioners has never been proven. Definite conclusions "must await additions to the database," the general council said. A report by the CMA's board of directors opposed any involvement by nurses in primary care. The board suggested that nurses would be sacrificing their traditional tasks if they gained an expanded role in health care. The CMA even found a way to attack the studies that have shown that doctors could spend more time with their patients if they hired nurse practitioners to handle their routine medical work. "Council questioned whether quality or even quantity of care is necessarily a function of number of minutes in face-to-face contact with the patient," the official report of the 1983 meeting said.

In 1984 the Manitoba Medical Association released a document which argued that there was "little justification" for allowing nurses to perform any medical tasks. Diagnosis must always be performed by doctors, the MMA said. Nurses should work "under the ultimate supervision of a physician," the association said.

Individual doctors, in their daily practices, have also resisted the introduction of nurse practitioners. Very few of the fee-for-service physicians have ever hired nurse practitioners. In 1979, when the Sault Ste. Marie community health centre attempted to provide medical coverage by nurse practitioners in isolated communities in northern Ontario, local doctors effectively scuttled the experiment by expanding their services to replace the nurse practitioners.

Every provincial government in Canada has clearly understood the views of the medical profession on the question of whether nurses should have a greater role in health care. Medical associations have sent a strong message to the provinces: any government that attempts to replace some physicians with highly trained nurses would risk the wrath of organized medicine. Faced with the united opposition of a powerful profession, the provinces have decided to avoid a confrontation. None has dared to battle the physicians on an issue that is obscure to the average voter.

The resistance from physicians should not be surprising. In an era of massive doctor surpluses in Canada, the medical profession cannot afford to surrender any of its territory. Under the fee-for-service system, even the most routine medical services must be kept within the doctors' control because each service is a money earner for them. No matter how minor the procedure, it can be billed to the health-insurance plan. By contrast, doctors cannot submit bills for tasks they have delegated to nurses. The training and expertise of doctors is wasted on these mundane medical services, but who can expect them to surrender any of their money-earning powers?

The Politics of Nursing

The resistance from physicians is also based on a historical tradition. Until recently, nurses were taught to obey doctors blindly. In the early days of the 20th century, for example, nurses were always expected to stand if a doctor was present in the room. The motto of Canada's first school of nursing was: "I see and am silent."

An early article in a Canadian nursing magazine summarized the nurse's relationship with doctors: "She owes to the attending physicians absolute silence regarding their professional demerits or blundering." The article noted that nurses must learn "implicit obedience to authority" and must practise this obedience "until it has become a habit of life." In 1906 an article in the *Journal of the American Medical Association* advised doctors to reproach a nurse for any initiatives she takes and to teach nurses that it would be dangerous to step beyond their "proper sphere."

Most of the nurse's activities, until the 20th century, were similar to a servant's duties. Health care was divided between "caring" and "curing." Only doctors could participate in "curing," and they gained all of the credit for a patient's recovery. Physicians deliberately discouraged any steps to organize nurses into associations or unions. In 1897, for example, the Ontario Medical Association opposed the establishment of the Victorian Order of Nurses, the first national nursing organization in Canada. In its argument against the founding of the VON, the OMA said that "in all work of public health and preventive medicine, the medical profession should never surrender its right to lead." In western Canada, the Winnipeg Medical Society also opposed the VON. Doctors were always represented on the advisory boards that supervised the nursing profession in the 19th and early 20th centuries. The nursing profession in Ontario did not gain the power of self-regulation until 1951 — more than 80 years after the medical profession received the same power.

The hospital hierarchy has tended to reinforce the doctor's

dominance over the nurse. The nurse must follow the doctor's instructions, and rarely is she asked to comment on a patient's condition — even though the nurse is often closer to the patient than the doctor is.

But nurses have become much more independent and self-assertive in the past two decades. In their relationship with doctors, they have ceased to be submissive handmaidens. They see themselves as advocates for patients' rights and health promotion. They are willing to testify against doctors in malpractice suits, they have gained managerial powers in some hospitals, and they are raising their educational standards. Nurses are now convinced that they have a unique role in the health system: they are the guardians of health maintenance and self-care by patients, since the doctors are preoccupied with illness and injury. They believe their responsibilities are perhaps even more important than those of the doctor, since the prevention of sickness (through lifestyle counselling and patient education) is widely regarded as the biggest priority in health care today.

The Canadian Nurses Association, which has 170,000 members across the country, became active in politics and public policy issues in the late 1970s. The association was inspired by the World Health Organization, which had urged nurses to increase their role in primary health care. In 1979 the CNA began its political work by submitting a brief to Emmett Hall's inquiry into the Canadian health system. The brief made several recommendations that contradicted the official views of organized medicine. Among the CNA's recommendations: nurses should be permitted to perform activities currently defined as medical acts; provincial health-insurance plans should be expanded to cover the services of nurses and other non-physicians; and all health personnel (including doctors) should eventually be paid by a fixed salary.

In his final report, Emmett Hall said the CNA brief was one of the most impressive of the 450 submissions he received. Hall said he was "in general agreement" with the CNA's recommendations and concluded that "the plea for a greater utilization of nurses and nursing skills is amply justified." He added that the CNA submission "demands close study by all governments and I recommend that this be done in a serious and objective way."

Three years later the CNA escalated its battle for independence. Under the leadership of its president, a tough-minded university professor named Helen Glass, the association launched a massive lobbying campaign to seek improvements in the proposed Canada Health Act. The association hired a full-time lobbyist to coordinate the campaign. The CNA supported the proposed ban on extra-billing by doctors, but it also wanted the federal legislation to include the CNA's 1979 recommendations, especially the concept of allowing nurses to submit bills to the provincial health-insurance plans.

The nurses mobilized a national lobbying effort. In September 1983 more than 120 nursing organizations sent telegrams to a meeting of provincial health ministers. The CNA's provincial leaders went on a media blitz, appearing on television and radio to promote their views. The CNA issued bulletins to tell its members how to lobby politicians and distributed lists of key politicians who were major lobbying targets. The nurses also enlisted the support of influential women's groups and consumer organizations. There were petitions, letter-writing campaigns, speeches, telephone blitzes and meetings with members of Parliament.

All of this was a new experience for the nurses. They were not as sophisticated as the Canadian Medical Association, which had been lobbying in Ottawa for decades. Eventually they realized they had to abandon their more radical recommendations, and they concentrated instead on their proposal that non-physicians should be covered by health insurance. Finally they gained a victory. In a last-minute amendment, clearly designed to appease the nurses, the federal government revised the Canada Health Act to include a new definition of health-care practitioners. The amendment effectively permitted a province to give billing privileges to non-physicians. Helen Glass called it "a conceptual breakthrough." The amendment did not compel the provinces to expand their insurance plans, but it did provide some recognition of the expanding role of nurses.

Meanwhile, the Canadian Nurses Association was taking a tougher stand against the medical associations. When the Canadian Medical Association established a task force to study the future of health care in Canada, the nurses refused to cooperate. Helen Glass declined to participate in the task force because she felt it was dominated by the physicians. At the same time, the CNA refused to cooperate with the CMA's committee on allied health personnel. The CNA strongly opposed the committee's attempt to create a "medical perspective" on the role of other health occupations. When the CMA published a book that defined a restricted role for nurses, the nurses fired off angry letters of protest. When the CMA urged breastfeeding mothers to consult their doctors two weeks after the birth of their child, Helen Glass accused the doctors of encroaching on the nurses' territory. And when the Canadian Nurses Association unveiled its new code of ethics, observers noted that the code made no mention of loyalty to doctors.

Provincial nursing organizations are becoming equally aggressive. The Ontario Nurses Association and the Registered Nurses Association of Ontario were both strongly opposed to the Ontario Medical Association during the dispute over Ontario's legislation to prohibit extra-billing by physicians. The ONA placed a series of large advertisements in 13 major daily newspapers in Ontario in 1985 and 1986. The advertisements called for the banning of extra-billing, an increased emphasis on preventive health, a bill of rights for patients, and the transfer of resources away from expensive health care by hospital-based physicians. The ONA also commissioned an opinion survey by Goldfarb Consultants to demonstrate the public support for its views.

The Ontario nurses lobbied in the provincial legislature to push for a prohibition on extra-billing. They submitted briefs, wrote letters and joined a coalition of groups opposing the Ontario Medical Association. When the doctors went on strike, the nurses accused them of "holding the community to ransom" and jeopardizing the safety of their patients. They questioned whether the doctors had a moral right to go on strike.

In other provinces the story is the same. The Saskatchewan Registered Nurses Association has sponsored "political action workshops" to train their members in the fine art of lobbying. The Manitoba Association of Registered Nurses revised its statement on medical-nursing responsibilities without any attempt to consult the Manitoba Medical Association. And several nurses have entered politics as candidates for major political parties in recent provincial elections.

For the doctors of Canada, all of this is an alarming trend. Nurses are undermining some of the traditional power of the medical profession. "The doctors feel threatened," says Glenna Cole Slattery, chief executive officer of the Ontario Nurses Association. "Nobody thinks they're God any more. When they ask the nurse to get the chart, the nurse says, 'Get it yourself.' The doctors long for the good old days."

Cole Slattery is an experienced lobbyist and unionist. One newspaper described her as "a tough-talking, chain-smoking feminist." Hired by the ONA in 1986, she has directed her energies at the Ontario legislature, where the nurses have become a frequent sight in the committee rooms. She is determined to make the politicians pay attention to the 46,000 members of her association. "There's only two roads to power — money and numbers," Slattery says. "We don't have the money but we've got the numbers." Nurses today are "products of the 1960s and 1970s — the women's movement — and they know how to get what they want." As for the doctors, "We're going to go over them and around them," she says. "The nurse is still viewed as the doctor's assistant, but she has an independent body of knowledge and an autonomous learning centre. We have our own enabling examinations and our own registration system. I could sue a doctor for practising nursing."

On another occasion, Slattery phrased it this way: "I don't view doctors as my superiors and I don't view them as subordinates. I'm just as important to the patient as a doctor is, and that fact hasn't been reiterated enough to the patient."

In newsletters to her association's membership, Cole Slattery urges nurses to stop being "the silent pawns of the physician and hospital administration." She tells her members to "view nursing from the perspective of power and politics, rather than service and self-sacrifice."

It will be a long struggle. So far, doctors have not suffered any serious losses in their political conflicts with the nursing profession. The nurse-practitioner concept has been effectively suppressed. No province has allowed nurses to submit their own billing claims. Nurses have failed to make any permanent moves into primary health care (except for their traditional duties in the North and on the night shift in hospitals). The nurses associations are still inexperienced and considerably less influential than the medical associations, despite their much larger membership.

The Paramedical Workers

Nurses and midwives are just two of the estimated 665 health occupations in North America. There are a vast array of specialized technologists in the large teaching hospitals. In addition, there are a host of paramedical workers in private practice. These range from the well known (chiropractors, acupuncturists, physiotherapists, optometrists) to the obscure (osteopaths, homeopaths, clinical ecologists, neuropsychologists). Conflict between these groups and the medical profession is increasing every year.

In chapter 3 we saw the success of doctors in protecting their medical monopoly in the 19th century and most of the 20th century in Canada. In the "golden age" of the Canadian physician, no competing group was strong enough to mount a sustained challenge to the medical monopoly. But in the past decade, the "allied health" workers have pecked away at the doctors' turf. Physicians are still dominant, but the limitless expanse of their territory is finally under attack. Skirmishes are becoming more common. Doctors are fighting back by criticizing the skills of their competitors. They are working hard to undermine the credibility of their new rivals. If they succeed, the consumer's freedom of choice will be limited and the physician's income will be maintained. Dr. Robert Gourdeau, the 1977–78 president of the Canadian Medical Association, rallied his troops by urging them "to confound those who strive to expropriate, for their own profit, a greater share of our domain." He told the doctors to repel "this invasion" by paramedical workers. He acknowledged that the paramedicals might be cheaper than the medical profession, but he argued that the "continuous and systematic erosion" of the doctor's territory was a threat to society. "The financial savings often prove illusory and the quality of medical care is jeopardized," Dr. Gourdeau told a CMA annual meeting in 1978. He suggested that the paramedicals are motivated by ambition and the desire for prestige and wealth.

Other physicians made the same accusation against the paramedicals. "It's a rush for status and money," Dr. Augustin Roy told the CMA meeting. After listening to Dr. Gourdeau and Dr. Roy, the CMA decided to establish its allied health committee to define the role of non-physicians. The committee's first chairman, Dr. Parker Chesney, clearly viewed the paramedicals as a subordinate group. He called them "those technologists and technicians who have responsibility for supplementary areas of medicine."

In its clashes with the allied health workers, the CMA has consistently portrayed itself as the defender of the ordinary patient. But the CMA's behaviour also serves the self-interest of the doctor, and most observers think this is hardly a coincidence. Ake Blomqvist, an economist at the University of Western Ontario, has described Dr. Gourdeau's 1978 speech as "a very thinly veiled statement of the medical profession's determination to protect their economic interests by resisting competition from outsiders." Blomqvist added: "The ostensible motive has been to protect the patient against faulty diagnosis or treatment by insufficiently qualified personnel; but again, it is difficult to believe that a concern for the demand for the services of doctors and hence their potential income, has not been an important motive as well."

In 1983, Dr. Murray McAdam, president of the Ontario Medical Association, accused the paramedicals of undermining Canada's health-care system. In his speech to an OMA meeting, Dr. McAdam placed the chiropractors and nutritionists in the same category as "aura balancers, finger-pressure massagers and brain clearers."

Each of the medical specialties has its own particular rivals in the allied health professions. The opthalmologists, for example, frequently attempt to limit the independence of the optometrists and the opticians. In 1978, when the provincial legislature in New Brunswick proposed an act to permit optometrists to use muscle-relaxant drugs for the purposes of diagnosis, the opthalmologists were angry. The New Brunswick Medical Society submitted a brief to oppose the legislation. According to the medical society's brief, the legislation was "not in the best interests of the general public." The medical society warned that the muscle-relaxant drugs could cause "temporary madness, hallucinations, fits and even death." However, the drugs were already in use by optometrists in Ontario at the time of the medical society's brief. There were apparently no reports of madness or death in Ontario.

As recently as 1985, some opthalmologists in Alberta were refusing to accept referrals from optometrists. After a series of complaints, the Alberta College of Physicians and Surgeons was forced to issue a warning to the Alberta Opthalmological Society to ensure that the opthalmologists would accept referrals from optometrists.

Doctors who specialize in foot problems have usually opposed any increase in the autonomy of podiatrists. In the late 1960s the Alberta Medical Association tried to convince the Alberta government that podiatrists were overtrained. Dr. Robert Clark, executive director of the AMA, said the medical association "concluded that foot-care technicians with two years training, working under the supervision of physicians, could fill the role quite adequately."

In the late 1970s the AMA fought against a provincial regulation that allowed Alberta's podiatrists to prescribe antibiotics and steroids. "The AMA believes that this decision was not in the best interests of the health of Albertans," Dr. Clark said. "We are not convinced that podiatrists know when to use a systemic drug, which one to use and how to use it. We are not convinced that they can recognize drug interactions or the complications of drug therapy; nor do we feel that they can adequately deal with these interactions or complications." But by the end of the 1970s, despite the opposition of doctors, three provinces allowed podiatrists to use drugs and do minor surgery.

Acupuncturists have encountered the same kind of resistance from physicians. "For years the medical authorities have been trying to regulate the practice of acupuncture and for years the acupuncturists have disputed being controlled by the doctors," Quebec education minister Claude Ryan remarked in 1986. Ryan was forced to arrange a ceasefire between the doctors and the acupuncturists.

The Chiropractors

But of all the health professions in Canada, one occupational group has always suffered the harshest attacks from physicians. These are the chiropractors. "Organized medicine has been more hostile towards the practice of chiropractic than towards the practice of any other major healing group," the Ontario Committee on the Healing Arts reported in 1970 after its four-year inquiry. "Innumerable spokesmen for organized medicine have contended that the practice of chiropractic should be sharply limited or abolished." Two sociologists from the University of Toronto have described how the chiropractic profession has been forced to endure "the most strenuous efforts of the medical profession to destroy it."

In chapter 3, we saw the historical conflict between doctors and chiropractors. In the 19th century and the first half of the 20th, physicians were generally successful in suppressing chiropractors. But in the past 25 years chiropractors have finally managed to establish themselves. As chiropractors' popularity increased, doctors escalated their attacks on the practice of chiropractic. Many physicians refused to refer any of their patients to chiropractors, and they discouraged their colleagues from participating in the education of chiropractors. Many hospitals refused to allow any X-ray information to be given to chiropractors, even when the patient requested it.

Indeed, in their attempts to hamper the chiropractors, doctors were actually increasing the risks to their patients. The Ontario Committee on the Healing Arts concluded that the refusal to provide X-ray information to chiropractors was "an example of the medical profession's somewhat unreasonable attitude towards chiropractors, as well as an imposition of undue expense and, more important, an unnecessary exposure to radiation for the patient."

Medical organizations have tried to convince the public that chiropractors must not be permitted to have an independent position in the health-care system. In 1967 the Ontario College of Physicians and Surgeons argued that chiropractic theory is founded on false premises. The college insisted that patients should be prohibited from visiting any chiropractor unless they were specifically referred to the chiropractor by a medical practitioner who had diagnosed the patient. However, as the healing arts committee pointed out, most doctors would probably never refer their patients to a chiropractor. The college's proposal "would have the effect only of driving chiropractors out of the province and depriving patients of chiropractic services, results which are not in the public interest," the committee said. The committee noted that the medical profession has never done a scientific study of the benefits of spinal manipulation by chiropractors and that doctors have not provided any real evidence of harm done by chiropractors. Despite this lack of evidence, medical associations have attacked chiropractors with sweeping generalizations and inflammatory language. In 1969, for example, the Canadian Medical Association passed an official resolution describing the chiropractic profession as "health quackery."

In the same year, the Alberta Medical Association and the Alberta College of Physicians and Surgeons launched a major assault on the province's chiropractors. The rhetoric of the doctors was dramatic and clearly designed to alarm the public. "We do not believe that chiropractic can make any useful contribution to the health of Albertans," the doctors said in a submission to the provincial legislature. "In fact we believe that in some cases actual harm will result and premature death may follow." The doctors argued that the practice of chiropractic is merely a cult. They opposed the province's plan to include chiropractors among the practitioners who were covered by public health insurance.

Three years later the Saskatchewan Medical Association made the same argument when the Saskatchewan government proposed to include chiropractors under the health-insurance plan. The SMA described chiropractic as "a cult which is not based on scientifically demonstrated principles." The medical association charged that chiropractors "have contributed no significant scientific advance to humanity in the past 75 years." Dr. J. G. Monks, president of the SMA, stated publicly that the approval of medicare coverage for chiropractors "could indeed prove dangerous to the public health."

In 1984 the British Columbia College of Physicians and Surgeons reminded the province's doctors that they should not rent any of their office space to chiropractors. The college's registrar, Dr. John Hutchison, said a ruling by the college made it clear that "physicians should not deal with or recognize chiropractors."

The unrelenting opposition of the medical profession has failed to diminish the popularity of chiropractors. Today there are more than 2,200 chiropractors in Canada, more than double the number since 1971. In the province of Alberta alone, chiropractors annually receive nearly one million visits from patients. Chiropractors are covered by medicare in British Columbia, Alberta, Saskatchewan, Manitoba and Ontario.

A survey in British Columbia in 1983 found that 24 per cent of the population had visited a chiropractor at some point in their lives.

Two years later another survey in B.C. found that 40 per cent of the population had visited a chiropractor at some point. When asked who they consult for back pain, 27 per cent said they would first consult a chiropractor. A survey of the patients in a large health-service organization in Ontario found that chiropractors received 10 per cent of all the patients' visits to specialists. That meant that chiropractors were the third most popular of the specialists. They were more popular than the psychiatrists, dermatologists, obstetricians, gynecologists and pediatricians.

Several independent inquiries have concluded that the services of chiropractors can be beneficial to patients. The independent studies have generally agreed that the technique of spinal manipulation is valid and useful for some specific conditions, even though the traditional philosophy of chiropractic might be unsound. A provincial inquiry in Quebec found that chiropractic therapies often produced positive results that could not be duplicated by purely medical treatment. The Quebec inquiry recommended that chiropractors be allowed to practise their therapies after the patient has been diagnosed by a doctor.

The Ontario Committee on the Healing Arts concluded that "chiropractive manipulative technique has value and should be preserved." The committee received submissions from a variety of medical organizations, but it reported that it had heard "no conclusive evidence of significant harm" from chiropractic therapy. Indeed, the committee criticized the medical profession for ignoring the therapeutic benefits of spinal manipulation techniques. The committee recommended that patients be permitted to consult a chiropractor directly, without referral from a doctor. It also recommended that a patient be required to obtain a diagnosis from a physician before a chiropractic treatment is started, although the committee said that a doctor should not be allowed to prevent a patient from receiving chiropractic therapy if the patient so desires. Moreover, the Ontario committee recommended that the provincial health department "undertake a continuing surveillance of relations between medicine and chiropractic to ensure that physicians do not interfere with the right of patients to seek chiropractic treatment."

More recently, the 1980 report of Emmett Hall's special commission on Canadian health issues concluded that chiropractic has established itself as a valid health service. "It is time the discriminations against it were removed and forgotten," Hall wrote.

In recent years, chiropractors have audaciously struck back at the medical profession. The Alberta Chiropractors Association, at a news conference in early 1987, argued that physicians should be prohibited from practising spinal manipulation unless they have undergone special training for a year. The chiropractors alleged that some patients have been injured by physicians who attempted to manipulate their spines.

The clashes between physicians and chiropractors are bound to continue for many years to come. Physicians still frequently refuse to provide X-ray information or patient referrals to chiropractors. "Often I have to X-ray someone who has already had an X-ray," says Henri Marcoux, a Winnipeg chiropractor. "It still bothers me. I can't get any cooperation from most physicians. I get insults. I remember talking on the phone to a physician about a case. He said we were all quacks. I just let him talk. Finally he reluctantly gave me the information I needed."

Ken Harrison, president of the Alberta Chiropractors Association, has experienced the same problems. "I've had patients come in and say that doctors advised them that they were risking their life if they come to me. They run the risk of being ostracized by the doctors for coming here. Patients have told me that they were chastized by a doctor and told never to do it again."

Chiropractors feel vindicated by the patients who keep returning to see them. Several physicians are now willing to refer patients to Henri Marcoux, for example, and other physicians are grudgingly tolerating the profession of chiropractic. "They're learning to accept the fact that we're here to stay, no matter what they do or say," Marcoux says.

Ken Harrison works in the Alberta town of Edson, where five or six of the 20 local physicians have sometimes referred patients to him. "Twenty-four years ago, when I started in this profession, that was unheard of," Harrison says. "There was a time when they wouldn't consider it at all. We've made some tremendous strides."

Freedom of choice is still a fragile liberty in the Canadian health-care system. The health consumer of the 1980s has a few more options to choose from, but the influence of the medical profession is still a dominant force. Even though doctors have failed to restrict the independence of the major paramedical professions in some provinces, they have been remarkably successful in others. As of 1985, for example, podiatrists and chiropractors were unable to claim medicare privileges in New Brunswick, Nova Scotia, Newfoundland, Prince Edward Island, Quebec, the Northwest Territories and the Yukon Territory. And most of the smaller paramedical professions were completely frozen out of the health-insurance system. The turf of the medical profession may be somewhat diminished in the 1980s, but it remains by far the largest territory. Doctors have defended their borders with skill and determination.

CHAPTER 6

MEDICAL HERETICS: THE CAMPAIGN AGAINST SALARIED DOCTORS

If you need to see a doctor in the northern Ontario city of Sault Ste. Marie, you will probably find yourself in a sunny, spacious building on McNabb Street. It is a cheerful place. There are colourful paintings on the wall, and plants are hanging in the atrium. The doctors and nurses who work in this building are the primary source of health care for more than 40,000 people — about 45 per cent of the local population. The Group Health Centre of Sault Ste. Marie is one of the biggest success stories in Canadian medical history. And its philosophy is based on a simple principle: patients should not become addicted to doctors.

The Group Health Centre contains virtually all the services of a standard hospital (except for beds — overnight surgery is not performed here). But unlike a hospital, the health centre is not enveloped in institutional gloom. The emphasis is on health, not sickness. This is reflected in the wide-open design of the building's interior. More importantly, it is reflected in the treatment of patients. The patient is taught to become an independent person who knows how to cope with many of the most common health problems in society today.

Patients who visit the Group Health Centre often leave with a copy of a self-help manual called *Take Care of Yourself*. The manual provides a list of symptoms of common health problems and the recommended course of action for each symptom. If the health problem is minor, the manual explains how it can be treated at home.

In many cases, patients who visit the health centre will end up talking to a highly trained nurse or social worker. The counselling sessions run for 30 minutes or even an hour — much longer than a doctor could afford to spend with a patient. The nurse or social worker helps the patient understand the causes and proper treatment of common conditions such as pre-menstrual syndrome, depression or stress. According to one study at the Sault Ste. Marie health centre, the counselling sessions reduced the average patient's use of mood-altering prescription drugs by 45 to 62 per cent. The counselling also helped reduce the average patient's visits to the doctor's office by 27 to 40 per cent. And there were similar reductions in the number of laboratory tests and X-rays.

Essentially, the Group Health Centre weans its patients away from their reliance on doctors. "They should know when they should see a doctor, when they should see a nurse, and when they should apply home treatment," said Dr. Tom Ferrier, who has worked at the health centre since its birth in 1963. "There's a tendency for most doctors to make patients too dependent. As we face an increasing supply of physicians, there's going to be an increasing utilization of physicians. For example, a patient with hypertension will see a physician month after month after month. And he's given just enough medication so he'll have to come back. Whereas here we'll see the patient frequently at first, then cut it down to every three months, then every six months, then once a year. It's a stable, chronic condition which the patient can manage."

The crucial difference between the Sault Ste. Marie health centre and the traditional doctor's office is a difference in financial incentives. The ordinary doctor is paid on a fee-for-service basis: the more services provided, the greater his or her income. But at the health centre, Dr. Ferrier and his colleagues are paid by salary. Their incomes are fixed, regardless of how many times they see a patient. "There's no incentive for a doctor here to build up his practice," Dr. Ferrier said.

Fee-for-service doctors cannot submit a bill to the medicare plan unless they have actually seen the patient. As a result, many doctors tend to see each patient briefly, then move on to the next patient, spending only a few minutes on each case. Fee-for-service doctors are unlikely to delegate a case to a nurse who can spend more time with a patient, since doctors cannot bill medicare for this. Under the fee schedule, doctors receive less money for talking and listening to a patient than for carrying out procedures. It is thus not surprising that fee-for-service doctors are unlikely to spend much time providing health information to their patients. A survey in 1986 found that 39 per cent of Ontario residents felt they received inadequate information from their doctor.

By contrast, at a community health centre such as the one in Sault Ste. Marie, routine cases can be handled by nurse practitioners, who can spend more time counselling the patients, while the doctor concentrates on more complex cases. "We're freed from the tyranny of the time constraint," said Fred Griffith, the president of the health centre.

On a typical day at the emergency department of the Sault Ste. Marie health centre, Dr. Ferrier saw only three of the dozen patients who arrived. The remaining patients — who were suffering from minor injuries, infections and abdominal pains — were treated by the nurses. "Each of us functions at our highest level of competence, which keeps us a little more alive," Dr. Ferrier said.

Because the health centre is not bound by a rigid fee schedule, it can create new programs to meet the needs of its patients. For example, the centre has created a special clinic to help patients cope with chronic back pain; there are programs to help people lose weight and stop smoking; the centre has a health-information telephone service that receives as many as 500 calls a day; and there is even a special prenatal class for unwed teenage girls.

The absence of fee-for-service medicine, combined with the emphasis on health education and counselling, has allowed the Sault Ste. Marie health centre to keep its patients away from surgical procedures in hospitals. Studies have consistently shown that the health centre's 40,000 patients are 25 to 30 per cent less likely to enter hospital than other patients in the same city. There are fewer surgical operations among the health centre's patients, and there are more preventive health measures such as immunizations.

The Battle against the Health Centre

When it officially opened its doors in 1963, the Sault Ste. Marie health centre was the first community health centre in Canada. It was established by the local branch of the United Steelworkers of America. (The Algoma Steel Corporation is still the biggest employer in the Sault today, and the Steelworkers continue to hold five of the 11 positions on the health centre's board of directors.)

From the beginning, organized medicine has waged a long and bitter campaign against the health centre. The fight began in 1960, when the doctors realized that the Steelworkers were serious in their plans for a health centre in the Sault. The president of the Sault Ste.

Marie Medical Society wrote to the union in March 1960 to declare the society's unanimous opposition to the proposed health centre, and the local doctors warned that they would refuse to participate in it.

They repeated the threat a few days later in a full-page advertisement in the local newspaper. The medical society proclaimed a five-point statement of principles, including the principle of fee-for-service payment for doctors. Three weeks later the doctors arranged another full-page advertisement. This time they tried a different strategy: they attempted to drive a wedge between the union leaders and the union membership. The medical society's advertisement suggested that "our accumulated knowledge of medical care may be of help to the union members in preventing their executives from leading them into a very unhappy and costly experiment."

In February 1961 the Canadian Medical Association declared its opposition to the health centre. Three months later the Ontario Medical Association published a pamphlet for distribution to patients in the Sault. The pamphlet warned that a health centre "could endanger the welfare of a community." The pamphlet also predicted that a health centre would increase the cost of medical services and would be "alien" to "the best practice of medicine" and to "the democratic rights of free people."

The local medical society continued its campaign in March 1962 with an official statement that the health centre was "not in the best interests either for the union members and their families or the community at large." The statement warned that the centre would "result in deterioration of the quality of medical care provided to the community." In July 1962 an Ontario doctor backed out of an agreement to become the centre's medical director. The attacks by the local and provincial medical associations were a major factor in his decision.

Despite the fierce opposition from organized medicine, the Steelworkers voted to proceed with the health centre. By 1963 the centre was guaranteed a base of more than 12,000 patients. The fee-for-service doctors still refused to end their battle. It was clear that they would cease to refer their patients to any physician who joined the health centre. They also threatened to stop providing consultations to any doctor who joined the centre.

The medical society's president, Dr. Walter Zaharuk, wrote to the health centre in February 1963 to warn that "none of the local doctors in private practice will join the Union Clinic on a full or part-time basis. This clearly denotes that consultative and other assistance will not be available." In March Dr. Zaharuk said the health centre would provide "assembly-line treatment" and its medical staff "will pull out as soon as they have paid off their debts and saved some money to establish themselves. . . . Not many will stay long enough to establish any kind of personal relationship with their patients." He predicted that the only doctors who would work in the centre would be "young graduates, misfits and a few true believers."

Meanwhile, many of the fee-for-service doctors were urging a local hospital to refuse to give hospital privileges to the health centre's doctors. (The hospital rejected this suggestion.) Private physicians tried to convince local nurses to refrain from applying for jobs at the centre. Because of complaints from private physicians, nurses were denied the use of meeting rooms in the local hospitals when they wanted to meet the health centre's administrators. After the centre recruited 12 doctors (mostly recent graduates), the medical society decided to ostracize these doctors. Fee-for-service physicians urged their colleagues to refuse to speak to the centre's doctors and to walk away if one of them entered their office. When the health centre's doctors wanted a tour of a local hospital, they were forced to accept a janitor as their guide.

The health centre opened its doors in September 1963. Three months later the medical society placed an advertisement in the *Canadian Medical Association Journal* to warn all doctors to contact the medical society for advice before making any commitments to the centre. Fee-for-service doctors continued to ostracize the centre's doctors. Virtually no patients were referred to the centre by the private physicians. The health centre's doctors were unable to gain membership on hospital committees, and their applications to join the medical society were rejected. They were even excluded from cultural and recreational organizations in which the private doctors were influential.

Fred Griffith was the director of a major charity organization and a respected member of the community in the early 1960s. When he became the administrator of the health centre, everything changed. "I was blackballed at a club where I'd been a member for years," he recalled. "The community was really polarized."

There was intense hostility from the medical society. One of its members physically assaulted Dr. Ferrier and another doctor at the centre. Dr. Ferrier, who was the health centre's medical director at the time, said his wife was attacked publicly "with a verbal assault of extreme viciousness" by the society member. In 1965 one doctor who resigned from the health centre said his resignation was prompted by the hostility of the fee-for-service doctors. "I do not choose to spend my life in an atmosphere of hate, vindictiveness and paranoid delusions," the doctor said in his letter of resignation.

In 1966 the chief of medical staff at a local hospital threatened to remove the hospital privileges of all health centre doctors if the centre did not give its patients the option of visiting a fee-for-service doctor. The centre agreed to allow its patients to visit any physician they wanted. But when it asked the medical society to help provide anesthetists for the health centre, the medical society refused.

Two years later the medical society again refused to provide any anesthetic services for the health centre, except in emergencies. Since the centre was temporarily unable to recruit its own anesthetists, it was effectively prevented from conducting any non-emergency surgery. The centre was forced to take legal action to gain assistance from anesthetists in the Sault.

By the 1970s the health centre was still receiving only 2 to 3 per cent of all patients referred by private physicians in the Sault, even though the centre had more than 30 per cent of the city's physicians. "Anything we did was opposed," Dr. Ferrier said. "Everything we did was looked upon as a threat."

Today some of the fee-for-service doctors still refuse to talk to the veteran doctors at the health centre. "At the meetings of the medical academy, usually after a few drinks, tempers sometimes flare," Dr. Ferrier said. When a local newspaper printed a story about the health centre's plans for a women's health unit, some local doctors complained to the Ontario College of Physicians and Surgeons. The doctors said the centre was violating the college's rules against advertising. "It's an unending guerrilla war," Fred Griffith said. "You never know what tree they're going to pop out of."

The St. Catharines Health Centre

The second community health centre in Ontario's history was created in St. Catharines in 1967. Here too there was hostility from the local doctors. But this time the health centre did not survive.

The St. Catharines health centre began as a modest centennial project by the United Automobile Workers. The UAW raised $500,000 through weekly donations of $1 each for three years from the union membership. They set up a community board of directors, hired a handful of doctors on fixed salaries and launched their experiment. There were obstacles and difficulties, but within a few years the community health centre was a popular success. Union members were not the only people who enjoyed the centre's medical services. By 1978 the centre was serving about 20,000 patients from across the city. Indeed, it was threatening to take business away from private medical practices. Then the Ontario government pulled the plug. The province terminated its financial support, and almost immediately the centre was dead.

Who killed the St. Catharines health centre? The provincial bureaucrats insisted that it was a case of suicide. The centre was just too expensive to survive, government officials said. But a closer investigation suggests a more complicated picture. The UAW and the bureaucrats were not the only players in the story. The behaviour of the medical establishment was a crucial factor in the demise of the centre.

It must first be understood that there was no overwhelming logic in the province's decision to withdraw its financing from the St. Catharines health centre. True, the centre was more expensive than a private fee-for-service clinic. A provincial study in 1975 had established that the cost per patient at the St. Catharines centre was higher than the cost for the average patient at a comparable private clinic in Brantford. But the study had also revealed that the average patient in the St. Catharines centre spent 20 per cent less time in hospital than the average patient in Brantford.

The doctors in the St. Catharines health centre had no financial incentive to put their patients in a hospital. They received the same salary, regardless of how many medical services their patients consumed. Their emphasis was on preventive medicine. The centre had a family counsellor, prenatal classes, obesity clinics and education programs. The provincial study in 1975 had found that the quality of care at St. Catharines was slightly higher than the quality of care at Brantford (although the Brantford clinic was adequate). The doctors in St. Catharines kept better medical records than the Brantford doctors, the study said, and unlike the Brantford clinic, the St. Catharines health centre provided evening and weekend services.

There were some legitimate reasons for the higher costs in St. Catharines. For example, the board of directors at the St. Catharines health centre believed in giving the support staff the same salary structure as unionized workers in hospitals. The support staff in the Brantford clinic were not unionized. As a result, the salaries in St. Catharines were 30 per cent above the salaries of the Brantford clinic. The province admitted that this could account for part of the difference in the cost per patient in St. Catharines and Brantford.

There was another major reason for the financial problems of the St. Catharines health centre. Under the regulations of the province's health department, the St. Catharines centre was given a monthly payment for every patient in its care. However, some of these patients saw private doctors in addition to the health centre doctors. Curiously, the province required the community health centre to pay the cost of the medical services provided by these private doctors. In many cases, the cost of the private doctors exceeded the regular payment to the centre from the province. For example, the province might have been giving the centre a monthly payment of $20 for every patient enrolled in the centre. But some of these patients might have been receiving $100 worth of medical services from a private doctor. The $100 cost was deducted from the provincial payments to the health centre. Eventually these outside costs began to weaken the finances of the St. Catharines centre.

The province eventually admitted that the health-insurance regulations needed to be reformed. The regulations were amended so that the outside costs would not be deducted from provincial payments to community health centres — but by then it was too late. By 1978 the St. Catharines health centre had expired.

It was an unnecessary death. The province argued that the St. Catharines health centre was too expensive — yet on closer examination the higher costs had a reasonable explanation. The province failed to consider the better quality of medical care at the St. Catharines clinic, or the fact that its own regulations had seriously damaged the finances of the health centre.

It is hard to believe that the province could have overlooked these factors when it decided to terminate its support of the St. Catharines clinic. One suspects that there must have been another reason for its decision. What was happening in the backrooms of the Ontario Ministry of Health in the mid-1970s?

The senior officials of the health ministry were feeling some heavy pressure in the second half of the 1970s. The province's doctors were unhappy with the rise of the community health centres. The vast majority of private physicians have always believed strongly in the fee-for-service system. It allows them to set their own hours of work, see as many patients as they want, and effectively control their incomes (as we saw in chapter 4). Private physicians, and particularly the physicians who serve as the leaders of the national and provincial medical associations, are committed to the preservation of this system. Community health centres are a threat to the fee-for-service system. And in the mid-1970s this threat appeared to be growing in Ontario. In addition to the St. Catharines health centre, there was already the well-established health centre in Sault Ste. Marie. Moreover, the province had approved a series of "health-service organizations" (HSOs), similar to the community health centres except for the absence of a community board of directors.

The Ontario Medical Association began to lobby hard to protect the fee-for-service system. The OMA sent delegations to visit the provincial health minister to express concern about the growing number of community health centres and HSOs. A delegation in 1975 was particularly successful. The medical association's delegation was able to persuade the health minister, Frank Miller, to freeze the development of HSOs and health centres. The freeze was eventually lifted, but the HSOs and health centres were given below-inflation budget increases (or no increase at all) for several years.

A former health ministry official who worked with HSOs when they were started told the *Globe and Mail* in 1979 that the community clinics were suppressed by the hostility of the medical profession and by the free-enterprise ideology of Frank Miller and his successor, Dennis Timbrell. The former health official noted that Miller and Timbrell were sympathetic to the doctors' views on the subject of community clinics. Miller and Timbrell are both Conservatives — and the Conservatives have traditionally been closer to the doctors than any other political party in Ontario.

In this context, it is easier to understand the province's decision on the St. Catharines question. No-one is suggesting that the pressure from the OMA was the only reason for the government's decision to terminate its support. But clearly it must have been a factor — perhaps the biggest factor.

Another factor was the hostility of individual doctors in St. Catharines. They disliked the competition from the health centre, and some of them did their best to hinder it. The simplest way for the doctors to undermine the health centre was to increase the medicare expenses of patients who were enrolled in the centre — because these expenses would be deducted from the provincial payments to the centre (as described earlier). Since thousands of the centre's patients were also visiting outside doctors, these doctors controlled a large proportion of the centre's expenses. Ted Goldberg, a union official who helped establish the St. Catharines health centre, described the outside expenses as "an impossible situation" for the centre. "It allowed the competition to simply provide services that made the health centre unfeasible," said Goldberg. "It allowed the opposition to do away with the centre. And that's really what happened."

The failure of the St. Catharines community health centre is a symbol of the continuing dominance of the fee-for-service physician in Canada. Only a tiny fraction of Canada's population are served by salaried doctors. In Ontario, for example, just 2 per cent of the population are served by physicians in health-service organizations or community health centres. The proportion is even smaller in most other provinces. Quebec is the only province with a significant number of community health centres, but even there the fee-for-service model predominates.

The American Experience

Canada may be the last frontier for the fee-for-service doctor. Even in the United States — the heartland of the free-enterprise ideology — the private doctor in fee-for-service practice is becoming an endangered species. A steadily increasing number of American patients are switching to health-maintenance organizations (HMOs) — a concept similar to the Canadian HSOs and health centres, where doctors are prepaid by an organization that gives them a lump-sum payment for every patient under their care. Today about 24 million Americans are enrolled in HMOs. The number of HMO members has jumped by 14 million since 1981. Experts have predicted that one-half of the American population will be enrolled in HMOs by the mid-1990s. One-quarter of all practising doctors in the U.S. were participating in HMOs in 1986, an increase of 84 per cent over 1980. In the near future, half of the doctors in the United States will be salaried.

Why are the HMOs so popular in the United States? They were originally encouraged by President Richard Nixon, who introduced legislation in 1973 to provide federal grants to HMOs. Nixon was a critic of the fee-for-service system, recognizing that fee-for-service doctors had a financial incentive to provide an endlessly increasing number of medical services. "The more illnesses they treat — and the more services they render — the more their income rises," Nixon noted. By contrast, the income of HMO physicians depended solely on the number of patients enrolled. Regardless of how many medical services each patient was given, the HMO doctor got the same payment per patient. Clearly there was a strong potential for cost savings in an HMO.

The history of the past 14 years has vindicated the advocates of the HMO. When the federal subsidies ended, the HMOs continued to grow and prosper. As predicted, they did succeed in reducing the cost of health care — primarily by reducing the number of unnecessary hospital admissions. The evidence is overwhelming. Some 40 comparison studies have concluded that HMOs and other prepaid plans cut the cost of medical care by 10 to 40 per cent. They reduce the level of hospitalization by as much as 45 per cent, the studies show. For example, the average HMO in Minneapolis sends its patients to hospital at a rate of about 500 days per 1,000 members, compared to a rate of about 850 days per 1,000 patients in fee-for-service practices in the same area.

One of the most comprehensive and careful studies of the HMO concept was a 1984 randomized study by the Rand Corporation, a major U.S. think-tank. The Rand researchers decided to examine a large HMO in Seattle. A group of 1,580 people was divided into two subgroups: some were randomly assigned to an HMO doctor, and others were randomly assigned to a fee-for-service doctor. The health care of both subgroups, for the purposes of the study, was provided free of charge. The researchers found that the health care of the average HMO patient cost 28 per cent less than that of the average fee-for-service patient. Furthermore, the rate of hospital admissions for the HMO patients was 40 per cent less than the rate for the fee-for-service patients.

The Rand Corporation concluded that this sharp contrast could not be explained by any differences in the health characteristics of the two subgroups of patients. The physicians in the HMO "were simply practicing a different style of medicine from that of fee-for-service physicians," the researchers said. The HMO patients were getting a larger amount of preventive health care, they were receiving fewer prescription drugs, and they were spending more time with nurse practitioners and physiotherapists. The researchers concluded that the average fee-for-service physician was practising a more "hospital-intensive" style of medicine than is necessary.

The evidence also suggests that the health of HMO patients is not affected by the reduced hospitalization rate. They are not being underserviced by their HMOs. Indeed, the popularity of HMOs would surely decline if their members felt they were receiving inadequate care. The popularity of HMOs has, in fact, continued to rise. "It seems unlikely that there can be large deleterious health effects from their style of medicine," the Rand Corporation has reported. Alain Enthoven, the Stanford University health economist, has reached the same conclusion: "I have been unable to find any documented case of a pattern of underservice among HMOs." Joseph Califano, the former U.S. secretary of health, education and welfare, is another expert who agrees that the patient's health is unaffected by HMOs. When the financial incentives of the fee-for-service system are eliminated, the rate of surgery drops sharply "and the patients are just as healthy without enduring the risk and pain of the operation," Califano has said.

One of the biggest benefits of the HMOs is that they improve the efficiency of the health-care system by providing competition to fee-for-service physicians. Without fair competition, any system is bound to become wasteful and inefficient. "The only way to find good methods of organization and good incentives is through experience in a system of fair economic competition among alternative delivery systems," Alain Enthoven has pointed out.

The Canadian Evidence

Despite the limited number of community health centres and HSOs in Canada, the evidence here is already confirming the American experience: the fee-for-service system is sending an unnecessarily large number of people to hospital. A typical example is the community health centre in Sault Ste. Marie. Throughout its history, the patients at the health centre have enjoyed much lower hospital rates than other patients in the same city. A preliminary study in 1966 found that the health centre's annual rate of hospitalization was 680 days per 1,000 people, compared to a rate of 1,850 days per 1,000 people in the rest of the city.

A few months later the World Health Organization and the Ontario government agreed to support a more comprehensive study. This careful study, which took four years to complete, compared two groups of steelworkers: those who went to the health centre and those who went to fee-for-service doctors in Sault Ste. Marie. The two groups of patients had basically similar characteristics, yet the study found that the rate of hospital utilization by the health centre's patients was one-quarter lower than the hospital rate among the fee-for-service patients. The study said the health centre seemed to put more emphasis on preventive health rather than medical intervention. The health centre's patients had fewer surgical operations, and they were more likely to receive immunizations and health education. They were less likely to be treated by an inappropriate specialist, and they were more likely to receive laboratory tests and radiology examinations as out-patients rather than as hospital in-patients.

In the 1970s the evidence continued to confirm the advantages of the Sault health centre. The annual rate of hospital utilization among the centre's patients in the late 1970s was about 1,200 days per 1,000 people, compared to a rate of about 2,000 days per 1,000 people in the rest of the surrounding district. Meanwhile, the popularity of the health centre was steadily increasing. A consumer survey in the Sault revealed that the centre's patients believed they had greater accessibility to certain diagnostic services and shorter waiting periods before seeing a doctor.

The same kind of evidence was accumulating in Quebec, where community health centres are common. A study in 1978 by four sociology students in Montreal showed that the health care in the community clinics was "significantly better" than in the traditional fee-for-service system. The community doctors spent more time with their patients (an average of 30 minutes per patient) and regarded them as participants in the treatment — not simply as recipients.

In the 1980s, studies showed that the patients of Ontario HSOs were 20 per cent less likely to enter hospital than the patients of fee-for-service doctors. In 1983 alone, for example, the HSOs saved Ontario taxpayers a total of $2,268,000 in hospital charges. (These savings were achieved despite the small size of the average Canadian HSO compared to the average American HMO. The much larger HMOs were able to gain economies of scale that are unavailable to a small health centre.)

A study for the Ontario Economic Council in 1981 estimated that community health centres and HSOs had the potential to save as much as $143 million in hospital costs alone. This estimate was based on 1974 dollars, and the potential savings would be considerably higher today.

In 1982 Larry Grossman, the Conservative health minister in Ontario, finally acknowledged the evidence. He announced a program of financial incentives to encourage the development of HSOs and community health centres. It was a low-budget program, but it was still an improvement over the province's negative attitude towards health centres in the 1970s. Grossman, in his speeches in 1982 and 1983, criticized the fee-for-service system for its "revolving-door syndrome" — the tendency for patients to be pushed through the doctor's office at a rapid rate, since the doctor is paid for each visit. Doctors in health centres usually avoid the revolving-door syndrome, Grossman said. "The physicians who have chosen to practice in this way have, in many cases, a distinct orientation toward health promotion," he said.

The brave words from Larry Grossman could not conceal the fact that Ontario has been a laggard. A decade earlier — in the early 1970s — a host of government reports had urged the Canadian provinces to encourage the growth of health centres. Task forces and government inquiries all reached the same conclusion: health centres would encourage doctors to keep their patients healthy, since the centres would receive no extra money if their patients visited doctors more often.

In 1971 a conference of provincial and federal health ministers agreed to finance a full investigation of community health centres. The inquiry was headed by John Hastings, a professor at the University of Toronto. His study recommended that the provinces take steps to encourage the development of a significant number of community health centres. The Hastings Report said the provinces would be encouraging "flexibility and innovation" if they promoted the growth of health centres. It noted that the community health centres "are increasingly seen as an important means for slowing the rate of increase in the cost of health services." The report said the health centres would be a good location for a wide range of social and health services, including the services of nurse practitioners, social workers, psychologists and nutritionists. The report also noted that salaried doctors would be more likely to delegate their routine work to less-expensive nurses and paramedicals, allowing the doctors to concentrate on more complicated tasks.

In the first half of the 1970s, community health centres were advocated by major reports in Quebec, Nova Scotia, Manitoba, Ontario and British Columbia. Federal health ministers also recommended the development of community health centres. And the Lalonde Report, the landmark study by former federal health and welfare minister Marc Lalonde in 1974, threw its weight behind the concept of community health centres. All these reports and recommendations emphasized two major advantages of community health centres: first, their efficiency in delivering medical services; and second, their ability to provide an integrated program of preventive health care in which a team of physicians and other health professionals can ensure that the social and psychological needs of the patients are given as much attention as their medical needs.

Manitoba's 1972 white paper on health policy described both of these advantages. It concluded that community health centres could "restore unity of health care, providing within a single framework the services and professionals to assist people over a broad range of health and social problems. Such centres reduce the distorting incentives inherent in the fee-for-service system, and fill the vacuum where no incentives to efficiency exist." The Ontario Economic Council, in a 1976 report, confirmed the lack of efficiency in the fee-for-service system: "Of all the conceivable financial combinations, the current system is the one most devoid of incentives to induce efficiency in the production of health care services and to encourage economy in the consumption of those services."

Despite this consensus of opinion among the most knowledgeable analysts of health care, the fee-for-service system continues to dominate Canadian medicine. There are about 150 community health centres in Quebec, but most of them are serving a small population. Less than 10 per cent of Quebec's general practitioners are employed at the health centres. There are about 32 health centres and HSOs in Ontario, but they serve only a tiny portion of the provincial population. In the rest of the country, the number of health centres is even smaller. An informal survey in 1985 found a total of five in British Columbia, four in Saskatchewan, eight in Manitoba, two in Alberta and a half-dozen in the Maritimes and the North.

The Role of Organized Medicine

There are several reasons for the failure of the health centre movement in Canada, but the hostility of the medical profession has certainly been a major factor. Medical associations across North America have fought tenaciously to preserve the dominance of the fee-for-service system. They have opposed every attempt to introduce an alternative to the traditional payment mechanism.

Once, in the early 1960s, the president-elect of the Ontario Medical Association pointed out that the oath of Hippocrates does not say anything about the fee-for-service system. The president-elect, Dr. William Wigle, recalls the hostile reaction to his comment: "One volatile group of physicians interpreted this as a rejection of the fee-for-service principle, which to them meant only one alternative, a salaried service. So at the next meeting I addressed, in North Bay, a busload of these doctors insisted that I withdraw my statement or resign as president-elect of the OMA."

To understand the conflict between medical associations and community health centres, we must begin by looking at the basic ideology of the medical profession. The notion of professional independence is the most important element in the doctor's ideology. By instinct and by training, the average doctor insists on the freedom to determine his or her own income and his or her own style of practice. The concept of a salaried practice and a community board of directors is totally alien to this ideology.

Jonathan Lomas, who wrote the definitive history of the Sault Ste. Marie health centre, has analyzed the reasons for the medical ideology: "Professional status represents the zenith of achievement in today's specialized society, and maintenance of personal and professional autonomy ensures recognition as one of these privileged achievers. Not only is this attitude taught in medical schools, but the very concept of independence and freedom is one of the major attractions for many medical school applicants."

Community health centres also expand the opportunities for non-physicians to replace physicians in the health-care system. Again, this contradicts the self-interest of doctors. Community health centres "present a threat to the physician's share of the health budget," Lomas pointed out.

Thus it is not surprising that organized medicine would strongly resist the introduction of a new system that challenged the fee-for-service system. In the United States, the resistance began as soon as consumers introduced the earliest alternatives to fee-for-service. The ancestors of the HMOs were born in the state of Washington in 1910. The first "medical cooperative" was created in rural Oklahoma in 1927. Many others were founded in the 1930s and 1940s. Organized medicine immediately went on the attack. By the end of the 1940s, medical associations had persuaded most state legislatures to approve restrictive laws that effectively prohibited any consumer-controlled health plan. Doctors who joined a prepaid plan were ejected from medical societies and lost their hospital privileges.

Here in Canada, organized medicine has behaved in exactly the same manner. The medical leaders were unable to prevent the growth of the Sault Ste. Marie community health centre, but in most regions of Canada they have succeeded in restricting the development of similar health centres.

In 1939 a group of consumers in Regina made one of the earliest attempts to establish a medical cooperative in this country. The organizers succeeded in persuading 1,500 families to join the cooperative. While eight doctors applied to work for a salary in the new medical clinic, the vast majority of Regina's doctors were opposed to the cooperative. They quickly formed their own medical-insurance program in an effort to forestall the establishment of the cooperative. And they applied strong pressure to discourage the doctors who had applied to join the cooperative. As a result, all eight of the original applicants decided to withdraw their applications. None of the local doctors would agree to work for the cooperative, and the consumers were forced to switch to an orthodox health-insurance plan in which doctors were paid on the usual fee-for-service basis.

A medical cooperative in Saskatoon was somewhat more successful, but the Saskatchewan doctors hampered its growth by establishing their own health-insurance agency in 1946 to lure patients away from the co-op. Doctors in northern Saskatchewan urged their patients to join the doctor-controlled agency. Within a few years the medical agency had overtaken the consumer cooperative.

During the strike by Saskatchewan's doctors in 1962, a number of community health centres were established in Saskatchewan. These were fee-for-service clinics, but they were controlled by consumers. Each clinic had a community board of directors. Organized medicine immediately attacked the community clinics. The Saskatchewan College of Physicians and Surgeons accused the community clinics of being "centrally directed and politically inspired." Many doctors refused to accept referrals from the community clinics. They often refused to share medical information with the community doctors. Some anesthetists refused to give an anesthetic to a patient whose surgeon was employed by a community clinic. The community doctors were ostracized socially, and many were unable to obtain hospital privileges. One British doctor had been the assistant to Queen Elizabeth's personal physician, but he was unable to gain hospital privileges when he joined a community clinic in Saskatchewan. Finally the province had to appoint a royal commission to study the hardships imposed on the community doctors.

The royal commission concluded that the community doctors were being unfairly treated by the medical profession. One of the worst cases involved Dr. Reynold Gold, a community physician who had arrived from Britain during the 1962 strike. The medical advisory committee at Saskatoon City Hospital refused to give him hospital privileges because his training was "deficient" and "below Canadian standards." The royal commission concluded that the medical advisory committee was influenced by political considerations. The commission questioned the objectivity of the medical advisory committee.

In the early 1970s the Saskatchewan government began to give the community clinics an annual budget. This allowed the clinics to abandon the fee-for-service system and switch to a system similar to the Sault Ste. Marie health centre. Once again organized medicine was hostile. The Saskatchewan Medical Association warned that the development of community health centres could be "enormously expensive." The SMA said the health centre concept was being promoted by "radical health planners." The fee-for-service system is "the most equitable method of payment," the SMA said.

There is only a handful of community health centres in Saskatchewan today, but their financing is relatively stable. However, some tensions still exist. Even in the 1980s some medical specialists in Saskatchewan have refused to accept patients who are referred from the community health centres.

In Manitoba the leaders of organized medicine were successful in blocking a proposed expansion of the province's network of community health centres. In the early 1970s the provincial government announced a plan to establish 20 community health centres in Manitoba. The Manitoba Medical Association reacted with outrage. It produced a long list of objections. Health centres "could work to the disadvantage of patient care and could be more expensive per item of service rendered," the MMA warned in 1973. "Fee-for-service is the best mechanism for relating the reward to the workload and encouraging the doctor to strive to satisfy the individual patient," the MMA said. It argued that the establishment of community health centres would be "an untried system, possibly more costly and with greater bureaucratic control."

Faced with the strong opposition of the medical profession, the Manitoba government abandoned its plan to establish 20 community health centres in the province. Ever since this episode, the health centre movement has foundered in Manitoba.

One of the biggest weapons wielded by organized medicine is its ability to prohibit advertising by the community health centres. In the United States the growth of HMOs has been boosted by high-profile advertising campaigns. Television and radio commercials and billboard advertisements have ensured that the public is aware of the alternatives to the fee-for-service system. By contrast, in Canada the medical profession has effectively banned the use of advertisements by community health centres or HSOs.

In 1963, for example, the Ontario College of Physicians and Surgeons filed a charge of professional impropriety against Dr. Ferrier, the medical director of the Sault Ste. Marie health centre. The reason? The centre had mentioned the names of its doctors in a newsletter to its members. The college decided that this was a violation of its rules against advertising by doctors.

Similarly, when the South Riverdale Community Health Centre distributed a pamphlet in its neighbourhood in east-end Toronto, the Ontario college sent a warning letter to the health centre. The pamphlet, which simply mentioned the centre's 24-hour emergency service, was distributed by the centre's board of directors — not by the doctors. Nevertheless, the college decided that the pamphlet came within its legal jurisdiction. Another doctor was called before the Ontario college when he described his health centre in an interview in a neighbourhood newspaper. And in Saskatchewan, the growth of community health centres was restricted when the Saskatchewan College of Physicians and Surgeons prohibited any advertising by the health centres in the mid-1960s.

The rules of the provincial colleges have made it almost impossible for provincial governments to promote the use of community health centres or HSOs. Yet these centres cannot survive if the community is unaware of their existence. A health centre must have a sufficient supply of patients to attract financing from the provincial governments. By prohibiting any advertising by the health centres, the medical profession has jeopardized their existence.

Across the country, medical associations have consistently attacked the health centre concept. The Canadian Medical Association, in a 1967 report, strongly urged its members to stay away from community health centres. The 1970–71 president of the CMA described the health centres as "white elephants" that cannot survive without "generous government support." Even after the Ontario government finally endorsed the concept in 1982, the Ontario Medical Association continued to insist that the health centres are "still in the experimental stage." The OMA argues that there is still insufficient evidence to prove that health centres are as good as the fee-for-service system.

The Quebec Federation of General Practitioners criticized the network of community health centres which was introduced in Quebec in the early 1970s. The federation encouraged its members to establish private medical clinics to compete with the community health centres. More than 400 private "polyclinics," operating on a fee-for-service basis, were created. The Quebec government had intended the community health centres to serve as the major gateway to health services in the province, but the existence of the polyclinics has helped to block this goal.

Dozens of neutral studies and reports have concluded that community health centres could improve the efficiency and quality of health care in this country. Governments have endorsed the concept in principle, but the politicians recognize that they would face a major battle with the medical associations if they attempted to establish a significant number of community health centres. Consequently, the community health centres are still relegated to the fringes of Canada's health-care system. The medical associations realize that because the health centres are contained and limited, they are no longer a serious threat to the fee-for-service system.

Even the existing health centres are, in some cases, moving away from the basic principles of their idealistic beginnings. The oversupply of doctors in Canada has forced many conservative doctors to accept jobs at community health centres, and the influx has moderated the philosophy of some of the centres. Indeed, the medical staff at several community health centres actually supported the OMA during the 1986 dispute with the Ontario government. Instead of providing a fundamental challenge to the fee-for-service system, community health centres are perhaps becoming simply a convenient source of employment.

CHAPTER 7

LICENCE TO PRACTISE: THE CLOSED SHOP

Dr. Halina Sroczynski has applied for work at 35 Canadian hospitals every year since 1983. Ordinarily it would be a simple matter for Dr. Sroczynski to obtain an internship in this country. She is a Canadian citizen, she has passed her qualifying exams, and she is completely eligible for an internship. But Dr. Sroczynski graduated from a medical school in Poland. When internships are allocated, most hospitals in Canada are required to give preference to the graduates of Canadian medical schools. And so Dr. Sroczynski's applications are rejected. Hospital after hospital turns her away.

Dr. Sroczynski, who is 33, had worked as a general practitioner in Poland for a year before immigrating to Canada. But her medical experience is no help in this country. She considered herself fortunate when she finally persuaded another doctor to let her serve as an unpaid medical observer in the emergency department of a Toronto hospital. She worked part time as a computer clerk to support herself. After 18 months of unpaid work in the emergency department, she thought she might have a chance at an internship in the hospital.

Dr. Sroczynski received a good reference from the doctor in the emergency department. But when the internship interviews were held, she found that the doors were still closed to her. "They ignored me completely," she said. "I felt really sad."

Four years after she began applying for internships, Dr. Sroczynski is working as an admitting clerk at the same hospital in Toronto. She is tantalizingly close to the medical world, yet she is still firmly on the outside. She registers the patients who arrive — but she cannot treat them.

Dr. Sroczynski is one of about 40 Polish immigrant doctors — all of whom were fully qualified doctors in their homeland — who continue to search for internships in Canada. Some of the doctors have been seeking a medical position for five years. But they cannot get a licence to practise medicine in Canada until they have completed an internship. And in the 1980s, an internship is almost impossible for a foreign-trained doctor to obtain.

Most of the immigrants were specialists who had practised medicine for many years in Poland before their arrival in Canada. Some were leading experts who had taught medicine all over Europe. Today they are driving cabs in Toronto or working at other low-paying jobs. Some are working as unpaid "clinical fellows" in Toronto hospitals. They perform all the duties of a doctor, but they receive no salary.

"It's very frustrating," Dr. Sroczynski said. "Nobody ever gets used to it. You have a feeling that everything you ever did is all for nothing. We're not even being given a chance to prove ourselves."

Meanwhile, as the Polish doctors struggled to find a path into the promised land of Canadian medicine, remote communities in northern Ontario were crying out for doctors. More than 100 physicians were needed in towns such as Elliot Lake, Dryden and Fort Frances. Some communities had been searching for medical specialists for years.

The Polish doctors were willing to work in the North. In a proposal to the Ontario government, they promised to serve their two-year internships in northern towns that had doctor shortages. The suggestion had no effect. The barriers stayed up.

The plight of the Polish immigrant doctors is not a unique situation in Ontario — or in the rest of the country. By 1986 more than 500 foreign-trained physicians were looking for jobs in Ontario alone. Dr. Rocco Ferro, an Italian-trained physician who has been in Canada since 1981, failed to find any internship positions for three consecutive years after he passed his qualifying exams. Five years after his arrival in Canada, he was still looking for an opening. Similarly, a landed immigrant from India found herself working part time as a nurse's aide, even though she had graduated from a medical school in India with eight years of medical training. The immigrant, a 34-year-old Hamilton woman, applied to 32 hospitals in 1981 and again in 1982. No internships were available.

Further examples were uncovered by a Winnipeg newspaper in 1983. The newspaper found that Dr. Tran Hien was working as a sewing machine operator and Dr. Phan Tuan was working as a nurse's aide. Both were trained medical doctors from Vietnam. Both had passed their qualifying exams. Neither was able to find an internship at a Canadian hospital. They were just two of a group of more than 120 Indo-Chinese doctors seeking internships across Canada at that point.

In 1986 the Polish doctors launched a court action to challenge the constitutionality of policies that made it almost impossible for them to get an internship. Among their affidavits were copies of official resolutions from 13 municipal councils in northern Ontario, unanimously urging the provincial government to give internships to the Polish doctors.

The immigrants lost their court case in 1987, but by then the battle had shifted to the forum of public opinion. A municipal committee on race relations in Toronto concluded that the immigrant doctors were the victims of "blatant discrimination." The committee's co-chairman said the medical profession had created "an old boys' network" to "protect what is theirs." Nothing so obviously discriminatory had ever come to the attention of the committee before, the co-chairman said. Toronto Mayor Arthur Eggleton agreed, calling it "a disgraceful situation."

Many of the immigrant doctors are willing to sign long-term contracts with provincial governments to commit themselves to working in remote towns or rural areas suffering from a shortage of physicians. But the governments — and the leaders of organized medicine in Canada — are opposed to this idea. Indeed, the Canadian medical profession is campaigning for further restrictions on foreign medical graduates. The Canadian Medical Association, with the support of its provincial divisions, is urging the federal government to reduce the number of foreign doctors immigrating to Canada. The CMA and other voices of organized medicine have complained that the foreign medical graduates are threatening to take jobs away from Canadian-trained doctors.

Dr. John O'Brien-Bell, the 1986–87 president of the British Columbia Medical Association, has argued that Canada should prohibit any foreign medical graduate from entering the country to practise medicine. "That would give us control," he told the *CMA Journal*. At its annual meeting in August 1986, the CMA passed a series of resolutions aimed at limiting the number of foreign graduates who are permitted to enter the medical profession in Canada. "We must give priority to our own people," said Dr. Augustin Roy, president of the Professional Corporation of Physicians of Quebec (the provincial licensing body).

If the CMA succeeds in its current campaign, Canada will be turning its back on a key source of supply for its small towns and rural regions. Without the foreign-trained doctors, the rural and northern areas would have suffered a serious crisis in medical care in the past 30 years. Outside the major urban centres, most patients have relied on foreign-trained physicians because Canadian doctors were reluctant to work in rural communities. For example, about 90 per cent of the doctors in solo practice in rural Saskatchewan are graduates of foreign medical schools. An estimated 58 per cent of the physicians in rural Manitoba are foreign graduates. Overall, Canada permitted an average of 914 foreign doctors to enter the country every year from 1961 to 1971. (By comparison, an average of only 919 students graduated from Canadian medical schools each year in the same decade.)

The supply of foreign-trained doctors helped Canada save millions of dollars in education expenses. It costs more than $100,000 to produce a medical graduate from Canadian schools. According to one estimate, the immigration of foreign doctors allowed Canada to save $771 million in medical education costs in the period from 1965 to 1970 alone. Foreign-trained doctors are also valuable in providing medical services to immigrant Canadians who do not speak English or French.

In the 1980s, however, it has become obvious that Canada has an oversupply of urban physicians. The medical profession has responded to this by insisting that foreign-trained doctors must bear the entire burden of the manpower reductions. Yet today the Canadian medical schools are by far the largest source of new doctors in this country. Indeed, enrolment in Canadian medical schools continued to rise rapidly in the 1970s, even as the number of foreign-trained doctors was being reduced. Since the early 1980s, there has been a slight reduction in enrolment, but this has failed to stem the growing surplus of doctors in Canada. Further cuts in enrolment have been strongly recommended by research studies and manpower experts, but the medical associations and the medical faculties have stubbornly resisted any attempt to reduce enrolment by a significant amount. Instead, they want drastic reductions in the ranks of the foreign-trained doctors.

The Doctor Glut

The surplus of doctors was first detected by Canadian health experts in the early 1970s. By 1982, government-sponsored studies were recommending that medical school enrolment be reduced by 10 to 30 per cent. The surplus of doctors has grown so large that a reduction in foreign-trained doctors is simply not sufficient to solve the problem. Even if the inflow of foreign doctors were completely halted, the glut of Canadian doctors would hardly be affected.

The glut is a product of the massive expansion of Canada's medical schools in the 1960s and 1970s. Because of faulty population projections, the need for doctors was disastrously overestimated. Four new medical schools were built. The total enrolment in Canadian medical schools jumped from 3,875 in 1965 to 7,350 in 1985. As a result, the supply of Canadian physicians doubled from 1968 to 1985, even though the country's population rose by only 33 per cent in the same period. And the rapid increase in medical manpower has continued in the late 1980s.

Today there is widespread agreement that Canada has far more doctors than it needs. Canada's 1964 Royal Commission on Health Services suggested that a reasonable goal was to maintain a ratio of one doctor for every 857 people. The World Health Organization has estimated that the optimal level of medical manpower is one doctor for every 667 people. Yet by 1985 there was one doctor for every 491 Canadians.

A study by Peat Marwick and Partners, a management consulting firm, concluded that 22 per cent of the doctors in British Columbia are unnecessary. The same study (which looked at only the western provinces) found significant surpluses of doctors in each of the other provinces in western Canada. Another study, by a federal-provincial advisory committee on health manpower, reported that 300 unnecessary doctors are entering the Canadian medical profession every year. If the trend continues, there will be a surplus of 6,000 doctors in Canada by the year 2000, the committee warned. This surplus will cost billions of dollars in unnecessary expenditures by provincial health departments. In addition, the surplus will encourage doctors to perform unnecessary surgery, putting patients in danger of injury or death.

The surplus is particularly severe among certain kinds of medical specialists. Because the fee schedule tends to provide larger fees for high-technology procedures, specialists can usually maintain adequate incomes even when they are relatively underemployed. Indeed, the surplus of some specialized surgeons is so extreme that they cannot perform enough surgery to maintain their skills at a high level.

Since 1983, several health experts have recommended the complete closure of one or more of Canada's medical schools. Even the mainstream political parties and medical regulatory agencies have finally acknowledged the glut of doctors. As early as 1981 the

Conservative government of Ontario was musing about a cutback in medical school enrolment, although no major action was taken. The Alberta College of Physicians and Surgeons confirmed the existence of the manpower surplus in Alberta in early 1986. Ontario Health Minister Murray Elston, a Liberal, echoed the same words in a speech in the fall of 1986. He warned that the surplus was causing an increase in unnecessary medical treatment.

The federal-provincial advisory committee on health manpower, in its 1985 report, strongly recommended an immediate 20 per cent reduction in first-year enrolment in Canadian medical schools. It also called for a 20 per cent reduction in postgraduate medical training by the early 1990s. The committee suggested that physicians be prohibited from setting up new practices in areas where they are not needed.

The surplus of doctors has been obvious to almost everyone since the early 1980s, but the supply of doctors has continued to soar. Medical faculties are reluctant to reduce the size of their departments. After all, the medical schools realize that their prestige and public image depend on the size and resources of their departments. No administrator or professor wants to see his or her medical school suffer a decline. Thus, the level of enrolment has remained high, despite the warnings of the health researchers. For example, first-year enrolment at the University of British Columbia's medical school rose from 80 to 130 in the period from 1977 to 1981, and remained at that level until 1985, when it dipped only slightly to 120. Yet the surplus of doctors in B.C. is the worst in the country.

The Association of Canadian Medical Colleges, representing the country's medical schools, has argued against any substantial reduction in medical school enrolment. Eva Ryten, the association's research director, has maintained that a cutback in enrolment would be a disservice to young Canadians who are interested in medical careers. Instead, she wants a quota to be imposed on foreign-trained doctors in postgraduate training positions.

Likewise, the Canadian Medical Association has resisted the notion of a major reduction in medical school enrolment. The CMA has consistently called for a drastic slashing in the number of foreign-trained doctors before the Canadian medical schools are touched. In 1981, for example, an editorial in the *CMA Journal* said that a reduction in enrolment would be "based neither on logic nor on common sense."

Since 1982, the provincial governments have refrained from any expansion in the number of government-funded postgraduate training positions. The provinces are aware of the doctor surplus and they realize that postgraduate positions are as important as undergraduate enrolment in determining the level of medical manpower in Canada. However, the medical faculties have thwarted the intentions of the provincial governments by expanding the number of non-government-funded residency (postgraduate) training positions. The number of such positions almost doubled from 1981 to 1985.

Dr. David Gass, a former CMA official, has acknowledged that the medical faculties are refusing to accept the latest data on the surplus of doctors. "The medical community, by its actions, seems resolved not to proceed beyond the projections of the 1970s," Dr. Gass has written.

The increasing size of postgraduate training programs has failed to provide much help for foreign-trained doctors. More than 400 foreign graduates apply for first-year postgraduate positions each year, but an average of only 27 are accepted. Among the 878 residents in first-year and second-year family medicine programs, only eight are foreign trained.

Rural and Northern Shortages

Canada's surplus doctors are concentrated in the major cities. The number of doctors per 1,000 residents is often three or four times higher in the cities than in rural areas. For example, the number of doctors per capita in Winnipeg is 3.4 times greater than the number of doctors in the rural and northern regions of Manitoba. The number of physicians in Saskatchewan's urban centres rose by 73 per cent from 1974 to 1984, while the number of physicians in rural areas of Saskatchewan increased by only 17 per cent in the same period. There are serious shortages of doctors in most of Newfoundland, in the northern regions of New Brunswick and in many other non-urban regions of Canada. Quebec estimates that it needs about 250 specialists in rural areas. Rural residents find that their tax dollars are funnelled into the cities to pay for the surplus of urban physicians. Organizations such as the Saskatchewan Health Care Association have reported that rural residents feel unfairly treated: they are paying for the cost of educating doctors, but they receive only a tiny share of the graduates.

There is a strong possibility that the restrictions on immigrant doctors will worsen the problems in the rural and northern communities. "Restricting the entry of foreign doctors will likely aggravate the shortage of physicians in a number of remote communities," says Dr. Reynaldo Pagtakhan, a professor of pediatrics at the University of Manitoba's faculty of medicine.

Only two provinces — Quebec and British Columbia — have taken forceful action to try to solve the shortages of rural and northern doctors. In 1982 the Quebec government introduced a system of rewards and penalties to encourage doctors to practise in areas where they are needed. New doctors who located in Quebec's cities received only 70 per cent of the normal amount of their fees for a three-year period. Those who located in rural communities were given a bonus payment of as much as 20 per cent. Quebec has also made it clear that medical graduates will not be automatically entitled to submit bills to the provincial medicare plan.

The British Columbia government, meanwhile, has placed restrictions on medical graduates — prohibiting some of them from billing the health-insurance plan if they locate their practice in an urban area with a surplus of doctors. However, other provincial governments have refused to introduce these kinds of forceful measures, relying instead on voluntary plans under which a doctor can get a financial bonus for locating in a rural or northern community. These plans do not penalize a doctor who chooses to practise in urban centres where a surplus exists.

The rural shortages have been exacerbated by the provincial colleges of physicians and surgeons, which are responsible for deciding whether a doctor is qualified to practise medicine. The colleges have often adopted an extremely strict attitude towards foreign-trained doctors. Consider this example: in 1984 the small Saskatchewan town of Esterhazy, after searching for a doctor for many months, persuaded an Ontario doctor to join an established practice in the town. However, the Saskatchewan College of Physicians and Surgeons refused to let the doctor practise in Saskatchewan because he had been trained in Mexico. Even though the doctor had passed the Canadian licensing exams and had completed a one-year internship and an 18-month residency in Ontario, the college barred him from Saskatchewan because it felt the doctor had insufficient practical experience.

The residents of Shaunavon, another small Saskatchewan town, suffered a similar experience in 1984. The town had persuaded a British-trained doctor to become the partner of an overworked local physician. The Saskatchewan college ordered the British-trained doctor to leave the province because he had missed a deadline for filing an application form by four days. He had missed the deadline after being asked to make a correction on the form. As a result, the local physician had to return to working solo in a practice covering 10,000 square miles and 7,000 patients.

Traditionally, the licensing rules are strictest for doctors from non-Anglophone countries. For many years the Ontario College of Physicians and Surgeons established easier licensing rules for doctors who were trained in Canada, the United States, Britain, Ireland, Australia, New Zealand or South Africa. These doctors could write their licensing examinations after a one-year internship. But doctors who were trained in other countries had to complete a two-year internship. The discrimination was finally ended as a result of intervention by human-rights officers.

Overall, foreign-trained doctors have obtained just 4.5 per cent of the internships in Canadian hospitals since 1971. At the same time, immigration to Canada by foreign physicians has been severely restricted. Less than 300 doctors were permitted to immigrate to Canada annually in the early 1980s, compared to a total of 1,347 who were allowed to enter the country in 1969.

Thus we have a paradox: the vast majority of foreign-trained doctors are locked out of the system, but the number of Canadian medical students and postgraduates remains at extremely high levels. The foreign medical graduates are much more willing to fill the rural and northern vacancies than Canadian doctors are; yet the number of foreign doctors is declining, while Canadian graduates are still pouring out of the medical schools in this country. As a result, the surplus of urban doctors is still a serious problem in Canada and the people who live in rural and northern regions are still suffering from a shortage of doctors. And the candidates who are the most willing to fill the vacancies — the foreign doctors — are bearing the burden of the cutbacks.

The Quality-Control Problem

The plight of foreign-trained doctors illustrates another paradox in the politics of medical licensure: it can be extremely difficult to break into the Canadian medical profession, yet it is almost impossible to be thrown out of the profession for incompetence or negligent behaviour. Once a doctor has overcome the barriers to entry, he or she is almost guaranteed a life-long tenure in the profession. The strict examinations and the difficult licensing procedures are an effective obstacle at the start of a doctor's career, but the barriers are non-existent in the middle or the end of the doctor's professional life.

The medical licensing system is supposed to ensure the quality and competence of Canada's doctors. In fact, it merely ensures that brand-new doctors are reasonably competent. If a doctor's professional habits have deteriorated over the years, if the doctor has failed to keep up with the latest medical information or has become sloppy or careless — he or she can continue to practise medicine. In almost every province of Canada, there is no mechanism to check the quality of a licensed doctor. Patients lack the technical expertise to assess the quality of care they receive from doctors. Yet most provincial licensing bodies do not evaluate the practice of a licensed doctor, unless a patient has complained about the doctor or the doctor's actions have been criticized by a coroner or a judge.

This serious flaw in the medical licensing system has provoked criticism from many experts. The 1970 report of the Ontario Committee on the Healing Arts concluded that the licensing bodies are "quite inadequate" for ensuring the continuing competence of doctors. A study by Dr. Samuel Wolfe and sociologist Robin Badgley remarked that the official scrutiny of licensed doctors is "minimal or non-existent." Even a former president of the Canadian Medical Association, Dr. Peter Banks, has acknowledged the problem: "New knowledge accumulates and changes in management occur so rapidly that the idea is ludicrous that you can examine a person at the beginning of his career and on the results of that examination give him a license to practise forever. There has to be a system of re-evaluation."

The same point was made by Milton Friedman, the prominent U.S. economist, in his classic critique of the North American system of licensure. Friedman pointed out that "a man's ability to pass an examination 20 or 30 years earlier is hardly assurance of quality now." He added that "licensure is not now the main or even a major source of assurance of at least minimum quality." Robert Evans and W. T. Stanbury of the University of British Columbia have compared doctors unfavourably with other professionals in this regard. "It is taken for granted that airline pilots, for example, are subject to periodic examination of both physical and occupational capabilities," Evans and Stanbury have noted. "Anyone suggesting lifetime licensure for airline pilots would be greeted with derision. Yet for surgeons, demonstration of competence at the beginning of the career is considered adequate."

There is plenty of evidence to suggest that the current licensing system does not guarantee a high quality of medical care for every patient. As mentioned in chapter 4, iatrogenic disease is a frequent event in North America. Some of these illnesses are caused by adverse drug reactions and hospital infections, but a large percentage of iatrogenic illnesses are simply the result of doctors' mistakes.

Autopsies have revealed the large number of errors that doctors make. One study of post-mortems at a U.S. hospital, reported in the

New England Journal of Medicine in 1983, found that doctors had wrongly diagnosed nearly one-quarter of the patients who died in the hospital. The study concluded that the diagnostic mistakes may have contributed to the death of 10 per cent of the 300 patients who were examined in an autopsy. A similar study at a hospital in Winnipeg, published in 1985, found that physicians had wrongly diagnosed 35 per cent of the patients who were examined in post-mortems. In more than one-third of these cases, the error probably shortened the life of the patient, the study said. Another study in Winnipeg found that diagnostic mistakes had been made in 24 per cent of the patients who were examined in autopsies.

Several other studies have confirmed that the quality of medical care in Canada is often inadequate. An intensive evaluation of 85 physicians in Ontario and Nova Scotia, published in 1963, found serious deficiencies in the medical practices of 28 per cent of the Ontario doctors and 52 per cent of the Nova Scotia doctors. "The deficiencies in these men's practices were thought likely to expose their patients to serious risk," said Dr. Kenneth Clute, who supervised the study. A 1977 study in Kingston, Ontario, found that the quality of medical care was considered adequate in only 40 per cent of the cases handled by family physicians.

Peer Review

Clearly, the original licensing examinations are not sufficient to ensure that a doctor will continue to provide a satisfactory level of medical care. Confronted with this evidence, what is the medical profession doing? In most provinces the medical licensing bodies make no systematic attempt to review the daily practices of physicians. The colleges of physicians and surgeons in Ontario and Quebec are the only regulatory bodies that have tried to assess the quality of care provided by doctors in their provinces.

These assessment programs have a limited scope. For example, only a small percentage of Ontario's doctors are evaluated in any single year. The assessors do not interview a doctor's patients or test his or her knowledge of medicine. They merely examine the doctor's medical records and conduct interviews with the doctor.

The first detailed review by the Ontario college, in 1979, involved an assessment of the medical records of 98 doctors. The review found that one doctor was judged to be practising at an unacceptable level, three had questionable patterns of practice, and three had such scanty records that it was impossible to assess their medical practices. In

1981 and 1982 the college reviewed a total of 391 doctors, most of whom were family practitioners. After reviewing the medical practices, the college had concerns about 12 per cent of the family practitioners. The college was worried about their standards of medical care or their record-keeping habits. In one case, the college had serious concerns about the safety of the patients of a doctor.

A further 200 doctors were assessed in Ontario in 1984. The assessors had concerns about the quality of care or medical records of 30 of the 200 doctors. The assessors were particularly worried about the practices of older doctors; in the first three years of the evaluation program, they had concerns about 49 per cent of doctors who were 70 or older. A total of about 650 doctors older than 75 are licensed to practise medicine in Ontario.

Peer-review programs have two major benefits. First, they can identify doctors who are risks to their patients. Second, they tend to improve the quality of medical care among almost all of the doctors who are assessed — including the competent doctors. The Ontario college, in its assessment of 98 physicians in 1979, found that 41 per cent of the physicians intended to make improvements in their medical practices as a result of the college's review.

Another study, involving doctors in Nova Scotia and New Brunswick, found that an appraisal of a doctor's patient care tended to produce a significant improvement in the doctor's treatment of his or her patients. Wolfe and Badgley have reached the same conclusion: "Peer review and ongoing review in a group setting may be key factors in preventing lapses that lead to missed diagnoses of what is not routine on an average busy day amidst the flow of patients with routine or mundane problems."

Despite this evidence, Ontario and Quebec are still the only provinces with a formal system of peer review for physicians in private practice. There are no indications that the licensing bodies in other provinces are planning to introduce an assessment program.

Continuing Education

The provincial colleges have also refused to establish regulations to require doctors to continue their medical education after they are licensed. Many experts believe that a system of mandatory continuing education can help to ensure that a licensed doctor is providing a high quality of medical care. Studies in the United States have shown that continuing medical education often produces an improvement in the performance of physicians. A total of 28 states in the U.S. have established rules to require doctors to take a certain number of educational courses every year. In 1970, after a four-year inquiry into the provincial health-care system, the Ontario Committee on the Healing Arts urged the provincial government to introduce a system of mandatory continuing education. Yet no such system has ever been approved in Canada, despite the studies and despite the U.S. precedent.

Essentially, the provincial governments have allowed the medical licensing bodies (the colleges of physicians and surgeons) to decide whether to require doctors to take educational courses, but the licensing bodies have shied away from the issue. In Manitoba the provincial college asked the Manitoba government to amend its legislation to make it clear that the college had the power to introduce a system of mandatory continuing education. But the college then decided not to invoke this power. "We have a voluntary code," says Dr. James Morison, registrar of the Manitoba college. "We try to be persuasive. We were ahead of the other provinces — that's one reason why we didn't implement it." A survey in 1980 by the Manitoba Medical Association found that the vast majority of Manitoba's doctors were opposed to the idea of mandatory continuing education. The survey of 427 doctors (one-third of the MMA membership) showed that 77 per cent were opposed to a system of compulsory education.

A similar stalemate has occurred in Alberta. The Alberta Medical Association decided to support a system of mandatory continuing education in 1972, but the Alberta College of Physicians and Surgeons has blocked the proposal. Dr. Roy le Riche, registrar of the Alberta college, has argued that the mandatory education programs are "useless."

The Royal College of Physicians and Surgeons of Canada (the national certifying body for medical specialists) has consistently opposed the idea of mandatory continuing education. The College of Family Physicians of Canada, by contrast, requires its members to participate in continuing education courses. However, a family practitioner can practise medicine in Canada without belonging to the national college, so its rules are not particularly effective. Only about half of Canada's family practitioners are members of the college.

On the issue of continuing education, Canada's doctors have fallen behind the members of other professions. In several provinces the licensing bodies for dentists and pharmacists have required the members of the profession to complete a specific number of hours of continuing education in order to qualify for a licence renewal. Even the associations of registered dietitians have established mandatory continuing education programs in some provinces.

Instead of establishing a mandatory education program, the Canadian medical profession has supported a voluntary system. In a few provinces, the medical associations have persuaded the provincial governments to provide financial incentives to doctors who complete a continuing education course. These payments tend to be around $600 per doctor per year. If a doctor does not take a continuing education course, he or she does not qualify for the financial bonus. There is no other penalty.

Other Solutions

Given the general absence of peer-review and mandatory education programs in Canada, how else can the quality of medical care be safeguarded? There are several other possibilities, but each has its weaknesses. One alternative is the system of medical audits that exists in many Canadian hospitals. These audits can sometimes be an effective method of reviewing the performance of doctors in hospitals. However, a study at one hospital, published in 1986, revealed that the audits are not always conducted properly. The study looked at 39 medical audits at the hospital. It found that a high proportion of the audits were unfinished or poorly structured. More than 90 per cent of the completed audits failed to compare their results with the medical literature. In many cases, the recommendations of the audits were never implemented. The study concluded that 76 per cent of the audits were not rigorous enough to improve the quality of health care in the hospital. The failure of the audits was "partly due to the physicians' lack of interest," the study said.

As mentioned earlier, an autopsy can be a good way of monitoring the quality of medical care. Of course, the findings of an autopsy are of little use to a dead patient, but the post-mortem can help identify a problem in a doctor's practice. Until the early 1970s, the Canadian Council on Hospital Accreditation required hospitals to perform autopsies on a minimum of 50 per cent of the patients who died at the hospital. But in recent years, there has been a steady decline in the number of autopsies performed at many Canadian hospitals. A survey of five hospitals in Winnipeg found that the number of autopsies had decreased from 1980 to 1985 in each hospital. By 1985, pathologists were examining less than 30 per cent of the patients who died in hospitals in western Canada.

Another method of maintaining a high quality of medical care is to issue a limited licence to a physician. Instead of allowing the doctor to be licensed to perform any kind of medicine or surgery, the licence could be restricted to a specific kind of specialty or a limited scope of treatment. This would help ensure that a doctor is highly trained for the treatment he or she is providing. The Ontario Committee on the Healing Arts concluded that "we favour the concept of limited licensing and would like to see it universally endorsed." In 1974 a leader of the Alberta Medical Association mused about the benefits of limited licensing. "Perhaps in the future we will tell graduates they can practise medicine and do a restricted amount of surgery, rather than giving them a licence to do everything medical," said Dr. Robert Hatfield, the AMA's president-elect.

However, limited licensing has never been adopted in Canada. Nor has any province introduced a program of periodic re-licensing for doctors, requiring them to pass examinations at regular intervals. Thus, a negligent or incompetent doctor will continue to practise medicine, undetected and unpenalized, unless a patient notices a problem and files a lawsuit or an official complaint. Yet patients do not have the technical knowledge to monitor the quality of their medical care. Only a doctor has the expertise to tell whether a colleague has provided adequate care. And many experts have noted that doctors tend to be reluctant to blow the whistle on a colleague.

Dr. Charles Culver of Dartmouth Medical School has studied the factors that discourage a physician from reporting a deficiency in the medical care provided by a colleague. He uses the example of a physician, Dr. A, who believes that a patient has suffered an injury as a result of negligence by another physician, Dr. X. In some cases, Dr. A will feel protective of Dr. X and will be reluctant to expose Dr. X to a malpractice suit because of the emotional turmoil it would involve. Moreover, Dr. A might also be afraid of losing patient referrals from Dr. X. "It is little wonder that physicians in Dr. A's position, balancing out the above pressures, so often choose the easy path and say nothing," Dr. Culver told a conference at Queen's University in 1983.

The Code of Ethics of the Canadian Medical Association requires a doctor to inform the provincial licensing body of any questionable conduct by a colleague. However, there is no legislation or ethical code to require a patient to be informed of questionable conduct by a doctor. Some experts in the United States have recommended that doctors be found guilty of malpractice if they fail to inform patients about medical mistakes that affect the patients' health.

"When a patient is injured through preventable error, he is morally entitled to recompense," Dr. Culver has said. "If patients have incurred temporary or permanent damages, the involved physicians snould take whatever steps are within their power to help with reparation of these damages," he added. "Beginning in medical school and throughout training and practice, there should be more open recognition that even the best of physicians make preventable mistakes."

There is some anecdotal evidence in Canada to confirm Dr. Culver's observations. Dr. Morton Shulman witnessed a medical cover-up in the early days of his career. He wanted to perform an autopsy on a patient because he believed the patient's death was due to medical negligence. The chief coroner, Dr. Smirle Lawson, ordered him to cancel the autopsy. "Dr. Lawson said I was never to order a post-mortem like that again," Dr. Shulman recalled. "He took all those cases himself after that. He felt that if such cases were made public, it would undermine confidence in the medical profession — and he was right. I didn't agree with him. But I went along with him. Everybody in the city knew you had to, or you wouldn't be there."

Martin O'Malley has described a similar case in his recent portrait of the Canadian medical profession. In this case, a physician who reported the reckless conduct of another doctor quickly found himself ostracized and then sabotaged by his colleagues. The chief of surgery at the local hospital, who received the doctor's report on the reckless conduct, never replied to the letter. Instead the chief of surgery considered the report to be a malicious attack on his colleague.

It seems clear that the voluntary behaviour of the medical profession is insufficient to guarantee the continuing competence of a doctor. There are too many pressures militating against a voluntary system. Unless a program is mandatory, it is likely to be disregarded by some doctors. Indeed, the doctors who ignore a voluntary program are probably the very doctors who are the greatest risk to patients. However, the Canadian medical profession has resisted the idea of a mandatory system for checking the quality of a licensed doctor. Instead, the medical profession has concentrated its attention on the licensing procedures that determine whether a medical graduate can enter the profession. For many graduates, the barriers to entry are tremendous. But once a licence is acquired, the barriers disappear. Most doctors will escape scrutiny for the rest of their careers.

CHAPTER 8

POWER POLITICS: THE MEDICAL ASSOCIATIONS

Less than two blocks from the Alberta legislature, the medical lobbyist is relaxing in his office. Dr. Robert Clark, the executive director of the Alberta Medical Association, is just a short walk from the corridors of power. His government connections are impeccable. The senior decision makers of the provincial medicare system are within the reach of his fingertips. "I can pick up the phone at any time and talk to the deputy minister," Dr. Clark says calmly. "The president [of the AMA] can pick up the phone at any time and talk to the minister. We have no problem with communication."

In a suburban home near Vancouver, the former health minister of British Columbia is describing his own relationship with the medical leaders of his province. James Neilsen, the health minister from 1981 to 1986, is proud of his friendship with the leaders of the B.C. Medical Association. "There was constant communication between the president, the executive director, myself and the deputy. We all got to know each other personally. I had dinner at the former executive director's house this week, along with three or four other doctors. He was my family doctor 25 years ago. The former president has been a house guest here. I got to know most of those people very, very well. I consider them all friends."

Organized medicine still enjoys a special relationship with Canada's top politicians and bureaucrats. No other health profession can match the influence of the doctors in the hallways and backrooms of the provincial and federal health ministries. Indeed, the doctors may be the best-organized and best-connected profession in Canada. In some provinces they still dominate the health ministry's decision-making process. In other jurisdictions they exercise an effective veto. The political and financial resources of the Canadian medical profession are unrivalled among occupational groups in this country.

It began with Sir Charles Tupper in 1867. Sir Charles, a physician, was the first president of the Canadian Medical Association. Later, he became prime minister of Canada. "His political experience was of the greatest value to the Association in the early stages of its development," an official history of the CMA noted. It was an impressive beginning for the CMA. For any lobby group, the ascendancy of one of its leaders to the most powerful political job in the country is perhaps the ultimate coup.

Today leaders of the medical profession are still prominent in the top levels of government. Consider the example of Dr. Bette Stephenson. In the 1960s and the early 1970s she served one-year terms as the president of the Ontario Medical Association and the Canadian Medical Association. Shortly afterwards she entered provincial politics as a Progressive Conservative. After gaining election to the Ontario legislature in 1975, Dr. Stephenson was quickly appointed to the provincial cabinet. She entered the cabinet just a few months after completing her term as the 1974-75 president of the CMA. She remained an influential member of the Ontario cabinet until 1985. There can be little doubt that Dr. Stephenson was a strong advocate of the viewpoint of organized medicine when the cabinet was debating the fee schedules of the doctors and other health-policy questions. Reflecting on the relationship between Ontario's doctors and the provincial Conservative government, Dr. Stephenson once said: "I have enjoyed thoroughly being a part of this medicine-government arrangement which has always been very friendly, very congenial and very conciliatory throughout the years and I hope it will continue to be so."

The same kinds of close connections are particularly visible in Alberta. A classic example is Dr. T. Alex McPherson, who was the president of the AMA in 1981-82. He became the president of the CMA in 1984-85, and then, while serving as the head of the CMA, he was appointed as the deputy minister of hospitals and medical care in Alberta. His appointment became effective on September 1, 1985 — as soon as he completed his term at the CMA. With barely a pause, Dr. McPherson moved smoothly from the medical lobbying group to the top position in Alberta's health bureaucracy. Needless to say, the AMA finds it useful to have Dr. McPherson in a senior governmental post. "He understands our philosophy and our concerns very, very well," Dr. Clark says. "Certainly it helps us to have him understand the issues as well as he does."

Dr. McPherson's appointment would be an overwhelming achievement for any special interest group. Yet it was not the first such success for the AMA. A previous deputy minister of hospitals and medical care was Dr. L. C. Grisdale, who had been the president of the AMA in 1967–68 and had also been the president of the CMA. For the medical associations, success breeds success.

The Canadian Medical Association

The medical profession began to organize itself officially in the early 19th century. Local medical societies were formed as early as 1826. The CMA was created at a conference of physicians in Quebec City in October 1867, and its first resolution made its main objectives clear: the medical association "will give a frequent, united and decided expression of the medical opinion of the country." Another major objective of the CMA, according to the founding resolution, was the task of "directing and controlling public opinion" towards the "medical men" of Canada.

The CMA today has an annual budget of $5.5 million, and it employs about 100 people in its headquarters in Ottawa. It represents four out of every five Canadian physicians. Political lobbying and public relations are still prominent in the association's daily activities. The CMA has six full-time employees who work on communications with the government and the public. The head of this division is a lobbyist who regularly meets with members of Parliament and bureaucrats. He also monitors federal legislation, attends hearings of parliamentary committees, attends the annual conventions of all three federal political parties and maintains an information file on every member of Parliament. The CMA has regular communication with the federal health minister, including four or five formal meetings every year. And the association submits briefs to parliamentary committees several times a year.

Perhaps most important of all, the CMA has organized a system of personal contacts between MPs and doctors. Several hundred doctors are participating in this scheme. In most federal ridings, two or three doctors were chosen to lobby the local MP and keep him or her informed of the CMA's views on proposed legislation. The doctors were chosen on the basis of their personal connections with the MP. The CMA recruited doctors who socialized with the MP in local clubs or organizations, or who were personal friends of the politician. Most of the provincial medical associations have organized a similar system of personal contacts. It is regarded as a valuable lobbying technique.

The CMA was directly involved in the 1984 federal election

campaign. The association's president, Dr. Everett Coffin, sent a letter to each of the CMA's 38,000 members to urge them to become active in their local campaigns. He suggested that they become members of local constituency associations, volunteer to work for political candidates, help raise funds for candidates and make donations of at least $100 to a political party. The CMA targetted 25 to 30 ridings for special attention. In these ridings the CMA gave its members specific information about a local candidate who seemed to be pro-doctor or anti-doctor. Several MPs who had opposed the CMA's viewpoints were targetted by the medical association, so that the doctors knew who to vote against. Candidates who were physicians by occupation were targetted for strong support. The CMA also backed candidates who were (in the words of the *CMA Journal*) "known allies of the profession." This included Jake Epp, the Manitoba MP who was the Conservative health critic before the election. The CMA's strategy succeeded: Jake Epp was re-elected and became the federal health minister in the Conservative government. Once again the medical profession had a strong ally in the highest levels of government.

The CMA recognizes that the greatest strength of the medical profession is its influence over its patients. This is an advantage that is unavailable to any other interest group. Patients have a great deal of faith in their doctors. They implicitly trust the advice of their doctors. This personal faith has spilled over to benefit the medical associations. According to a 1982 opinion poll, more than 80 per cent of Canadians trust the public statements of CMA officials. The survey found that the CMA was trusted more than consumer associations, labour unions, banks, telephone companies, oil companies, business associations and industry associations. Of crucial importance was another finding: the number of people who trusted the CMA was much greater than the number who trusted the provincial governments. And the CMA was trusted by more than twice as many people as the federal government.

The CMA has made certain that the medical profession uses its influence with its patients. "Every day of the week we should have some 35,000 PR men and women at work across Canada selling the medical profession to the Canadian people," said the 1981–82 president of the CMA, Dr. Leon Richard, in a speech to physicians in 1981. Another CMA official, David Woods, made the same point in an editorial in the association's journal in 1984. He noted that the physicians of Canada do not have enough votes of their own to influence a federal election. "But they do have some 25 million patients. About half of these can vote." He urged each doctor to "carry your message to the voters."

Dr. John O'Brien-Bell, the 1986–87 president of the British

Columbia Medical Association, is another medical leader who urges physicians to send political messages through their patients. "Politicians often forget that their public is our patients," he told a Vancouver newspaper. "That's our edge. It is in the privacy of our offices that we can best influence the climate of opinion."

All of the CMA's political weapons came together in a single campaign in the early 1980s, when the medical association fought the federal government's proposed Canada Health Act. The Canada Health Act authorized Ottawa to reduce its transfer payments to any province that tolerated the practice of extra-billing by physicians. The conflict began in 1980 when a federal report, written by former Supreme Court justice Emmett Hall, recommended the termination of extra-billing. The CMA was outraged. Its first reaction was to threaten to transform itself into a medical union. A few weeks later it threatened to launch a work-to-rule campaign if extra-billing was prohibited. Under this plan the doctors would refuse to work outside hospitals, and they would stop performing many non-essential medical services.

The federal government ignored the threats and began to prepare a draft of the Canada Health Act. The CMA decided to try another tactic. Instead of resorting to brute force, the CMA now offered a compromise. It proposed that welfare recipients and low-income patients be issued special "medicare cards" to identify themselves to doctors. These cards would exempt the patients from extra-billing. Doctors would promise to honour the cards if Ottawa refrained from an official ban on extra-billing.

Recognizing that the CMA's proposed compromise would have been degrading and embarrassing to low-income patients, the federal government rejected the proposal. The Canada Health Act was soon introduced in the House of Commons. The CMA responded by organizing a massive protest against the legislation. More than 1,200 physicians wrote letters to Health Minister Monique Bégin to express their opposition. The CMA held a series of meetings with the Liberal and Conservative caucuses in Ottawa.

Meanwhile, the provincial medical associations lobbied their local MPs to try to persuade them to oppose the legislation. The Ontario Medical Association organized a series of 11 "study sessions," in which doctors closed their offices to protest the Canada Health Act. The OMA provided signs for medical offices warning that the legislation was threatening the medicare system. Many Ontario doctors wore buttons that said: "Canada's new health act may be dangerous to your health."

Medical societies in some communities took similar action. For example, the members of the Kitchener-Waterloo Academy of Medicine distributed 20,000 letters to their patients, urging them to oppose the Canada Health Act. The letters were clearly designed to frighten the patients. "The Act will serve to eliminate the present independent professional status of medicine, leading to decisions regarding your health being made on the basis of political expediency or availability of funds," the letter said. The physicians also spent money on radio and newspaper advertisements to promote the same alarming message.

The CMA was unable to block the Canada Health Act. The legislation was approved by Parliament in 1984. However, the CMA did secure some amendments that helped the medical profession. One amendment established that the provincial medicare plans must provide "reasonable compensation for the services of physicians." Another amendment allowed the use of binding arbitration to settle fee disputes between a province and a medical association. This was a significant victory for the medical associations, and the provincial governments were upset at the clause. Arbitration decisions in 1986 and 1987 in Manitoba and Alberta have confirmed that binding arbitration tends to protect doctors from provincial restraint programs.

Despite the passage of the Canada Health Act, the battle is not yet over. The CMA is spending more than $250,000 to hire a crack team of legal experts to challenge the constitutionality of the legislation.

The Underfunding Campaign

In recent years, the CMA's lobbying and public-relations efforts have emphasized two major themes: the "underfunding" of health care in Canada and the need for "patient participation" in the financing of medicare. These two themes are inextricably linked. If the CMA can convince Canadians that the health-care system must have more money pumped into it, the association will find it easier to argue that patients should dip into their own pockets to pay for the extra costs. Both themes are connected to the self-interest of the medical profession. If more money is poured into the medicare system, a large portion of the money would filter through to the doctors. At the same time, both of the CMA's major themes would help to protect doctors from government restraint programs. If Canadians are persuaded that the health system is underfunded, they will not permit their governments to reduce the cost of the system. And if Canadians are taught to accept the need for patient participation, a restraint-minded government could transfer the burden of health costs to the patients without causing any reduction in medical incomes.

In 1981 and 1982 the CMA complained that Canada was spending only 7.3 per cent of its gross national product on health care. The medical association argued that the percentage of GNP spent on medicare in Canada had failed to increase for more than a decade and that other countries were spending a greater percentage than Canada. The CMA alleged that the underfunding of health care in Canada "has reached crisis proportions" and "threatens the integrity and quality of health care for Canadians." The medical association recommended that Canada spend at least 8.2 per cent of its GNP on health care.

Early in 1982 the association hired a writer to find examples of underfunding in the Canadian health system. The CMA also gave the media a guide on how to find cases of underfunding in local hospitals. The CMA's 1981–82 president, Dr. Leon Richard, embarked on a cross-country tour to promote the concept of underfunding. He gave speeches in the capital of each province, describing the problems caused by a lack of money in local hospitals.

To dramatize his argument, Dr. Richard often used the phrase "health-care rationing." He made newspaper headlines by suggesting that certain groups in society (perhaps key industrialists and politicians) should be given first priority for medical services in this rationed system of medical services. The Ontario Medical Association, following in the footsteps of Dr. Richard, conducted an elaborate survey of Ontario surgeons to publicize the waiting lists that are sometimes established for non-emergency surgery in the province. Medical leaders claimed that some patients were dying while they waited for an operation.

The campaign against underfunding suffered a setback in 1983 and 1984. First, the latest statistics revealed that Canada was now spending 8.4 per cent of its GNP on health care — more than the CMA's original target of 8.2 per cent. Then, when the CMA established a task force to study the "rationing" of health care in Canada, the medical association was embarrassed to learn that the task force could find no clear evidence of underfunding. "Because the evidence is contradictory and inconclusive, the Task Force does not support the contention that there is underfunding generally in Canada," the final report concluded.

After a discreet silence for several months, the CMA soon began to revive the underfunding argument. By 1986 the medical association was back in full throttle, repeating the same argument as if the task force had never existed. "At present, the health care system in Canada is dangerously underfunded," the CMA said in an official policy statement in 1986. "Increased use of private funding within the health care system is essential if Canadians are to be assured adequate service levels." Today the CMA continues to call for extra-billing, user fees and other devices to ensure that patients are required to pay a portion of their health costs. It refuses to accept the results of several studies which found that extra-billing and user fees prevent some low-income people from obtaining all the medical care they need.

In almost all its campaigns, the CMA has relied heavily on a single basic strategy: the exploitation of people's fear of losing their access to physicians and medical services. The CMA has constantly warned that the Canadian health system will be rationed or damaged if doctors are unhappy with their financial resources or their working conditions. When the CMA talks of work-to-rule campaigns or possible rationing of medical services, it is clearly hoping to shock and frighten patients who are dependent on their personal physician. The same tactic is evident when the CMA urges its members to lecture their patients on the negative consequences of government actions. Such scare tactics were employed again in the 1970s and early 1980s, when the CMA repeatedly warned that Canadian doctors were fleeing to the United States. For years the CMA alleged that Canada was suffering from a mass exodus of doctors. It was a throwback to the strike by Saskatchewan doctors in 1962, when the doctors claimed they would abandon the province if medicare was introduced.

The CMA continued to raise fears of a tremendous exodus of Canadian doctors — until it finally became clear that the number of emigrating physicians was not increasing at all. In fact, the emigration of doctors actually declined after 1978. The CMA then began to argue that Canada was losing its "elite" doctors — its best specialists and top surgeons.

Most of the provincial medical associations have similarly relied on a strategy of fear-mongering. When a medical association is engaged in a dispute with a government, the temporary walkouts by the association's members are designed to make ordinary patients dwell on the possibility of losing their doctors for an extended period of time. The medical associations realize that there is a major difference between a strike by ordinary workers and a strike by doctors. When the postal workers go on strike, for example, the public is annoyed and angry. When doctors shut their offices, people worry about their personal health. The fears are deeper and much more unsettling.

Each province in Canada has a provincial medical association or medical society to represent its physicians. Officially, these associations are divisions of the CMA. In effect, they operate with complete autonomy from the national association. However, the CMA is quick to provide assistance to the provincial associations if they are embroiled in a major conflict. We have already seen that the CMA provided large sums of money to the Saskatchewan physicians during the 1962 doctors' strike. The CMA provided strong support for the Quebec medical specialists who went on strike in 1970. And in 1986 the CMA spent about $65,000 to support the striking doctors of Ontario.

The Alberta Medical Association

Of all the provincial medical associations, the Alberta association is certainly the strongest and the most successful. The AMA has a history of effective lobbying at the provincial legislature. In the early 1960s it convinced the province to adopt a system of voluntary health insurance, under which the government provided subsidies to low-income people to help pay for their insurance coverage. The doctors regarded this system as the best alternative to a fullfledged medicare program. The Alberta doctors enjoyed the benefits of their close relationship with the provincial health minister, Dr. Donovan Ross, who was himself a member of the medical profession. Dr. Ross remained the health minister for 12 years. When Alberta finally joined the national medicare program in 1969, Dr. Ross resigned his cabinet portfolio in protest.

The bargaining power of the AMA was vividly displayed in the early 1980s. The association obtained a fee increase of 15.5 per cent in 1980, followed by another increase of 12.8 per cent in 1981 and an amazing increase of 21 per cent in 1982. The huge increase in 1982 was approved by the Alberta government after the doctors organized a sophisticated series of pressure tactics. The AMA arranged for some doctors to withdraw non-essential medical services, such as telephone advice to patients. The AMA also organized massive "study sessions" in Edmonton and Calgary, in which the participating physicians closed their office doors and cancelled all non-emergency surgery. An estimated 600 physicians in Calgary and 600 in Edmonton participated in the study sessions. In effect, 40 per cent of the province's doctors were briefly on strike. The government quickly surrendered, and the doctors got their 21 per cent increase.

In recent years the AMA has received much smaller increases, but

Alberta doctors are still enjoying the highest incomes in Canada. According to Revenue Canada, the average Alberta doctor had a net income of $105,000 in 1984. Revenue Canada said the Alberta physicians earned more than any other group of professionals in the country. The income of the average Alberta physician was 4.2 times as high as the income of the average Canadian taxpayer. Moreover, the Revenue Canada statistics underestimated the actual income of the average Alberta physician, since they failed to include many of the highest-paid doctors — those who have incorporated themselves to take advantage of tax breaks for private corporations. (The physicians of Alberta are the only doctors in Canada who have won the right to incorporate themselves for tax purposes. This is yet another indication of the political strength of the Alberta medical profession.)

Until late in 1986, the AMA was successful in persuading the provincial government to preserve the practice of extra-billing. The rate of extra-billing in Alberta was higher than in any other province. In 1980, for example, 38 per cent of Alberta's doctors were extra-billing their patients. That compared to 18 per cent of Ontario physicians and 7 per cent of Manitoba physicians.

Furthermore, Alberta physicians enjoyed the most favourable system of extra-billing in Canada. In other provinces, doctors who extra-billed were not guaranteed any payment at all. Their patients were partially reimbursed by the government, but the doctors had to collect their fees from the patients. In some cases, fee collecting was a difficult process. In Alberta, however, any doctor who extra-billed a patient was guaranteed to receive a payment from the government. Only the amount above the provincial fee schedule had to be collected directly from the patient. This drastically reduced the risks of bad debts for doctors who extra-billed. In addition, Alberta doctors could decide which patients to extra-bill and which services to extra-bill. This gave them more flexibility than doctors in other provinces.

The AMA used the threat of extra-billing as a tactic to put pressure on the provincial government during the 1981–82 fee dispute. The AMA was dissatisfied with its pay increase, so it asked all its members to begin extra-billing their patients. The number of extra-billing doctors rose by 7.5 percentage points by mid-January of 1982. The increase was a shock to many patients. One woman, in tears, told the *Calgary Herald* that she had been told to bring $60 when she arrived for an appointment with her surgeon.

Research in 1982 by Professor Richard Plain of the University of Alberta found that the practice of extra-billing added about $1,550 to the monthly income of the average Calgary physician. Extra-billing was so pervasive in Alberta that many patients found it impossible to avoid. In some medical specialities, 75 to 100 per cent of the physicians were extra-billing their patients. In January of 1984, for example, 87 per cent of Alberta's plastic surgeons were extra-billing. So were 82 per cent of the ear, nose and throat specialists, and 80 per cent of obstetricians and gynecologists.

Moreover, many doctors extra-billed patients who were poor or elderly, despite regulations explicitly prohibiting the extra-billing of patients who are receiving social assistance. The 1984–85 annual report of the Alberta College of Physicians and Surgeons revealed that about 800 Alberta physicians had extra-billed patients who were receiving social assistance. (The college chose to ignore most of these incidents. Only one doctor was disciplined for extra-billing a welfare recipient.) Provincial statistics showed that 1,482 welfare recipients were extra-billed by Alberta doctors in the first quarter of 1984. During the same period a further 6,089 low-income people and 3,523 senior citizens were extra-billed by the province's physicians.

In 1986, facing severe pressure from the federal government (including the prospect of financial penalties under the new Canada Health Act), the Alberta government was finally forced to terminate the practice of extra-billing. However, the AMA negotiated an agreement guaranteeing that doctors would not suffer any financial losses. First, the doctors obtained an extra $10 million a year from the government through an increased fee schedule. Second, they obtained a $1.24-million disability-insurance fund to pay doctors who are unable to work because of illness or accident. Third, they obtained an "Extraordinary Medical Services Assessment Fund" that will provide an additional $3 million annually to doctors judged to have spent extra time or effort on a patient. In effect, this fund allowed extra-billing to continue, although it is now the government, not the patient, that pays the extra amount. Fourth, the doctors obtained a system of binding arbitration to resolve fee disputes. And finally, the doctors obtained a guarantee that the government would not impose harsh penalties against doctors who extra-billed. For the first extra-billing offence, a doctor would merely forfeit the amount of the payment. For a second offence, the doctor might be investigated by the college (or might not be investigated — nothing would be compulsory). And for a third offence, a doctor might be deemed to be opted out of the medicare plan.

The end of extra-billing in Alberta was hardly a severe blow to the medical profession. The AMA secured an agreement protecting the doctors from any significant decline in their incomes. Indeed, the end of extra-billing was a financial boon for the majority of Alberta doctors.

Another example of the strength of the AMA was its successful battle against a provincial proposal to put a cap on health-care spending. Capping was suggested when some Alberta officials began to question the dramatic rise in health-care costs in the province. Other government departments were keeping their cost increases within the rate of inflation, but the Alberta health department's budget was increasing by as much as 20 per cent a year. Most of this rapid growth was due to massive increases in utilization of the health-care system by patients. (As we saw in chapter 4, doctors largely control the utilization of the health system.) A cap would have limited the annual increase in medicare payments in Alberta. Provincial cabinet ministers said they were considering the idea, but the AMA strongly opposed any cap. In early 1984 the AMA organized a high-pressure campaign to defeat the capping proposal. The association sent a series of letters to every MLA in the province. Hundreds of individual doctors lobbied their MLAs through meetings and letters. More than a dozen physicians attended the 1984 annual meeting of the Alberta Progressive Conservative party to spread their message among the politicians. The AMA president went on a speaking tour across the province. In the end, the AMA convinced the government to abandon the idea of capping the health budget.

Not surprisingly, Alberta's doctors are pleased with their relationship with the provincial government. "Alberta physicians have had the advantage of negotiating with a progressive, fair-minded government," said Dr. Douglas Perry, the 1985–86 president of the AMA. When the medical association held a reception and dinner for the members of the provincial legislature, about 35 MLAs accepted the invitation. One physician, Dr. Andrew Johnston, sent a letter to every Alberta doctor in 1986 to urge them to contribute money to the provincial Conservatives.

Despite their status as the best-paid doctors in the country, the Alberta physicians are still flexing their muscles. Late in 1986, the AMA complained that its members were inadequately compensated when they performed abortions. The AMA demanded an increase in abortion fees. When there was no immediate increase in the fees, most doctors who had previously performed abortions decided to stop the operations. An increasing number of Alberta women were forced to travel to clinics in Montana to obtain an abortion.

Meanwhile, the AMA announced plans for a high-profile

public-relations campaign in 1987. The campaign will focus on issues such as the AMA's argument that the health-care system is underfunded. The medical association has allocated a budget of $125,000 to $150,000 for the campaign. The AMA also began to argue that patients should pay a deductible fee for their medical services. It was a revival of the CMA's traditional belief in "patient participation."

The British Columbia Medical Association

In the hierarchy of the provincial medical associations, the British Columbia Medical Association is perhaps the second most powerful in the country. The doctors of B.C. have the highest fee schedule in Canada. Their average net income in 1984, according to Revenue Canada, was $102,500. These incomes were achieved despite the tremendous oversupply of physicians in British Columbia. No other province has as many doctors per capita as B.C., yet the competition has failed to drive prices down.

For most of the 1980s the BCMA has done extremely well in its negotiations with the provincial government. The medical association gained a fee increase of 9.7 per cent in 1980, a further increase of 20 per cent in 1981 and another increase of 14 per cent in 1982. Then the national recession struck, and the provincial economy was badly hurt. It became obvious that doctors had received too large an increase in comparison to the rest of the economy. The government threatened to roll back the 14 per cent increase to just 6 per cent. In order to avoid this fate, the doctors agreed to give the government an average of $8,000 each. Because Revenue Canada ruled that this could be considered a gift to the Crown, doctors were permitted to deduct the amount from their taxable income. In effect, the give-back was much cheaper than $8,000 each.

Recent fee increases have been considerably less than those from 1980 to 1982, but the fees of B.C. doctors are still 32 per cent above the Canadian average. The total increase from 1980 to 1985 was 118 per cent — twice as high as the local inflation rate in the same period. Two scholars from the University of British Columbia, W. T. Stanbury and M. J. Fulton, have concluded that the province's doctors "were not as hard hit by the recession and government restraint efforts as the average citizen."

The BCMA has a cozy relationship with the provincial government. Every six weeks, BCMA officials sit down with senior provincial officials for a private meeting. In addition, the BCMA sometimes holds weekend "retreats" with provincial officials. These events are two-day private meetings at exclusive resorts, with no interruptions to break the flow of discussion. Jim Gilmore, the BCMA's communications director, described a weekend retreat in late 1986 as "harmonious." The doctors are the only group of health professionals who enjoy the privilege of weekend retreats with the B.C. government.

The BCMA has not been completely immune to negative decisions by the provincial government. The association was unable to prevent the province from introducing a policy prohibiting recent medical graduates from submitting bills to the medicare plan if they choose to practise in urban communities that have a surplus of doctors. The physicians have challenged this policy in the courts.

Of all the medical associations in Canada, the BCMA is probably the most sophisticated in its public-relations techniques. During its 1980–81 fee negotiations with the provincial government, the BCMA spent $460,000 on an advertising campaign to promote its pitch for a large increase in fees. The theme of the advertisements was: "Help us help you."

More recently, the BCMA has hired a polling company to help doctors analyze the public mood. And in 1985 it launched a $2.1-million public-relations campaign. The three-year campaign is being financed by an annual contribution of $180 from each of the association's 6,000 members. The campaign, known as Project 2000, includes money for lobbyists and about $300,000 for a weekly television show on health and medical issues. As part of the campaign, doctors have distributed more than one million pamphlets in their waiting rooms. Project 2000 is the largest public-relations program ever attempted by a medical association in Canada.

According to the BCMA, the objective of Project 2000 is "to restore the strength of the profession and return it to its traditional role of being the senior health care providing group. It will attempt to decrease the influence and power of those individuals and groups, less qualified than physicians, who are making medical and health-care decisions." Jim Gilmore has said that the campaign is designed to make people realize the cost of the health-care system. This could make it easier for politicians to introduce a deductible health fee (perhaps as high as $200), which would pump more money into the health system.

The BCMA has a well-organized lobbying system. In addition to the association's professional lobbyists, the BCMA made certain that each of the province's MLAs was linked to a local doctor in the MLA's home riding. The medical association organized a training session for these doctors in 1985. Key politicians helped to teach the doctors the best lobbying techniques. More than half the province's MLAs attended a reception and dinner with the doctors at the end of the training session.

Other Medical Associations

The Nova Scotia Medical Society (NSMS) is another medical association that has given an impressive display of bargaining power in recent years. The incomes of the Nova Scotia doctors are the second best in the country. Their average net income in 1984, according to Revenue Canada, was $104,500. They were permitted to extra-bill their patients until the Canada Health Act threatened to impose financial penalties on the province. Faced with these penalties, the Nova Scotia government reluctantly prohibited extra-billing. To protect themselves from any loss of income, the doctors secured a 3 per cent increase in their fee schedule (in addition to their normal annual increase). The upward revision of the fee schedule provided $3.5 million to the doctors to compensate them for the termination of extra-billing. This was equal to the total amount of extra-billing. As a result, the doctors suffered no loss in income. The NSMS also obtained the government's approval for a system of final-offer arbitration to settle fee disputes.

The *CMA Journal* hailed the Nova Scotia agreement as proof of the warm relationship between the provincial government and the NSMS. The doctors and the government officials have a "traditional spirit of understanding and co-operation," the journal said. The 1981-82 president of the medical society, Dr. Murdoch Smith, had previously emphasized the same point. "We enjoy good relations with government," he said after the NSMS accepted a 6 per cent fee increase for 1983.

After the termination of extra-billing, some doctors were dissatisfied with the $3.5-million compensation package. They began to charge patients for uninsured services such as telephone consultations, home visits, injections, and prescriptions refilled by telephone. (This was a preview of the tactics later used by Ontario doctors after the banning of extra-billing in 1986.) The Nova Scotia health minister, Gerald Sheehy, offered sympathy to the doctors who charged patients for uninsured services. "I am sure that administrative justification can be made for this practice . . . and I am sure that in the cost-accounting scheme of things, this can be rationalized as a business-like way of doing things," he told the doctors.

In the rest of the Atlantic provinces, medical incomes are somewhat lower. However, in comparison to the average resident of their province, the doctors were still doing extremely well. For example, while the average physician in Prince Edward Island earned about 5 per cent less than the average Canadian doctor in 1978, the average resident of P.E.I. earned 33 per cent less than the average resident of Canada.

In Saskatchewan the provincial medical association used a series of rotating walkouts in 1986 to gain a $10-million agreement with the provincial government. The settlement included a 3.5 per cent increase in the fee schedule, as well as extra payments for some specialists. Saskatchewan's medical leaders enjoy the privilege of sitting on an executive committee in the provincial health department that discusses issues affecting doctors in the province. No other health professionals are given the right to sit on a similar departmental committee.

The Manitoba Medical Association used the threat of mass opting-out as a bargaining tool at several points in the 1970s. The tactic helped the association gain fee increases from the provincial government. Then the MMA resorted to the strike weapon in 1981 and 1982. The association held rotating walkouts in 1981 to obtain a larger fee increase, and in 1982 they adopted a similar strategy to seek a form of binding arbitration. The 1983 dispute included a weekly series of province-wide walkouts by Manitoba doctors. The MMA also spent $125,000 on a television and newspaper advertising campaign to gain public sympathy for their demands. The doctors eventually won a binding-arbitration mechanism, which was finally established in 1986. When the arbitrator awarded them a healthy fee increase, the government quickly decided to cancel the system.

The doctors of Quebec have been equally militant, but considerably less successful than the doctors in English Canadian provinces. The Quebec fee schedule is among the lowest in Canada. Extra-billing has been illegal since 1971. The Quebec government also established a regulation in 1975 to prohibit any more than a small percentage of the province's doctors from opting out of medicare at any given time. When the doctors tried to withdraw their services, the government passed back-to-work legislation in 1970 and again in 1982. Moreover, the government introduced financial penalties for physicians who settled in large urban areas with doctor surpluses. The government also set payment ceilings to limit the incomes of general practitioners and specialists.

Does the Quebec example suggest that the Canadian medical profession is not as strong as we suspected? Actually, Quebec is a unique case. The doctors of Quebec are weakened by special factors that do not apply in any other province. First, their bargaining power is limited by the language barrier. Most of the French-speaking doctors are unable to move to another province or to the United States if they are dissatisfied with conditions in Quebec. Without the power to threaten to leave the province, Quebec doctors cannot match the medical associations in the English Canadian provinces.

Second, the Quebec doctors are hampered by internal divisions. There is no unified medical association in the province. There is one federation for general practitioners, another federation for specialists, and a third group that is affiliated with the CMA. The two federations are legally empowered to negotiate with the province. Essentially, they are unions — and they have no formal connection to the CMA. The third organization, the Quebec Medical Association, was originally dominated by Anglophones. Without any internal unity to support itself, the Quebec medical profession never gained the strength it needed to battle an aggressive government.

But the Quebec situation is an isolated case. Elsewhere the medical associations are powerful, unified, increasingly sophisticated and generally successful. Even when the Liberals replaced the Conservatives as the government party in Ontario, the OMA was eventually able to build new connections to the government. A former OMA president, Dr. Robert MacMillan, was appointed as an assistant deputy minister in the Ontario Ministry of Health in 1987. Although he has no degree in health administration or health policy, he was chosen to oversee all programs related to community and public health. Just two years after Dr. Bette Stephenson found herself in the opposition ranks in Ontario, the OMA had another close ally in the senior levels of the provincial government.

CHAPTER 9

THE PRIVATE POLICEMEN

Debbie De Champlain, the mother of an infant son, entered Etobicoke General Hospital for a thyroid operation on November 7, 1979. She had a steady job as a microphotographer, and she was thinking about having two or three more children. But something went wrong. During the operation, Debbie De Champlain suffered a cardiac arrest. There was a delay in reviving her. By the time her heart had started again, she was blind and brain-damaged.

Her family decided to file a complaint with the Ontario College of Physicians and Surgeons, the disciplinary and regulatory agency for Ontario's doctors. There is a similar body in every province in Canada. Our provincial governments have placed their faith in the colleges to ensure the competence and professional standards of Canada's 45,000 physicians. The colleges are the private policemen who are entrusted with the crucial task of protecting Canadians from negligent physicians.

When it received the complaint from the De Champlain family, the Ontario college asked for an explanation from the surgeon who performed the operation. The surgeon sent the college a letter that provided no real clues. He suggested that the incident was a medical mystery, an unexplainable phenomenon. The college accepted this version of the events. Without interviewing the hospital staff who witnessed the incident, the college dismissed the complaint.

However, the Etobicoke surgeon had failed to mention a vital piece of information: the anesthetist, who is supposed to monitor the patient during an operation, had left the operating room just before Debbie De Champlain suffered the cardiac arrest. The case might have remained a mystery forever. But the family launched a malpractice suit, and eventually the anesthetist admitted his liability. In 1985, after a six-year struggle by her family, Debbie De Champlain was awarded $2.2 million in a malpractice judgment.

The award will not restore her health. "Debbie is legally blind," said Mr. Justice Robert Montgomery of the Ontario Supreme Court in his written decision. "She just sees shapes; at dusk she is completely blind. . . . She walks with a spastic gait, her balance is bad and she falls often. The feeling is gone from her fingertips and her toes. This means that she cannot learn Braille. . . . She is subject to temper tantrums and regresses into child-like behaviour. Sometimes she tears up her son's teddy bears."

The court award was not a windfall profit for Debbie De Champlain. Most of the money went to pay for the cost of her future care and her lost income. Her two-storey home had to be converted to a bungalow to allow her to move around the house safely. Her injuries proved to be a serious strain on her marriage. Her husband eventually left. A psychologist examined her son, Christopher, and concluded that "his situation is even worse than having lost (his mother) through death, in that he must now be exposed to the results of her personality change. . . . [She is] unable to give him consistent, wise judgment."

During a pretrial examination, a registered nurse who had worked with the Etobicoke anesthetist testified that the anesthetist had walked out of operating rooms 50 to 100 times before, during previous operations. Yet his conduct would never have been questioned if the victim's family had not persisted with the case for six years. The Ontario college was not concerned about the conduct of the medical staff. After a brief investigation, the college washed its hands of the matter. The college did not choose to discipline anyone involved in the operation.

The case of Debbie De Champlain is just one of many cases that raise serious questions about the disciplinary system for Canada's doctors. The medical profession has always argued that physicians can police themselves. Our provincial governments have accepted this argument. They have allowed a private group of doctors to govern the conduct of their medical colleagues. When a patient complains about a doctor's behaviour, the college acts as the prosecutor, judge and jury. Key disciplinary decisions are thus left in the hands of doctors who may not be completely impartial.

For several important reasons, the colleges are unlikely to function as completely neutral or independent enforcement agencies. First, the doctors who sit on a college's complaints committee and discipline committee may be dependent on their medical colleagues for patient referrals and consultations. "If you are in consulting practice and depend on other doctors to refer cases to you, you are not in a position to discipline them unless you are willing to have your practice reduced," said Dr. Peter Banks, a former president of the CMA.

Second, the governing councils of the colleges are elected by the medical profession. Any doctor who publicly advocates a crackdown on negligence and incompetence is unlikely to gain election to the college council.

The third reason, and probably the biggest factor, is the professional sympathy that tends to arise in a doctor who witnesses the plight of a medical colleague. It is a natural phenomenon among any group of people who share the same working conditions and the same occupational risks. When the college investigates a patient's complaint, most doctors tend to see the case from the viewpoint of the harassed colleague. "There but for the grace of God go I," the doctor muses. When the college members share an instinctive understanding of the feelings of the doctor, it is difficult for them to remain independent in a patient-doctor dispute.

Throughout the country, decisions by the medical profession's disciplinary bodies have been questioned by patients, lawyers and advocacy groups who believe there are serious weaknesses in the system of self-regulation. In many cases, the colleges (also known as medical boards or medical councils in some provinces) have refused to take disciplinary action against physicians whose conduct was severely criticized by civil courts, criminal courts, provincial coroners or expert witnesses. Here are some examples from across Canada:

- A coroner's jury in Alert Bay, B.C., ruled that Dr. H. J. Pickup was negligent in the death of an 11-year-old Indian girl. But the B.C. College of Physicians and Surgeons decided that Dr. Pickup was competent to continue his medical practice. Witnesses at the coroner's inquest in 1979 had testified that Dr. Pickup failed to follow the correct procedures for diagnosing the girl's appendicitis. The witnesses also testified that Dr. Pickup refused to consult another doctor or transfer the girl to another hospital when he was unable to discover what was wrong with her. In addition, the testimony indicated that the doctor improperly used painkillers that masked the girl's appendicitis symptoms. The girl eventually died of a ruptured appendix.

    Local patients accused Dr. Pickup of drunkenness and racism against Indians. But after testing Dr. Pickup, the college concluded that he had a satisfactory background of knowledge and more than adequate skills in diagnosis. Later, a federal inquiry was appointed. This inquiry investigated Dr. Pickup and concluded that he was "an alcoholic in need of treatment." The federal inquiry found that Dr. Pickup had been drunk on duty and was responsible for the deaths of two other people, in addition to the 11-year-old girl. The inquiry reported that the college had referred the case to the wrong committee. It said the college "acted inadequately and inappropriately in referring complaints of Dr. Pickup's drunkenness on duty and verbally abusive behaviour with patients to the committee investigating Dr. Pickup's competence."

- A lengthy provincial inquiry in Nova Scotia, headed by a judge, ruled that an anesthetist and a nursing superviser were culpably negligent in the death of 37-year-old Ann Dawe, who had died shortly after a breast operation in 1984. The same provincial inquiry found that a doctor was negligent in the death of six-year-old Diana Strickland, who died after a routine tonsillectomy in 1983. But when the Nova Scotia Medical Board looked into the matter, it cleared two of the doctors who were involved in the incidents. The medical board cited the anesthetist for two errors of judgment, but it imposed no penalty against him. The medical board also decided that a third doctor was guilty of professional misconduct in the Strickland death, but it gave him only a letter of reprimand. Debbie Strickland, the mother of Diana, was angry. "As far as I'm concerned, doctors should not be allowed to judge doctors," she said. The medical board defended its decision at a news conference. "A letter of reprimand is not a slap on the wrist," said Dr. Michael Banks, a member of the disciplinary committee.

- In 1984 two doctors in Winnipeg dumped several boxes of confidential patient records into unprotected garbage bins behind their office building. The patient records included sensitive information about pregnancy tests, syphilis and gonorrhea screening tests, and drug prescriptions. The files also included notes about the psychological and physical health of the patients. When the files were discovered by a newspaper reporter, many patients were outraged that the records had been left in open boxes in an easily accessible place: the doctors were supposed to incinerate or shred the medical files. The Manitoba College of Physicians and Surgeons looked into the incident and decided not to discipline the doctors. "I think those doctors got some publicity which was discipline in itself," the college registrar said.

- Another doctor in a Winnipeg hospital examined the victim of a motorcycle accident and decided to send him home. A few days later the victim was still in pain. He went to his family doctor, who ordered an X-ray. The X-ray revealed that the motorcyclist had spinal damage — one chipped and one cracked vertebra. He ended up spending six weeks in hospital. The Manitoba College of Physicians and Surgeons investigated the conduct of the first doctor. In its report the college concluded that "it is quite apparent that X-ray examination should have been performed." However, it decided not to reprimand the doctor.

The Ontario College

The College of Physicians and Surgeons of Ontario is widely regarded as one of the most progressive colleges in Canada. For instance, it has experimented with a system of random evaluations of the medical practices of Ontario doctors to encourage the physicians to improve their performance. It also worked hard to control the excesses of the Ontario doctors' strike in 1986. It has even maintained contacts with the Medical Reform Group. Yet the disciplinary decisions of the Ontario college have tended to follow the same pattern as the decisions of the other provincial colleges. Here are a few examples:

- The Ontario college dismissed a complaint by a woman whose infant son was left brain-damaged and blind after a forceps delivery at a Toronto hospital. The college said the method of delivery was correct, but the mother, Judy Paloheimo, filed a malpractice suit. Her lawyer found several doctors who were willing to give expert opinions that criticized the method of delivery. In an out-of-court settlement the mother eventually obtained $2.1 million in damages from the doctor.

- The college dismissed a complaint by an Ottawa woman who said her doctor had sexually assaulted her. The college had asked the doctor to respond to the complaint, and the doctor denied any wrongdoing. After receiving the denial, the college decided the complaint was unfounded. But later the doctor pled guilty to charges of indecent assault in connection with the same case.

- The college dismissed a complaint by the family of an eight-year-old boy who died at the Hospital for Sick Children in Toronto. A coroner's jury had heard evidence that the boy's abdominal pains and continual vomiting were wrongly diagnosed as psychogenic (of mental origin). Because of the incorrect diagnosis, the boy was forced to clean up his own vomit in the hospital. The boy eventually suffered a cardiac arrest after an intravenous feeding tube was wrongly disconnected. In addition, X-rays were misread and hospital records were stolen. The boy was also given 10 times more than the prescribed dose of antibiotics. The family filed a malpractice suit and settled for $40,000 in damages. But the college decided there was no negligence by the doctors.

- The college dismissed a complaint by the husband of a North York woman who died after waiting two and a half months to be admitted to hospital. The woman's condition deteriorated while she was waiting, and she eventually suffered a massive stroke. At an inquest into her death, the coroner said the death might have been avoided if her family physician and consulting physician had monitored her condition. The coroner told the jury that the responsibility rests on the doctor to ensure that the patient is monitored. He said the patient and family often cannot recognize the symptoms of a deteriorating condition. The jury said there was "a definite lack of communication between doctors." The college investigated three doctors and decided there was no evidence of professional misconduct.

- The college dismissed a complaint about a doctor who prescribed the strap for a 16-year-old girl who had just slashed her wrists. The doctor did not recommend hospital treatment for the girl, but he sold a strap to the girl's mother for $5. The mother consulted the head of a hospital's adolescent crisis centre, who was appalled at the doctor's recommendation. The college ruled that there had been no professional misconduct.

- The college refused to take any disciplinary action against a Toronto urologist who was found negligent in a malpractice suit. The Ontario Supreme Court had awarded damages to a Toronto couple after the husband suffered an atrophied testicle following a vasectomy performed by the urologist. The judge ruled that the doctor had performed the operation too soon after the man had experienced an infection near his testes. The judge said the urologist had failed to warn his patient of the increased riskiness of a vasectomy after an infection. The judge also ruled that the urologist should have prescribed an antibiotic and sent the patient to hospital after he complained of swelling in his testicles after the operation. Instead, the doctor told the patient to apply heat and continue to rest. The college investigated and decided to take no action. Interestingly, the urologist was the chairman of the college's complaints committee at the time of the investigation by the college officials. He was also a member of the college's executive committee, and he was the immediate past president of the college.

- The college refused to admonish a doctor who had neglected to inform a patient's family about the condition of the patient, who had undergone a complex heart operation. The Ontario Health Disciplines Board, the appeal body for college decisions, ordered the college to admonish the doctor, but the college refused.

- The college refused to issue a warning to a doctor who had sent a form to an insurance company describing one of his patients as a chronic alcoholic. The doctor had insufficient evidence of the patient's drinking. The Health Disciplines Board instructed the college to issue a warning to the doctor, but the college ignored the instruction.

- The college declined to follow the recommendations of a coroner's jury and the province's chief coroner, both of whom had urged the college to investigate a doctor who had refused to go to a hospital to treat a heart attack victim. The doctor had twice ignored requests from nurses who wanted him to see the victim. Later the same day, the patient died. The college took no action on the chief coroner's recommendation, until finally the Health Disciplines Board told the college to look into the case. Eventually the college reprimanded the doctor.

The Colleges and the Medical Associations

In theory, the colleges and medical boards in each Canadian province are neutral regulatory agencies, established to protect the public interest. They are not intended to act on behalf of the doctors. Theoretically, there should be no connection between the colleges and the provincial medical associations, which represent the political and financial interests of the medical profession. Yet historically the colleges have been closely linked to the medical associations. In some provinces the college and the medical association were merged into one organization for many years. This resulted in an obvious conflict of interest: the college was supposed to represent the public, yet it was actually representing the interests of the doctors.

The College of Physicians and Surgeons of Saskatchewan merged with the Saskatchewan Medical Association in the late 1930s. The two organizations were not officially separated until the early 1970s. This meant, for example, that the Saskatchewan college was representing the political and financial interests of the doctors during their 23-day strike in 1962. The health of Saskatchewan patients was jeopardized by the 1962 strike, but the college consistently defended the interests of the doctors, not the patients.

Similarly, the New Brunswick Medical Society was given the regulatory powers of a college in 1881. No separate college was created until long into the 20th century. In Manitoba a single doctor was simultaneously the registrar of the provincial college and the executive director of the provincial medical association in the 1950s and 1960s. In Prince Edward Island the Medical Society (the professional association) and the Medical Council (the regulatory body) are still intimately connected. The officers of the Medical Council are nominated by the Medical Society's nominating committee, and the Medical Council reports to the society's annual meeting. (By 1987 there were efforts to separate the two organizations.)

The same kinds of connections have been visible in other provinces as well. The College of Physicians and Surgeons of Alberta took over the lobbying and negotiating role of the Alberta Medical Association in 1922. This improved the position of organized medicine in Alberta because the college governed every licensed doctor in the province and collected annual fees from all of them. The college had greater financial resources and greater power over its members than the medical association could hope for. The Alberta college and the Alberta Medical Association ended their official connections in 1969. But the association continued to receive financial support from the college until 1975. Both organizations are still located in the same building in Edmonton.

The College of Physicians and Surgeons of British Columbia took over the lobbying and negotiating functions of the B.C. Medical Association in 1933. The B.C. college was not separated from the provincial medical association until 1952, when the BCMA took responsibility for finance and politics. Even today the B.C. college and the BCMA share the same office building in Vancouver. (Similarly, the Saskatchewan college and the Saskatchewan Medical Association continue to share the same building in Saskatoon.)

In many instances, the elected officials of a provincial college are former activists from the provincial medical association. The same is sometimes true of the appointed officials. Dr. Dennis Kendel, the current registrar of the Saskatchewan College of Physicians and Surgeons, is a past president of the Saskatchewan Medical Association. As the head of the SMA, Dr. Kendel fought hard to advance the financial and political interests of the medical profession in Saskatchewan. Now, as the registrar of the college, he is the senior administrative official of a regulatory agency that is supposed to be neutral and objective.

There is a similar case in Ontario. Dr. Michael Dixon, the current registrar of the Ontario College of Physicians and Surgeons, is a former employee of the Ontario Medical Association. And several other elected officials of the Ontario college were previously active in the OMA.

Political Activism by the Colleges

Many of the colleges have compromised their neutrality and impartiality by becoming involved in political issues. As late as the 1960s, the College of Physicians and Surgeons of Quebec was heavily involved in politics and economics. For example, the Quebec college served as the negotiating body for the province's medical profession when the doctors were negotiating the rules for hospital insurance in 1961. The Quebec college also submitted a brief to the Castonguay Commission, which was studying health care in the province. The college's brief, submitted in 1967, urged the province to ensure that there was "minimum government intervention" in any public health insurance plan.

Meanwhile, the Ontario College of Physicians and Surgeons continued to be active in medical politics until the mid-1980s. It opposed the Canada Health Act. It called for the introduction of user fees in the medicare system. And some of its members participated in physician walkouts in 1982, even though the college was supposed to protect the public during those walkouts.

The provincial colleges have frequently taken action on public issues completely unrelated to their official duties. The Manitoba college, for example, discouraged a Winnipeg physician from speaking to a holistic medicine conference. The Manitoba college also sought an injunction to prevent Dr. Henry Morgentaler from practising medicine in the province. In British Columbia, the provincial college instructed the province's doctors not to rent any office space to chiropractors.

Perhaps the best example of the political activism of the colleges is their history of support for extra-billing. Dr. Leroy le Riche, the registrar of the Alberta College of Physicians and Surgeons, has been a prominent defender of extra-billing. In 1984 he attended the annual meeting of the Canadian Medical Association and proposed a resolution that called for the CMA to take immediate legal action against federal or provincial governments that prohibited extra-billing. A few months later, in its annual report for 1984, the Alberta college said it strongly supported extra-billing "as a fundamental and inalienable right of physicians."

The Ontario college became involved in the extra-billing issue in 1982. The college refused to enforce an agreement that required Ontario doctors to give an advance warning to their patients if they were planning to extra-bill. When he learned of this decision, the provincial health minister asked the college to amend its regulations to prohibit doctors from extra-billing a patient who had not received advance warning. The college refused. Its 27-member governing council voted unanimously to reject the health minister's request. Finally, the provincial cabinet went ahead and amended the regulations itself.

In 1983 the Ontario college refused to discipline an anesthetist who had demanded immediate payment from a woman who was lying drugged on an operating table. The woman, who was scheduled to have four wisdom teeth removed, had been injected with the anesthetic before the doctor asked her to pay him. When the woman said her cheque was in her clothing in another room, the doctor sent a nurse to fetch the clothing. Then he watched as she filled in the cheque. "The patient stated that she felt tense and tight and wanted to cry," the college reported later. "When she recovered consciousness following the operation, she was crying and asked the nurse if the episode concerning payment had actually occurred in the operating room." The college dismissed the complaint. It said the anesthetist's actions were "an error of judgment," but it decided that the incident fell "just short of professional misconduct."

If the billing practices of doctors are not a major concern to the colleges, what kinds of conduct do they take a strict stand against? In the eyes of the colleges, advertising by a physician is among the worst possible offences. Most colleges have adopted a firm position against any advertising by doctors. They have ignored the recommendations of economists and consumer groups, who believe that advertising would provide valuable information for health consumers. In recent years, lawyers and other professionals have been permitted to advertise. The medical profession continues to be the exception. In some cases, doctors can advertise a change in their hours of operation. But in most provinces the colleges prohibit even the slightest form of advertising. Doctors who list themselves in boldface type in the Yellow Pages can be subject to prosecution by a college.

A Tradition of Secrecy

Many of the provincial colleges appear to believe that their decisions should be surrounded by secrecy. In Ontario the vast majority of doctors who receive reprimands from the college are never publicly identified. The college simply refuses to release their names. The complainant is the only patient who knows the outcome of the case. Other patients will never know whether their doctor has ever been guilty of professional misconduct.

The Ontario college has followed this policy of secrecy even in cases where a patient's death was partly due to the doctor's actions. In 1981, for example, the college refused to identify a surgeon who had failed to visit a seriously ill patient who eventually died. The patient was a 67-year-old woman with a perforation in her bowel wall. The surgeon did not visit the woman for 20 hours, despite repeated telephone calls from the attending nurses. The nurses told him that the woman's condition was becoming dramatically worse, but the surgeon continued to stay at home. He finally did visit the woman, but she died of kidney failure a day later. The college reprimanded the surgeon but decided to keep his name secret, arguing that the case was an isolated incident in the doctor's career. It also argued that the doctor "was under considerable pressure as the sole surgeon in a small hospital with limited staff."

In other provinces the colleges have traditionally operated with even greater secrecy than the Ontario college. The annual reports of the Alberta college were kept confidential until 1985, when pressure from consumer groups and the media finally persuaded the college to make its reports public. Even after 1985 the names of guilty doctors were kept secret, except when the college's disciplinary committee made a specific request to have the doctor identified. (The disciplinary committee rarely made such a request. Doctors were identified only when their offence was extremely serious.) The college's 1985 report explained that the public disclosure of the identity of a guilty doctor might "expose certain physicians to public criticism where that could in no way serve the public interest and only unjustifiably embarrass the physician and his family."

In one case, the Alberta college decided not to release the name of a psychiatrist who had sex with a patient. Many psychiatrists believe that a patient can be damaged by a sexual relationship with the patient's therapist. But the registrar of the Alberta college, Dr. Leroy le Riche, argued that the incident was merely "a little love affair." If the psychiatrist's name were disclosed, "all patients relying on him would be devastated by it," Dr. le Riche said.

The British Columbia college has traditionally been the most secretive of any self-governing body in the province. Until recently, its annual report was marked "not for publication." The names of guilty physicians were routinely kept secret, until a public controversy erupted in 1984. From 1976 to 1984, at least nine B.C. physicians were found guilty of engaging in sexual relations with their patients, but the college concealed the identity of all of them. The college provided no information about any of its disciplinary hearings. In some cases, doctors were continuing to practise while under suspension without their patients knowing about it. Finally, in 1984, a Vancouver newspaper obtained enough leaked information to publish a story about a doctor who had been suspended for engaging in sexual acts with four female patients. Public pressure forced the college to change its policies. It agreed to release the names of guilty physicians and a summary of their offences.

In Manitoba the provincial college decided in 1983 to stop compiling information on the number and type of complaints it received from the public. The registrar said the college had decided that this information "wasn't constructive." When a reporter contacted the chairman of the college's complaints committee in January 1983, the chairman said he couldn't talk to the reporter until March. Even then, he said he would talk to the reporter only if he was paid for his time.

The Ontario college, whose complaints committee is somewhat less secretive, has revealed that it receives about 1,000 complaints per year. The number of patients who complain to the college has increased dramatically in the past 10 years, but only a tiny fraction of these complaints are upheld by the college. For example, the college imposed penalties on 28 doctors in 1985, after investigating about 1,000 complaints from patients.

The number of annual complaints to the Ontario college has tripled since 1976, when there were about 350 complaints. At the same time, an increasing number of patients are dissatisfied with the college's rulings. The number of appeals of college decisions rose by 135 per cent in the early years of the 1980s — from 40 appeals in 1980 to 94 appeals in 1984.

Complaints from the public are reviewed by the college's complaints committee. If the committee decides that the case is serious, the complaint is referred to the college's discipline committee, which holds a private hearing and decides whether to punish the doctor. A study of the period from 1969 to 1977, conducted by the Patients' Rights Association, found that only 3 per cent of the written complaints to the Ontario college were passed on to the discipline committee.

A patient who is unhappy with a decision by the complaints committee can file an appeal with the Ontario Health Disciplines Board. But the board cannot hear new evidence and has no power to impose penalties. It simply reviews the college's action and decides whether to recommend a different action. If the board disagrees with the college's decision, it sends the case back to the college. In addition, the board cannot hear appeals of discipline decisions. Its jurisdiction extends only to the complaints committee.

A survey of one group of complainants — female patients who complained of sexual abuse by doctors or other health professionals — revealed a widespread dissatisfaction with the disciplinary system. The women felt confused and angry at their treatment by the system. They said they were ignored and subjected to long delays. They were upset at the secrecy in the disciplinary hearings. They felt that the system was unfair, biased against them and designed to protect the doctor and other professionals.

Weaknesses in the Disciplinary System

According to lawyers and advocates who have observed the Ontario college in action, there are some major weaknesses in its disciplinary system. Most of these weaknesses are also present in every other college and medical board in the country. Here are some examples of the weaknesses in the Ontario college:

- The original letter of complaint from the patient is the cornerstone of the college's investigations. Yet the patient is unaware that the original letter must be detailed and well prepared. This policy also tends to work against complainants who are uneducated, inarticulate, or immigrants whose command of English is poor. Because the college does not always interview the complainant, the college often overlooks key facts in the case. "Sometimes when you hear it from the person, you realize that the complaints committee didn't understand what the complaint was all about," says Ted Kerzner, a lawyer for the Health Disciplines Board.

- The college keeps such a low profile that many patients are simply unaware of its existence or its procedural rules. Particularly in northern or rural regions, patients can be unaware of their right to file a complaint. The college makes no attempt to publicize its existence.

- The college has no mechanism for monitoring the results of malpractice suits, unless the cases are reported in the media. Yet some patients do not file complaints in these cases because they assume that the college will automatically investigate a doctor who has been found negligent in a malpractice suit.

- When a complaint is filed, the doctor is allowed to know the details of the patient's grievance. But the complainant does not always have the right to see the complete medical records or the full response from the doctor. In some cases, the college does not give the complainant any details of the evidence it has gathered.

- Neither the patient nor his or her lawyer is permitted to observe a discipline hearing, except when the patient is giving evidence. The patient cannot hear the cross-examination of the doctor. Nor is the patient guaranteed the right to know the identity of expert witnesses who testify at the hearings. The patient has no opportunity to correct any errors in the evidence or to pursue new information that emerges at the hearing. (By contrast, the Law Society of Upper Canada has decided to hold open hearings in most discipline cases.)

    The chairman of the Health Disciplines Board, Hugh Mackenzie, recommended in 1985 that the college's disciplinary hearings should be open to the public. "There has to be more stringent accounting," he told a provincial legislative committee. In recent years the college has suggested that it might be willing to consider holding some public hearings, but it has steadfastly opposed the idea of allowing the complainant to participate in the hearings. "If the complainant was a party to the hearing, the complexity of the proceedings would be such that mistrials would be likely," the college argued in a 1985 brief to the provincial government.

- The college tends to rely on hospital records and letters of explanation from doctors, but these documents can conceal an act of negligence. In many cases, a denial is accepted at face value. The college usually does not interview hospital staff or other witnesses to check the doctor's version of events. (This policy was noticed as early as 1976, when a patient complained that Dr. John Porter had gained access to his hospital records without his consent. The college dismissed the complaint, accepting Dr. Porter's explanation that it was an isolated incident. Yet a royal commission later found that Dr. Porter had obtained records without the patient's consent on six to 12 occasions.)

- When a patient's testimony is pitted against a doctor's testimony, with no eyewitnesses on either side, the college tends to support the doctor. For instance, in a decision in early 1986, the college dismissed a complaint by a female patient who alleged that her doctor had started a sexual relationship with her. The doctor denied the charge. The college said the patient "appeared sane and gave straightforward evidence," while the doctor could not recall key details of the events. Nevertheless, the college found the doctor not guilty because there was no "clear and convincing evidence."

- Doctors hold 80 per cent of the posts on the college's discipline committee, even though most discipline hearings do not require any expert knowledge. Most cases involve sexual impropriety, billing practices or other matters that can be decided by lay persons.

  For many years, the Ontario college refused to allow any lay persons to sit on its committees. In 1965, when Dr. Morton Shulman was the chief coroner of Metro Toronto, he had the audacity to suggest that an ordinary member of the public should be allowed to sit on the discipline committee. His idea immediately sparked an uproar in the medical community. The Ontario supervising coroner, Dr. H. B. Cotnam, said Dr. Shulman's suggestion would be like "letting an ice cream vendor assess the actions of lawyers." Today the medical profession has finally accepted the notion that ordinary citizens should not be excluded from the college's committees. However, the non-doctors are kept to a small fraction of the membership of the key committees.

At the time of writing, some of the weaknesses of the Ontario college are on the verge of being remedied. A provincial review of health legislation is recommending several significant improvements in the college's procedures. The recommendations include steps to reduce the college's secrecy. The review also proposes to increase the Ontario health minister's power to intervene in college decisions. However, the college is fighting against the recommendations, and it is not clear at this point whether the government will approve the proposals.

Despite the tolerant attitude of the colleges in most provinces, they can occasionally be an annoyance to the medical profession. However, the profession has several weapons at its disposal to help undermine the strength of the colleges. One of the most effective weapons is the legal system. The B.C. College of Physicians and Surgeons was damaged by a 1985 court ruling which declared that the college did not have the authority to remove 70 patient files from a doctor's office to see whether the doctor had overbilled the provincial health-insurance plan. The court action was launched by Dr. Rodney Bishop of New Westminster, who was fighting the college's investigation. The college was merely intending to remove the files for two or three days, to allow them to be photocopied. But the B.C. Supreme Court ruled that the college had no such authority. The court said Dr. Bishop's patients had expected privacy, and Dr. Bishop's medical practice could be prejudiced by the college's actions. The B.C. Court of Appeal confirmed the ruling in 1986. "It was a very significant blow in terms of our role as a self-regulating profession," said Dr. J. R. LeHuquet, president of the B.C. college.

Doctors can use legal action to enable themselves to continue practising medicine after a college has decided to suspend them. For example, a doctor in a small town in Saskatchewan was allowed to continue practising for two months after the provincial college found her incompetent. The doctor obtained a ruling from the Court of Queen's Bench that permitted her to continue practising until an appeal of the college's decision had been heard. She continued seeing patients until another judge overturned the court ruling two months later.

In some cases, court appeals can take years, and a doctor can keep working until the case has ended. In 1982 a doctor in Metro Toronto, whose licence had been revoked after he was found guilty of prescribing drugs to addicts, continued to prescribe drugs to his patients while he appealed the Ontario college's disciplinary decision. The Ontario college recently gained the power to prohibit a doctor from practising medicine if he or she is believed to be a threat to the public, but this power is rarely invoked. Many colleges do not have this power at all.

Doctors can further weaken the colleges by putting political pressure on them. A group of British Columbia doctors tried to force the resignation of the elected council of the B.C. college in 1986. The doctors were upset about several disciplinary decisions by the college. (The decisions were later overturned by the courts.) In 1985 a group of doctors in Saskatchewan tried to persuade their colleagues to hold an annual vote on whether the college's registrar had the confidence of the medical profession. The physicians said the college had been conducting "witch hunts" against doctors. In both the B.C. case and the Saskatchewan case, the colleges managed to defeat these challenges. But the colleges cannot afford to ignore pressures from dissident doctors. The agitation and opposition from doctors is a constant reminder that the colleges are accountable to their members. If a college becomes stricter on disciplinary matters, it could face an open revolt from its membership.

Because the members of the college councils are directly elected by doctors, the colleges are often guided by the self-interest of the medical profession. "It is perhaps not unnatural that one who is elected to a position of prestige in his profession should see himself as having some obligation to his constituency," the Ontario Committee on the Healing Arts noted in its final report in 1970. "Our examination of the practices of the professions discloses an inclination on the part of the statutory governing body to see itself as the defender of the interests of its members and we believe this is due in large measure to the fact that their members are elected by the practitioners."

The Ontario Public Health Association has made the same criticism of the current system of electing a college's council members. The system "has led to situations where professionals have campaigned to become members of the regulatory body on a platform which is clearly not in the public interest," the association said in a 1984 brief to the provincial government.

The political pressures from the medical profession, combined with the natural tendency of college officials to have sympathy for their medical colleagues, are probably the biggest reasons for the weakness of the disciplinary system in Canada. But even when the college does decide to discipline a doctor, the penalties tend to be mild. In many cases, the penalty is merely a reprimand and the doctor is not publicly identified, even if found guilty of serious misconduct.

Malpractice lawyers who have had experiences with the Ontario college are sharply critical of its procedures. Theodore Rachlin, lawyer for Debbie De Champlain, said he is thankful that patients can go to the courts if they are not satisfied by the college. "Where would we be if we let doctors police themselves?" he asked after the De Champlain decision.

However, the courts cannot replace the colleges, since the function of the courts is completely different from the role of the colleges. In a malpractice case the civil courts are designed to provide compensation for victims. They cannot prevent a doctor from practising medicine. The colleges are supposed to protect the public by disciplining doctors who fail to maintain an acceptable standard of medicine.

When the Canadian medical profession was granted the right to self-regulation, the provincial governments were handing it a tremendous amount of power and responsibility. In return for this power, the doctors were required to act as the trustees for the public. The power to regulate their own affairs is not a divine right, but a delegated duty. Yet the politicians have permitted the provincial colleges to operate with complete autonomy. Governments have rarely made any effort to see whether the colleges are properly exercising the powers they were granted. It is not surprising that the private policemen are following their natural instincts. Nobody has told them that their natural instincts are not synonymous with the public interest.

In 1985 the Ontario college reprimanded a doctor for failing to monitor a patient who had signs of lung cancer; the doctor had "completely forgotten" the indication of cancer for three and a half years and the patient eventually died. Yet the college decided that the reprimand should not even be recorded in the college's official register. Today, the doctor's patients are unaware that they are being treated by someone who has already made one life-threatening mistake. As long as secrecy surrounds the disciplinary decisions of Canada's medical profession, patients will continue to be deprived of vital information.

CHAPTER 10

CONSUMERISM AND THE PATIENTS' RIGHTS MOVEMENT

Harold Coy was a retired accountant who lived in the suburban Toronto community of Etobicoke. His wife, Anne, was a music librarian at the Canadian Broadcasting Corporation. They were ordinary people who had faith in the basic institutions of society. Harold was an active and healthy man in his mid-60s. In the winter he skated and played badminton. In the summer he swam and sailed. And he loved to play golf. Meanwhile, Anne took French lessons, socialized with the neighbours and frequently joined Harold on the golf course. It was a good life.

One day in the spring of 1969, Harold Coy noticed that his golf game was being hindered by an ache in his shoulder. His doctor diagnosed it as a case of bursitis. It was a minor health problem, but a nuisance all the same. Coy asked for his doctor's advice. The doctor prescribed a drug called phenylbutazone.

Two days after he began taking the drug, Harold Coy felt weak and sick. In the ensuing weeks and months he felt nauseated almost constantly. His abdomen was bloated, his stomach was painful, and one day he suffered a blackout. But the doctor instructed Coy to continue taking the drug. "The stomach pain is not important," the doctor said.

One evening Anne Coy returned home from work to find Harold seated on a stool in their kitchen. His head was hanging over the sink. "The pain in my stomach is killing me," he whispered. "I feel like vomiting constantly." He was ashen-faced and perspiring heavily. Anne called an ambulance and took him to the emergency ward of Toronto Western Hospital. A surgeon examined Harold

Coy and ordered an immediate operation to repair an ulcerous perforation in his stomach. Several doctors at the hospital told Mrs. Coy that the ulcer had been caused by the phenylbutazone. Over the next 34 months, doctors performed a series of operations to remove ulcers from Harold Coy's stomach. During this period he developed cancer. Harold Coy died on October 15, 1972.

Mrs. Coy's niece, a nurse, found a standard medical textbook and checked to see what it said about phenylbutazone. The textbook warned of serious side effects, including nausea, vomiting, stomach discomfort, ulcers and perforations in the stomach. Some of these symptoms could result in death. The textbook emphasized that any use of the drug must be accompanied by close medical supervision of the patient. The drug should not be used for more than one week, and its use should be discontinued if side effects occurred.

Anne Coy consulted a lawyer and decided to file a complaint with the College of Physicians and Surgeons of Ontario. In her complaint, she noted that her husband had taken daily doses of phenylbutazone for eight months under the doctor's instructions. The medication was finally discontinued when Harold Coy underwent his first operation — but by then it was too late.

It took the college more than two months to acknowledge receipt of the complaint. It took another week of persistent telephone calls, plus the assistance of her lawyer, before Mrs. Coy was permitted to meet a college official to explain the details of her husband's death. The college official told her that only the doctor's evidence was admissible. Everything else — including a statement by a pharmacist, the comments to Mrs. Coy by the other doctors and the comments by Harold Coy to his wife — were considered hearsay.

Three months after this meeting, the college dismissed the complaint against Harold Coy's doctor. Anne Coy was notified in a brief, impersonal letter from the college in September 1973.

By this point, most patients would have given up and walked away. Instead, Mrs. Coy began to think about the powerlessness of the ordinary patient. She was determined to challenge the system. When a Toronto newspaper described the gruesome story of her husband's death, Mrs. Coy was flooded with telephone calls and letters from people who had similar experiences with doctors. In the summer of 1974 Mrs. Coy helped to found the Patients' Rights Association.

"Patients have to get together and figure out a way of getting a fair deal from the medical profession," Mrs. Coy told a reporter when the association was born. "The purpose of our organization is not to harass doctors but to protect patients against the small minority of physicians who fail to live up to the high standards of an honourable and difficult profession."

In the early days of the Patients' Rights Association, most doctors tried to ignore it. When patients telephoned the college of physicians and surgeons for information about the association, the college sometimes said it had never heard of the organization. College officials dismissed Mrs. Coy as "a bitter woman." They implied that the association was a one-woman organization. "There was an attempt to personalize it," she recalls.

As for the patients, many were reluctant to join the association. "When we spoke to people, they were fearful," Mrs. Coy says. "They were intimidated. It was an atmosphere. There was a fear of challenging anything." The Patients' Rights Association was perceived as a fringe group. "We started from nothing," Mrs. Coy says. "It was disconcerting to be seen as a radical movement."

Today the Patients' Rights Association has 300 members across Ontario. Despite its lack of any paid staff or full-time office, it is widely respected by government officials and health professionals. The Ontario Ombudsman and the provincial Ministry of Health have referred people to the association for assistance. Public health nurses have done the same. Even the College of Physicians and Surgeons of Ontario has occasionally referred a patient to Mrs. Coy for help. The association has been consulted by provincial task forces, government commissions, hospitals and even the Ontario Medical Association. Its spokespersons are frequently quoted in the media, and they are regularly invited to speak to other organizations. The association's advice is sought by hundreds of bewildered and baffled patients. In many cases, the association has helped injured patients gain redress through the regulatory agencies or the courts.

Anne Coy is 74 today, but she is still one of the key leaders of the Patients' Rights Association. Now retired from her long-time job in the CBC music library, she lives with her cats in a high-rise apartment in Toronto. She is the current president of the Patients' Rights Association, and her apartment is the mailing address for the organization. While she talks to a visitor, her answering machine is busy taking messages from patients and government officials.

Patients in the mid-1980s are much more willing to assert themselves, Mrs. Coy says. "People are eager to ask questions now, and to act on it. There's a recognition of the fact that patients' rights is not a radical idea any more. It is accepted now. We've been very instrumental in educating the public."

According to its 1986 annual report, the Patients' Rights Association provided advice and guidance to 115 patients in the previous 12-month period. The association was also involved in two appeals of college decisions, and its leaders were invited to speak to 16 organizations. The association received a total of 613 telephone calls from patients in the one-year period.

The Evolution of Patients' Rights in North America

The patients' rights movement is still a relatively recent phenomenon in North America. In the past, patients were expected to be passive and obedient. Indeed, the very word "patient" implies a person who is stoic and silent. In 1897 the Cornwall General Hospital published this instruction: "Patients must be quiet and exemplary in their behaviour and conform strictly to the rules and regulations of the hospital and carry out all orders and prescriptions of the various officers of the establishment." As recently as the 1960s, a malpractice lawsuit was still a rare event in Canada. In 1970 a total of only 80 malpractice suits were filed by Canada's 21 million patients.

North America's first consumer group for patients was launched in 1959 by James Donnelly of New York. The group, called the Patients Aid Society Inc., grew rapidly in the 1960s and 1970s. The society had 6,000 members by 1974, when James Donnelly travelled to Toronto to help provide advice to Anne Coy and the other founders of the Patients' Rights Association. He told Mrs. Coy: "Doctors are organized and hospitals are organized. Until patients are organized, nothing will happen for patients."

James Donnelly's group has pioneered many of the techniques of medical consumerism. Its members are assigned to pore over the medical journals to find studies of unnecessary surgery and other abuses by physicians. The society has also discovered that the medical journals contain useful legal opinions on recent malpractice suits. By reading these opinions, the patients have learned the kinds of legal arguments that are successful against doctors in court. Sometimes the legal opinions even provide the names of doctors who are willing to act as expert witnesses on behalf of patients.

Early in its history, the Patients Aid Society decided to expose a gynecologist who was known for his excessive rates of surgery. The society sent six women to the gynecologist for an examination. The gynecologist advised each of the six women that a hysterectomy was necessary. The society's medical consultant disagreed with the diagnosis. Most of the women eventually had children without any difficulty.

In another case, the society sued a Brooklyn hospital that had given injections of live cancer cells to a number of cancer patients as part of an experimental study. The society won the suit.

Meanwhile, in Canada, the patients' rights movement has quietly emerged as a major social force in the past 15 years. Doctors could not remain immune to the wave of consumer activism affecting every other profession and business sector. Patients' rights organizations were established in several provinces — including Nova Scotia, Quebec, Ontario, Manitoba, Saskatchewan and British Columbia. A steadily increasing number of patients began to file complaints with the provincial colleges of physicians and surgeons. The number of malpractice suits has climbed rapidly. The courts have confirmed that a doctor must obtain a patient's "informed consent" before treatment is commenced.

At the same time, patients have created dozens of self-help groups to reduce their dependence on the medical profession. The women's movement has challenged the authority of the physician by asserting a woman's right to control her body. The media have become more aggressive in their scrutiny of the medical profession, and many books have been published to help patients stand up for their rights. Patient advocates, hospital ethicists and hospital ombudsmen have provided protection to patients in institutional settings. Patients have learned to question the need for some surgical operations, such as Caesarean sections. Even the terminally ill patient has won the right to refuse medical treatment.

There is plenty of data to confirm the rise of consumer activism in the Canadian health-care system. The number of malpractice suits in Canada quadrupled from 1970 to 1979. Then, in the first half of the 1980s, the number of suits jumped by a further 163 per cent. In 1985 a total of 906 lawsuits were launched against physicians who belonged to the Canadian Medical Protective Association (the organization that provides malpractice insurance for the vast majority of Canadian doctors). The CMPA spent $14,240,126 on damages awarded by the courts to injured patients in 1985, and it spent a further $9,091,771 on legal expenses in the same year.

While an increasing number of patients are asserting themselves in the courtrooms of Canada, there is also a steady growth in the number of written complaints sent to the provincial regulatory bodies. The College of Physicians and Surgeons of Ontario received 941 letters of complaint from patients in 1985, compared to a total of 703 complaints in 1980. The Saskatchewan college reported that the number of complaints from patients climbed by almost 50 per cent in a single year in the early 1980s.

The largest patient organization in Canada is a group in Quebec called the Provincial Committee of Patients. Its founder and president is Claude Brunet, a 46-year-old paraplegic who has overcome tremendous handicaps. He has only one leg and one kidney, and he transports himself on a motorized stretcher. His organization, founded in 1972, specializes in representing the elderly and the chronic patients who must remain in institutions. The organization has about 200 affiliated committees in nursing homes and other institutions in Quebec. It began with a membership of just seven patients, but today it represents about 25,000. (Membership dues are not required, and patients are automatically represented by the provincial organization.)

Claude Brunet and other leaders of the Quebec group have taken a public stand on several important health issues. They have appeared on radio shows and have written letters to newspapers. They submitted a brief to the government on the problem of chronic patients who occupy acute-care hospital beds. They have lobbied doctors to improve the quality of medical care in Quebec. And they have strongly opposed strikes by doctors in Quebec. "Patients' rights are incompatible with strike action," Brunet says.

The Self-help Movement

The rise of the patients' rights movement has been accompanied by another important trend: the emergence of the self-help movement. At one level, this movement is manifested by people who monitor their own blood pressure and heart rates. A self-care program for diabetics in California achieved a 67 per cent reduction in the number of diabetic comas in a two-year period. Another self-care program, for hemophiliacs, reduced the cost of health care for the average patient by 45 per cent.

At a deeper level, the self-help movement includes the growing number of patients who have formed support groups to help each other cope with illnesses, health conditions, or diseases. In effect, these patients have learned to reduce their dependence on doctors. Self-help organizations exist today for people who suffer from schizophrenia, epilepsy, diabetes, blindness and dozens of other conditions. Senior citizens in Vancouver have organized a "Be Well" program to encourage each other to preserve their own health. Ex-psychiatric patients in Toronto have banded together to support their return to the community. The self-help movement also includes groups such as Alcoholics Anonymous and Weight Watchers.

Most recently, self-help groups have played a crucial role in the battle against AIDS. In many cases, Canadians who have developed AIDS have contacted the self-help groups before talking to a doctor. Medical authorities have acknowledged that the self-help organizations are the best vehicles for AIDS education and counselling programs. Without the self-help groups, doctors would find it almost impossible to fight the spread of AIDS.

Every self-help group has a common philosophy: its members believe that they can learn to cope with their lives without the constant guidance of professional health experts. "As soon as you have health professionals, people lose faith in themselves," said Jean Schnell, who coordinates a self-help program for people who are 55 or older. Her program, called Fully Alive, deals with topics such as fitness, nutrition, assertiveness and self-esteem.

H. L. Laframboise, a former assistant deputy minister in the federal Department of Health and Welfare, has pointed to the success of Alcoholics Anonymous as an example of the effectiveness of self-help groups. "The medical solution to alcoholism, as a disease, was found wanting by so many alcoholics that they struck out on their own, outflanking such professional counsellors as social workers, clinical psychologists and medical doctors, to devise their own methods for dealing with their problems." The power of the professionals has been undermined by these modest organizations, Laframboise says. "The advantage self-help groups have is that they are viewed initially as non-threatening by the elites they are designed to outflank, perhaps because they are perceived as fumbling amateurs. By the time the elites take notice, the movements have firmly woven themselves into the social fabric."

The federal government is now actively encouraging the growth of self-help groups. "Informal networks are recognized as a fundamental resource in the promotion of health," the Department of Health and Welfare wrote in a 1986 report. "There is strong evidence that people who have social support are healthier than those who do not."

One of the fastest-growing self-help organizations is the network of support groups for women who want to avoid Caesarean-section births. The skyrocketing number of C-sections in North American hospitals has alarmed many women, especially those who have experienced the extreme pain and discomfort of the procedure. Yet doctors have traditionally insisted that a mother who has given birth by C-section must continue to undergo the operation for every future birth. In response, women have formed Vaginal Birth After Caesarean associations in most of the Canadian provinces. The movement is less than a decade old, but it has already had an impact.

Its supporters helped push for a national conference of scientific experts in February 1986. The conference, in a bid to reduce the number of unnecessary operations, decided to set stricter rules for Caesarean sections.

The women's movement is having a tremendous impact on the attitude of patients in Canada. In many cases, medical issues have become women's issues. Thousands of women have been inspired by a popular self-help book called *Our Bodies, Ourselves*. Women's health clinics and childbirth clinics have been established in most cities. Female patients are no longer willing to obey their doctors blindly. In Vancouver, for example, the Women's Health Collective has kept an open file on patients' experiences with their doctors. This allowed other patients to get a sampling of opinion on the habits of local doctors.

Perhaps the best-organized women's health movement in recent years has been the campaign for midwives. Female patients have rebelled against the medical profession's attempt to suppress midwives who attend home births. The health consumers have been particularly successful in Ontario, where the government has agreed to legalize midwifery. More than 1,000 women joined an organization to support the legalization of midwives in Ontario. They worked hard to lobby the chairman of the provincial Health Professions Review in the mid-1980s. They prepared a series of briefs, and they sent thousands of telegrams to the provincial review. They got advice and support from several major women's organizations and labour unions. Before the 1985 provincial election the consumers met the opposition Liberal and NDP caucuses, gaining support from both parties. This became a crucial advantage when the Liberals formed the government with the assistance of the NDP in 1985.

Some doctors called the midwifery supporters "cold strategists." It was a sign of their frustration with the success of the consumers. By 1987 the women had convinced the Ontario government to legalize the practice of midwifery.

The Limits of Consumerism

Despite some notable successes, the victories by health consumers are still restricted to a handful of cases. The doctor-patient relationship continues to be dominated by the medical profession. The militancy of some patients cannot disguise the passiveness of most health consumers. Patients tend to feel vulnerable and intimidated by the medical system. Many patients are unhappy with their treatment, yet they are reluctant to complain for fear of antagonizing their doctor. They believe that their health depends on the goodwill of their physician.

This is particularly true in a hospital. The patient is "for all practical purposes, at the mercy of the hospital staff," says Lorne Rozovsky, a law professor at Dalhousie University who specializes in medical issues. "He often does not want to complain for fear of retaliation or lack of service."

As a result of this passivity, the number of official complaints and malpractice suits does not reflect the actual level of discontent among patients. "There is a tremendous subterranean dissatisfaction with medicine," says David Coburn, a University of Toronto behavioural science professor and a past president of the Patients' Rights Association. "There are few Canadians who cannot give their own personal medical horror story." Cynicism and a feeling of intimidation have pushed this discontent beneath the surface of daily life, despite the occasional outburst of activism.

In an article in 1980, Professor Coburn described some of the factors that continue to limit the patients' rights movement: "Doctors tend to come from middle or upper middle class families, and the profession is assumed to possess a monopoly of medical knowledge. Differential class position, an assumed knowledge monopoly, and expertise in the system (what is a crisis for the patient may be routine for the health worker) all have tended to produce patient passivity, a psychological as well as physical supineness."

This instinct for passiveness by most patients has hampered the consumer groups in the political arena. One prime example of the failure of health consumerism is the absence of a legislated bill of rights for patients in Canada. Many groups have called for a patients' bill of rights, but the call has gone unanswered in Canada. In the early 1970s the American Hospital Association adopted the first bill of rights for patients in the United States. Several state legislatures in the U.S. have approved their own versions of a bill of rights for patients. Many states have also enacted laws to require doctors to obtain their patients' consent for treatment. Some states even established the rights of a patient under specific diseases. For example, California requires doctors to inform their patients about various treatment options for breast cancer.

In 1973 a study commissioned by the Ontario Medical Association recommended the introduction of a patients' bill of rights in Ontario. The Ontario study, written by Edward Pickering, suggested that the bill of rights could include the following: the right to equal attention regardless of economic status and geographic location; the right to know what treatment is being prescribed, the reasons for the treatment, the side effects and the possible alternatives; the right to a second opinion; and the right to know the cost of medical services.

A survey by the Ontario Nurses Association in 1985 found that 82 per cent of Ontario residents were in favour of a legislated bill of rights for patients. But despite the views of the public, despite the U.S. examples and despite Edward Pickering's recommendation, no provincial government has ever established an official bill of rights for patients.

Health consumers suffered another defeat in the early 1980s, when they were unable to convince the Ontario government to guarantee a patient's right to see his or her own medical records. The 1980 report of the Krever Commission had urged the province to take action to ensure that patients could gain access to their medical records. The report, written by Mr. Justice Horace Krever, argued that patients would gain a better understanding of their treatment if they had access to their medical files. Such access would reduce the paternalism of the doctor-patient relationship, the study said. Judge Krever described the issue as a matter of fundamental human dignity. In his report, he documented many cases in which a doctor had put incorrect information in a patient's medical records. This inaccurate information was often given to employers and insurance companies, with disastrous consequences to the patient. Yet patients did not have the right to gain access to their medical records to make sure their records were accurate.

When the Krever Commission completed its report, the Ontario government decided to wait for reaction to its recommendations. The medical profession seized the opportunity to oppose the notion of allowing patients to examine their own medical records. The Ontario Medical Association and the Ontario College of Physicians and Surgeons argued strongly against Judge Krever's recommendation. In a submission to a provincial review of the Krever Report, the college insisted that "direct access to health records would not always be in the best interests of the individual." Patients are not "qualified" to correct the information in the medical records, the college told the provincial review. Individual doctors also opposed Judge Krever's recommendation. "I believe that, as a physician treating a patient, I have the right to confidentiality of thought process and records," Dr. C. L. K. McIlwaine told the provincial review.

Faced with this opposition, the Ontario government quietly shelved the Krever Report. As a result, patients in Ontario still have no right to examine their own medical records. Indeed, only three provincial governments — those of Quebec, Alberta and Nova Scotia — currently have laws to enable patients to gain some form of access to their medical records.

The Canadian Medical Association has done its best to discourage any other provincial governments from approving such a law. In 1983 the CMA approved an official policy of opposition to the notion of patient access to medical records. "Medical records belong to the health care institution or professional who compiled them or had them compiled," the CMA said. If patients want to see their medical records, the CMA advises its members to explain the medical information to them, without actually allowing the patients to examine the records. The CMA believes that patients cannot possibly comprehend their medical records except through a doctor's interpretation. According to the CMA's official policy, patients "do not have the right to demand a copy of the documents."

The CMA argues that its policy is based on consideration for "the well-being of the patient" and the need for "discretion." However, the CMA is certainly aware that doctors would be much more vulnerable to malpractice suits if patients were able to gain copies of their medical records. By prohibiting patients from looking at their medical records, doctors can make it difficult for patients to know whether there is any written evidence of problems in the medical care given by the doctors.

Patients in the Courts

The civil courts are still the major battleground for conflicts between doctors and patients in North America. A malpractice lawsuit is the ultimate weapon of an injured patient. The rapid growth of malpractice suits in the past 20 years has been a serious headache for the medical profession. Doctors would prefer their patients to accept the results of their treatment, regardless of how disastrous it might be. But an increasing number of patients are refusing to ignore the damage that sometimes results from medical treatment. In response to the lawsuits, doctors have complained loudly about the "malpractice crisis" in North America. They argue that the number of malpractice suits is excessive. They are asking the government to protect them from the rising cost of these lawsuits.

Dr. William Vail, the 1985–86 president of the CMA, has described the malpractice problem as "absolutely obscene." In 1986 he told his fellow doctors that the defendants in malpractice suits have frequently done no wrong — "there has been no negligence, no malpractice, we simply had a bad result — a medical misadventure." He blamed the problem on judges and juries who "feel sorry for the patient." Another CMA official, Dr. John Bennett, has complained that patients perceive a malpractice suit as "Lotto 6/49 — an opportunity to get a lifestyle they otherwise wouldn't achieve."

There has been no intelligent public debate on the malpractice issue. The medical associations have been permitted to define the crisis. Nobody has challenged their allegation that the lawsuits have reached epidemic proportions. Yet several little-known studies have concluded that the vast majority of physicians who commit an act of negligence are never brought to court.

One study in California found that one in 126 hospital patients has suffered an injury because of negligent medical care, but more than 90 per cent of the injured patients never launch a malpractice suit. Even when the patient suffered a major permanent disability, only one in seven filed a malpractice claim. Another study at two hospitals in the U.S. found that only one in 15 malpractice victims filed a lawsuit. A third study estimated that just one of every 60 injured patients launched a suit. Regardless of the exact percentage, it is clear that a malpractice suit is rarely launched by an injured patient. Most patients believe they have a good relationship with their doctors. When they are harmed by their medical treatment, they find it difficult to blame the doctor. Instead, they tend to blame their injury on bad luck or fate. Their faith and respect for the doctor makes them reluctant to file a malpractice suit. One cardiologist, quoted in the *Canadian Medical Association Journal*, put it bluntly: "If a patient knows and trusts the doctor, he or she will forgive practically anything." Even those patients who become angry are often unwilling to launch a suit. "They may be angry, bitter, and in pain, but the thought of lawyers, lawsuits and judges is enough to dissuade them," Professor Lorne Rozovsky says.

In those unusual cases where a malpractice suit is actually filed, there is no guarantee of success. Across the U.S. and Canada, more than half of all malpractice suits are abandoned or thrown out of court. The California study found that financial compensation was provided to only one in 25 victims of negligent medical care, after all the legal activity was over. Yet California has one of the highest rates of malpractice claims in the United States. And the rate of malpractice claims in the U.S. is almost 10 times higher than in Canada. (About 18 malpractice suits are filed for every 1,000 doctors in Canada, compared to a rate of about 160 malpractice suits for every 1,000 doctors in the United States.) Thus it can be estimated that only one in 250 victims of malpractice in Canada will ever receive compensation from the courts. If there is a "malpractice crisis" in Canada, it is the absence of any compensation for most patients who are injured by negligent doctors.

Why are malpractice suits so remarkably rare in Canada, particularly in comparison to the situation in the United States? Canadians may simply be more deferential to authority, as some observers have suggested. Americans, by disposition, may be more aggressive in their pursuit of justice. But there are several other important reasons for the small number of malpractice suits in Canada. One reason is the much smaller percentage of lawyers who accept contingency fees in Canada, compared to the United States. Under a contingency fee arrangement, a lawyer will agree to pursue a lawsuit on behalf of a client in return for a share of the eventual award from the court. If the lawyer fails to win the case, he receives no payment. A contingency fee makes it easier for a patient to obtain legal help, since the patient is not risking an expensive legal bill if the lawsuit fails. Contingency fees are common in every region of the U.S., but they are rarely used in most Canadian provinces. Contingency fees are prohibited in Ontario and strictly regulated in the Atlantic provinces. In addition, they are infrequently used in Quebec. Even in the western provinces, many lawyers are reluctant to work for a contingency fee. "Most lawyers in these provinces still are not prepared to gamble on the outcome of a case," Professor Rozovsky has noted.

Without a contingency fee, patients can be stuck with a debt of several thousand dollars at the end of a malpractice suit. It takes extreme determination to pursue a malpractice action when the result could be financial ruin for the patient. For example, a couple in Quebec had to mortgage their home to pay their expenses in a malpractice suit against the doctor who delivered their child. The doctor spent three days trying to induce labour with drugs, before finally performing a Caesarean section. The baby was not breathing at birth, had to be revived and ended up with cerebral palsy. The couple, who live in a small village on the lower St. Lawrence River, had to spend large sums of money on fees for their lawyer and for doctors who were hired to examine the hospital files. The legal action took several years. Trips to Montreal, along with a lengthy series of medical tests and cross-examinations, were required to settle the case. In the end, the court gave the child a multimillion-dollar award. But the couple would have suffered a serious financial loss if they had failed to win the case. Few patients are willing to take that risk.

Even when a lawyer accepts a contingency fee, the cost of a

malpractice suit can be prohibitive. Consider the example of Ray and Diane Quintal, a Saskatoon couple who sued two doctors for negligence in 1982. Their infant daughter, Crystal, had fallen victim to a rare metabolic disorder that eventually left her mentally retarded and blind. The Quintals believed the doctors had failed to diagnose and treat the illness. Their legal battle took four years to settle. Their lawyer agreed to a contingency fee, but the Quintals still needed to raise about $20,000 to pay for the cost of expert witnesses, court documents and other legal expenses. Ray Quintal had been laid off from his job, so the Quintals had to sell their house and borrow $10,000 from their parents. If they had lost the case, they could have been ordered to pay the costs of the defendants, probably totalling a further $20,000. Fortunately for the Quintals, they won the case in 1986 and were awarded $1.5 million. They later acknowledged that the legal battle had put a strain on their marriage. They called it an experience they wouldn't wish on their worst enemy.

In the Quintal case, the court decision was made by a six-person jury. This was a rare event in Canada. The vast majority of Canada's malpractice suits are decided by a judge, without a jury. This is another major difference between Canada and the United States. Jury trials are generally available for malpractice suits in the U.S., but they are infrequently permitted in most Canadian provinces. Physicians have been afraid that a jury might be too sympathetic to the plaintiff. As a result, they have persuaded Canadian judges that a malpractice suit is too technical and complex for a jury to understand. This argument rests on the assumption that a judge is more capable of comprehending the complexities of medicine than a jury would be. Yet judges have no special training in anything but the law. "Doctors seem to be a sacrosanct group," malpractice lawyer Richard Sommers has said. "For the life of me I have never been able to understand if you can try a complicated products-liability action with a jury, one that involves sophisticated new machinery and technical engineering matters, why can't you try medical malpractice with a jury?"

In the 19th century, most of Canada's malpractice suits were heard by juries. But the situation was reversed in the 20th century. In most cases, Canadian doctors have been granted immunity from the scrutiny of juries. Several experts have concluded that the absence of jury trials in malpractice cases is one of the reasons for the relatively small number of malpractice suits in Canada, compared to the United States. The absence of juries is also regarded as an explanation for the smaller size of the average malpractice award in Canada. The average award or settlement for a malpractice case in Canada is $88,500, while the average in the U.S. is about $340,000.

Canadian judges, unlike their U.S. counterparts, have put a ceiling on the amount of compensation that can be awarded for pain and suffering. This is another reason for the smaller size of the average malpractice award in Canada. "The pot of gold at the end of the lawsuit may exist in the United States, but it does not encourage litigation in this country," Professor Rozovsky has said.

Because of the smaller awards and the smaller number of lawsuits, Canadian doctors pay much lower insurance premiums than U.S. doctors. The average U.S. physician paid $8,400 in annual malpractice insurance premiums in 1984, and the average U.S. obstetrician paid $18,800 in premiums in 1984. By comparison, a family doctor in Canada paid only $650 for malpractice insurance in 1986 (although the premiums rose to $800 in 1987) and Canadian obstetricians paid $4,900 (rising to $8,250 in 1987).

In recent years, physicians in the U.S. and Canada have complained vociferously about the rising cost of their malpractice premiums. However, they have made no attempt to reform the premium structure to penalize doctors who are repeatedly negligent. One study of doctors in the Los Angeles area revealed that 46 of the 8,000 doctors were responsible for 10 per cent of the malpractice claims and 30 per cent of the malpractice awards and settlements. If the medical profession asked the insurers to increase the premiums for doctors who were proven to be a bad risk, the premiums for good doctors could be reduced. This would improve the fairness of the system and put the burden where it belongs: on the negligent doctor. The premiums would reflect the performance of the doctor, and the medical profession would have no reason to complain about the cost of insurance.

But instead of reforming the insurance system, Canada's medical associations have demanded that the provincial governments pay for the increased cost of malpractice insurance. In some provinces the doctors have been successful. For example, the Alberta Medical Association gained an extra 0.26 per cent increase in its fee schedule in 1986 to pay for the higher cost of malpractice premiums.

About 90 per cent of Canada's doctors are members of the Canadian Medical Protective Association, a voluntary non-profit organization that provides malpractice insurance for the medical profession. If a malpractice claim is filed against a CMPA member, the association will provide lawyers and expert witnesses to defend the member. If the patient wins the case, the CMPA will pay the damages on behalf of the doctor. Negligent doctors can thus escape without paying any direct financial penalty, even if they lose their suit.

The CMPA is a powerful, wealthy organization. Founded in 1901, it has grown to a position of strength. By the end of 1985 the CMPA had $54.5 million in its reserve fund. Its lawyers are the best available, and it usually has little difficulty in finding expert witnesses (usually a physician) to testify on behalf of its members.

Malpractice victims, on the other hand, often have trouble finding a doctor to testify on their behalf. Lawyers hired by injured patients have frequently described the "conspiracy of silence" that traditionally protects a physician in a malpractice suit. Indeed, some malpractice insurers in Canada have actually prohibited doctors from taking the witness stand against a fellow physician. Medical associations also discouraged their members from testifying against other doctors. This has diminished somewhat in recent years; a few doctors are now willing to testify for an injured patient. But this can still be a major problem for someone who wants to sue a doctor. "It is notoriously difficult for lawyers to persuade colleagues in a hospital to give evidence against each other," says Dr. David Surridge, chairman of the medical audit committee at Kingston General Hospital.

In some Canadian hospitals, doctors review the quality of medical care provided by their colleagues. However, these reviews often cannot be obtained by patients who have filed a malpractice suit. In several provinces there is legislation to ensure that the hospital reviews cannot be used in malpractice cases.

Another obstacle for injured patients is the deadline for filing malpractice lawsuits in some provinces. Patients in several provinces must file a suit within one or two years of their last treatment from a doctor. If the patients do not discover the damage until several years later, it is impossible for them to sue the doctor. Three recent cases demonstrated this problem. In one case, a woman in Manitoba became ill after a sponge was left in her abdomen during an operation in 1975. The sponge was not discovered until 1984, when a surgeon removed it. The woman filed a lawsuit, but the case was dismissed because provincial laws had required her to file a suit within two years of the original incident.

In the second case, part of a medical instrument was found inside the knee of a Halifax man in 1983. The metal object had fallen off the medical instrument during an internal examination by a surgeon in 1977. The man tried to sue the surgeon, but his case was dismissed because of a one-year deadline that had existed at the time.

In the third case, an Edmonton woman went to a doctor because she suffered from chest pains. The doctor treated her for bronchitis. In fact, the woman had cancer. Eighteen months later, when she moved to another city, her new doctor told her that the first doctor should have ordered a biopsy. By then the cancer was terminal, but because the original misdiagnosis had occurred more than a year earlier, no legal action could be taken.

To rectify these injustices, several provinces have amended their laws to allow a malpractice suit to be filed after the problem is discovered. The Canadian Medical Association is lobbying to restrict these laws, arguing that the "discovery" law is unfair and "places physicians in a position of indefinite risk." Four provinces still have no discovery law to protect patients from judicial deadlines.

Finally, there is another problem for the injured patient. The Canadian Medical Protective Association has a policy of rarely settling out of court. The association prefers to fight to the bitter end. Unless the doctor admits to negligence, or unless the evidence of negligence is overwhelming, the CMPA will force the plaintiff to pursue the case through a full trial — and frequently one or two appeals as well. Since the CMPA has far more resources than the average patient, it can afford to drag out a case. The longer a lawsuit continues, the greater the financial pressure on the patient.

In summary, a host of obstacles makes it difficult for an injured patient to obtain compensation from a doctor in Canada. Indeed, experienced malpractice lawyers refuse to accept the vast majority of cases offered to them. Barry Percival says he only accepts one in 25 patients who request his services in a malpractice case. Other lawyers say they reject 80 to 95 per cent of the patients who try to retain their services. Only the most blatant cases have a chance to succeed, the lawyers say. "Unless I feel that the injury itself would attract substantial damages, I recommend against proceeding because trials are very expensive," says Toronto lawyer Bob Roth. In a speech to his fellow lawyers, Barry Percival said: "Given the many defences available to the defendants, their phenomenal resources of expert witnesses for the defence, their intransigence in settlement negotiations, and their hard-line attitude in defending most actions to the bitter end, I can only promise you — a potential counsel for a plaintiff in a malpractice action — much hard work, a fascinating lawsuit and, on occasion, the reward of a successful result."

Patients have enjoyed one notable success in the malpractice field in recent years. In 1980 the Supreme Court of Canada handed down a pair of decisions clearly establishing the concept of "informed consent." These rulings, particularly the landmark *Reibl* vs. *Hughes* decision, were a major step forward for the patients' rights movement. Essentially, the Supreme Court said that doctors must inform their patients of the risk of a medical procedure or operation. If there is any possibility of serious injury, even if the risk is remote, doctors must inform their patients.

In the best known of the 1980 decisions, the court upheld an award of $225,000 to an automobile worker named John Reibl, who had suffered a stroke after a 1970 operation on a blocked artery in his neck. Reibl would have been eligible for a company pension if he had stayed on the job for another 18 months. But the stroke left him permanently disabled. Reibl said he would have postponed the surgery if the doctor had warned him that there was a 15 per cent chance of post-operative complications. The court ruled that any reasonable person in Reibl's situation would have postponed the surgery if informed of the risks. As a result of this decision, and subsequent decisions confirming this concept, doctors can now be required to establish that they gave enough information to their patients.

In the 15 years since the death of Harold Coy, the patients' rights movement has grown tremendously in Canada. Doctors are subject to greater scrutiny, and their power is no longer absolute. Checks and balances are emerging. Yet the medical profession's complaints about the "obscenity" of the malpractice situation have created a perception that the pendulum has swung too far. Doctors have succeeded in convincing many people that they are unfairly persecuted by malicious patients. The evidence suggests otherwise. The malpractice battlefield is still dominated by the doctor. Patients are still struggling against overwhelming odds in the courtrooms. And most doctors can avoid a malpractice suit by establishing good communications with their patients. The statistics clearly indicate that the average physician is unlikely to be penalized for an act of negligence.

Anne Coy has learned to be content with small victories. In 1987 she witnessed another small victory for health consumers. The Ontario Conservatives published a discussion paper entitled "Patients' Rights: Building a More Balanced System." The paper contained a number of favourable references to the work of the Patients' Rights Association. It was a symbolic breakthrough for the consumer movement. The Conservatives, who had governed Ontario from 1943 to 1985, had always maintained close connections with the province's medical profession. If the Tories had finally recognized the other half of the doctor-patient relationship, another barrier had fallen. Who knew what breakthrough might come next for health consumers?

CHAPTER 11

THE POTENTIAL FOR REFORM

The new symbol of the Canadian health-care system is the walk-in medical clinic in your local shopping mall. Doctors call it "mall medicine." The modern consumer drops in for a quick checkup or a prescription while grocery shopping. There's no waiting, no anxiety, no inconvenience, and few questions are asked. There are dozens of walk-in clinics in major Canadian cities, and the numbers are steadily increasing.

The walk-in clinic is a symbol of the overmedicalization of the Canadian health system. As the surplus of doctors grows worse, new medical graduates are turning to these clinics to gain a toehold in the market. The clinics are marketing themselves aggressively. They are recruiting patients who would otherwise postpone their trips to the doctor. The provincial governments, which ultimately pay the bills of the doctors in the walk-in clinics, have discovered that the clinics are not always a substitute for the hospital emergency department or the private practice of a family physician. Instead, the walk-in clinics are simply an added cost to the system. Patients visit the walk-in clinic and then visit their family doctor at a later date. Or they visit the clinic for a condition that is likely to disappear a day later. In most cases, these clinics merely increase the cost of health care without improving anyone's health.

At the same time, an increasing number of private physicians are marketing themselves in the same manner as the walk-in clinics. They're expanding their office hours and seeing more patients at more frequent intervals. To maintain their target incomes, many doctors are recalling their patients more often, expanding the number of medical services in each episode of care. Under the fee-for-service system, the doctor can bill the government for each of these medical services.

As Canadian doctors become more accessible and more likely to insist on increased medical services, patients are finding it easier to get treatment. It becomes almost like an addiction — patients become dependent on their doctors for increasingly minor treatments. The bottom line is this: the consumption of medical services is skyrocketing. For example, the average resident of Saskatchewan today is seeing a doctor 11 times a year, compared to six times a year in 1971. The cost of prescription claims in Ontario, under the provincial drug benefit plan, has escalated almost 300 per cent in the past seven years. The increased consumption of medical services is not a result of a sharp rise in the needs of Canadians. (Do the residents of Saskatchewan need to see a doctor twice as badly as they did in 1971? Are they twice as unhealthy?) Instead, the rising consumption is largely a result of the rising supply of doctors.

Canadians are spending about $40 billion annually on health care. Health expenditures amount to 8.5 per cent of Canada's gross national product. This is considerably less than the percentage spent in the United States, since a national medicare system is much more efficient than a disorganized system of private and public insurance. (The cost of health administration is several times higher in the United States than in Canada.) But the total health expenditure in Canada is rising rapidly. In 1970 only $6.26 billion was spent on health care in this country. The total has increased almost sevenfold in less than two decades. Yet the health literature suggests that a great deal of the additional medical care does not appear to have any positive effect on patients.

In recent years almost every provincial health minister has made agonized speeches about the rapid rise of health costs. When their cabinet colleagues are slashing the budgets of other major departments, the health ministers find it difficult to justify the soaring cost of health care. There is mounting pressure to find a solution.

The politicians realize that the doctors are the key to controlling the overconsumption of medical services in Canada. The doctors are the gatekeepers. They are the ones with their hands on the cash registers. And so the politicians have two choices: they can try to persuade doctors to put reasonable limits on the utilization of medical services, or they can regulate the doctors by imposing restrictions on the utilization of specific services.

The regulation of medical consumption is not a far-fetched idea. A survey in 1982 found that 38.4 per cent of Canadian physicians acknowledge that revolving-door medicine is a serious problem. Some provinces already limit the number of complete examinations that a doctor can perform annually on a patient. It would not be difficult to extend these limits to a large number of other medical services.

In the United States the cost of medical care has increased so tremendously that corporations and government agencies are finally taking steps to restrict the physician's clinical freedom. In some cases, review processes are being established to examine the doctor's decisions. Many U.S. companies now require a patient to obtain a second opinion before they reimburse the patient for the costs of surgery. Private insurance companies in the U.S. are hiring "utilization review" firms, which examine the consumption of medical services by insured patients and recommend ways to save money without violating good clinical practice. These are the kinds of regulations that could confront Canada's doctors if they refuse to take voluntary action to limit the consumption of medical services.

Ironically, the tremendous popularity of Canada's medicare system is helping to protect doctors from government regulation. The public perceives any proposed reform as a possible threat to medicare. In Manitoba, for example, anti-poverty groups and senior citizen associations were outraged when the provincial health minister raised the possibility of refusing to pay for unnecessary medical services. Yet an unnecessary service is a benefit to nobody except the doctor who receives a payment for it. It is perhaps the ultimate irony that the doctors, who originally fought bitterly against medicare, are now protected by the popularity of medicare.

So far, the provincial governments have refrained from taking any major steps towards the control of medical consumption. When they are forced to reduce their health budgets, they use a blunt instrument: hospital budgets are chopped, or fee schedules are frozen. These measures fail to address the fundamental pressures that have caused the rapid escalation of health costs. The surplus of doctors and the financial incentives of the fee-for-service system are the major reasons for the soaring costs.

As taxpayers, Canadians have a vital interest in the rising cost of medical care. But as patients, they have an even greater stake in the issue. A rising volume of medical services does not necessarily represent an improvement in health. To a large extent, the expansion of medicare is a result of an increase in medical intervention, intensified laboratory testing, the introduction of new medical technology, increases in the popularity of certain surgical procedures, and a general attitude that "more is better." Many of these clinical habits and surgical procedures have not been adequately studied in scientific trials. Their costs and benefits are often uncertain.

When a specific kind of medical service is carefully evaluated, it is often found to be overutilized. Recent research has suggested that some forms of medical examinations, for example, are performed more frequently than necessary. And a host of operations are performed more frequently in Canada than in countries that have ended the fee-for-service system. Since most clinical activities have a certain risk attached to them, patients should be concerned about the non-stop escalation in the volume of medical services in Canada.

The overmedicalization of Canadian society has helped to intensify our modern obsession with personal health. But there is a paradox here. Because people tend to equate health with medical treatment, this obsession means that Canadians are missing some real opportunities for improving their health. The Sault Ste. Marie experience has shown how a community can benefit from an integrated health centre where physicians are supplemented by nurse practitioners, social workers, health educators and other paramedical professionals. A balanced approach to health care is safer than high-technology medical intervention, and it teaches patients to become more self-reliant. Yet the benefits of a community health centre are unavailable in most regions of Canada, largely as a result of the strong lobbying efforts of the medical associations.

In 1974 the federal government's Lalonde Report described the dangers of the traditional perception of health. "The traditional or generally-accepted view of the health field is that the art or science of medicine has been the fount from which all improvements in health have flowed, and popular belief equates the level of health with the quality of medicine," the report said. "The consequence of the traditional view is that most direct expenditures on health are physician-centred, including medical care, hospital care, laboratory tests and prescription drugs."

The Lalonde Report questioned whether orthodox medicine should continue to consume an increasing portion of public resources. The report recommended a greater emphasis on eliminating the root causes of poor health, particularly the environmental and lifestyle hazards that are among the biggest contributors to health problems. It called for a new health-promotion strategy, including better education and information about health and increased use of nurse practitioners and community health centres. The report's recommendations contained almost no references to medical treatment. Instead, the report said Canadians must be encouraged to "take more individual responsibility for the health of their minds and bodies."

The Lalonde Report had a great influence on health experts around the world, but it failed to change much in Canada. Thirteen years later the Canadian health system is still overwhelmingly distorted towards medical treatment. There is a federal Health Promotion

Directorate, but the provincial medicare plans continue to revolve around the physician's decisions. Only a tiny percentage of Canada's health-care budget is spent on public health measures. In Ontario, for example, just 3 per cent of the provincial health budget is spent on public health. Less than 1 per cent of the health budget is spent on research studies to evaluate the medical procedures that are routinely performed in this country. And there are virtually no financial incentives to encourage doctors to practise preventive medicine.

Dr. Gustave Gingras, the 1972–73 president of the Canadian Medical Association, was one of the very few CMA leaders who had worked as a salaried physician for his entire career. Perhaps because he does not work on a fee-for-service basis, his view of today's medicare system is different from that of other CMA leaders. Here is his description of medicare: "It has become a monstrous and gigantic sick parade, where hundreds of people are being pushed through, each given seven-and-a-half minutes and no more, and a pill or a little advice."

Despite the Lalonde Report, Canadians still equate medicine and health. Dr. Gingras gave this example: "After the Sunday church service, Joe will come in with his family and say, 'Doctor, what about taking our blood pressure? Why not attend to the whole gang while we're here? What about medication for the bunch of us?' And the doctor wonders, 'What can I do? Can I tell them, "No, I can't do this because it is not professional"? Because if I do, they will go to somebody else who will do it anyway and I'll lose my patients and I can't afford to do that.'"

The Reform Agenda

For the past decade, politicians and bureaucrats have been aware of the need for health reform, but they have been reluctant to introduce the innovative techniques that would restore balance to the health-care system. Yet these innovations have been successfully demonstrated in the United States and in certain regions of Canada. Previous chapters in this book have described the experiments that have proven the potential for cost savings and improved health care. By integrating these innovations into a broad-based reform, the provincial governments could solve their cost dilemmas and strengthen the health system.

Perhaps the most important reform would be the expansion of the network of community health centres and health-service organizations in which the payment of doctors is linked to the total number of enrolled patients. There is overwhelming evidence that these organizations can reduce the cost of medical care by as much as 40 per cent while preserving or improving the health of the patient. Moreover, these organizations would provide a crucial element of competition in the Canadian health system. The fee-for-service system has always enjoyed a virtual monopoly in Canada. Monopolies tend to be inefficient. Community health centres and health-service organizations would challenge the monopoly of the fee-for-service system. And the competition would improve the efficiency of Canada's health system. By 1987 there were indications that the governments of Ontario and Manitoba were considering a significant increase in the number of community health centres, as a cost-saving technique. It remains to be seen whether these provinces are sufficiently determined to overcome the opposition of the medical associations.

Manpower policy is another crucial battleground. There is a consensus among independent health experts that Canada has a glut of physicians. The surplus cannot be reduced without significant reductions in medical school enrolment. In addition, new entrants to medical school must be warned that they might be prohibited from submitting bills to the medicare system if they choose to work in regions that already have a surplus of doctors.

A reduction in the supply of doctors would permit the provinces to expand the paramedical occupations. Midwives, nurse practitioners and other health workers can be cost-efficient substitutes for doctors. In some instances, they can also improve the quality of health care.

Community health centres, paramedical workers and preventive health measures have been recommended by a host of government inquiries since the early 1970s. Organized medicine has tended to reject these ideas, dismissing them as left-wing notions. Yet even the most conservative thinkers have criticized the lack of competition in the medical profession. For example, the U.S. free-market economist Milton Friedman and the right-wing Fraser Institute of Vancouver have both attacked the monopoly power of the medical profession. A chorus of voices, from all points in the ideological spectrum, have called for increased competition from paramedical workers and health-service organizations to challenge the dominance of the fee-for-service doctors.

Even the concept of preventive medicine has been resisted by the medical profession. The CMA has argued that funds must not be diverted from curative care to preventive programs. A national survey of Canadian doctors found that the doctors ranked public health programs as a lower priority than acute-care hospitals and the acquisition of new medical technology. The survey concluded that there was "widespread support in favour of curative, institutional responses to health problems" in the Canadian medical profession.

Finally, another important battleground will be the question of whether doctors should be subjected to closer scrutiny in their private medical practices. Stricter monitoring of the medical profession is needed for several reasons. First, it could reduce the overutilization of medical services — particularly if medical experts are asked to establish guidelines for the ideal level of service for each disease or injury. Second, closer scrutiny would help ensure the continuing competence of the licensed physician. And third, stricter monitoring would improve the professional disciplinary system, so that patients are protected from negligent doctors.

Of course, a bureaucrat is not qualified to determine whether a doctor is misusing his or her clinical powers. Only a fellow physician can make that judgment. The medical profession must monitor itself. But in most provinces the scrutiny is almost non-existent. If there is no prodding from the provincial governments, the profession will continue to take a lax approach to the responsibilities of self-government.

The College of Physicians and Surgeons of Ontario has shown some leadership on this issue in recent years. It has introduced a peer-review system, taken a tougher stand against strike action by doctors and improved its policing of disciplinary matters. The progress in Ontario has been slow, but it is still far ahead of the other provinces.

Organized Medicine in the 1990s

The agenda for reform is clear. And there is evidence that the provincial governments are seriously considering many of these reforms. But the medical associations will fight strenuously to preserve the status quo. Indeed, organized medicine has demonstrated its strength by blocking the proposed reforms for the past two decades. Moreover, the medical associations are girding their loins for future conflicts. After the turmoil of the 1980s, they are battle-hardened and their war chests are flush with money.

Ontario's doctors lost their 1986 dispute with the Ontario government because the vast majority of provincial voters were strongly opposed to extra-billing. But most health-policy questions are obscure to the electorate, and politicians cannot count on automatic public support in their future conflicts with organized medicine. Knowing this, the medical associations in many provinces will again be willing to withdraw their services for temporary periods to put pressure on the politicians. Patients will continue to be embroiled in the disputes between doctors and governments.

In recent years the medical associations have taken several major steps to strengthen themselves. First, they have improved their financial resources by establishing compulsory dues payment rules. The medical associations of Manitoba, Newfoundland, New Brunswick, Nova Scotia and Quebec have persuaded their provincial governments to approve legislation requiring every doctor in the province to pay membership dues, even if the doctor doesn't belong to the association. The medical associations of British Columbia and Saskatchewan are also considering the same kind of rule. In addition to improving the revenue of the medical associations, the compulsory dues payment rules are allowing the associations to tighten their political control over the medical profession in each province.

Second, the medical associations are becoming more sophisticated in their public-relations techniques. They have learned that their public image is perhaps their strongest weapon in their conflicts with governments. The British Columbia Medical Association is spending millions of dollars on a communications campaign that includes a weekly television program. Other medical associations are launching anti-smoking campaigns and taking a vocal stand on issues such as AIDS education and automobile seatbelts. Instead of campaigning for the right to extra-bill, the top officials of the Ontario Medical Association are ceremoniously signing their organ donor cards and discussing the importance of physical education in high school. It is a different technique for achieving their traditional goal: to be perceived as society's leaders.

Finally, the medical associations are realizing the advantages of hiring outside consultants as expert advisors on the techniques of lobbying and negotiating. Ben Trevino, a prominent labour-relations lawyer from Vancouver, has been hired as a negotiator for the medical associations of British Columbia, Manitoba, Saskatchewan and Ontario in the 1980s. The Ontario Medical Association recently retained the services of John Laschinger, a well-connected Conservative political strategist, to help them improve their communications with the provincial government and the public at large.

Because organized medicine recognizes that the provinces cannot ignore the soaring consumption of medical services, the medical associations are preparing for the possibility of future conflict. They will be doing their best to discourage the reforms in the political backrooms, before the reforms can enter the arena of public debate. Given their remarkable record of success in the past, it would be unwise to assume that the reform of Canada's health-care system is inevitable.

SOURCES

A Note on Sources

Much of the information in this book comes from personal interviews with the people who are quoted in the text. In some cases, quotations are taken from the official publications of the national and provincial medical associations, particularly the *Canadian Medical Association Journal (CMAJ)*. The *New England Journal of Medicine (NEJM)* was another important source of data. The annual and interim reports of provincial colleges of physicians and surgeons and the Canadian Medical Protective Association were also valuable sources. Various media reports (including my own reports in the *Globe and Mail*) were useful. Chapters 2, 8 and 9 were based largely on the preceding sources. For the other chapters, the key sources are listed below.

Chapter 1

General sources: *International Journal of Health Services*, 1983, pp. 407–32; *Canadian Forum*, April 1981, pp. 5–9, 31; Ivan Illich, *Limits to Medicine* (Penguin, 1976); *Canadian Journal of Economics and Political Science*, February 1960, pp. 108–27; Robert G. Evans, *Strained Mercy: The Economics of Canadian Health Care* (Butterworth, 1984); and Marc Lalonde, *A New Perspective on the Health of Canadians* (Lalonde Report, 1974).

Quotations from medical associations: See the OMA's official response to the report of the Krever Commission (1981); C. David Naylor, *Private Practice, Public Payment* (McGill-Queen's University Press, 1986), p. 256; *CMAJ*, vol. 125, p. 768; and *Interviews with Past Presidents of the Canadian Medical Association* (CMA, 1980).

Studies of medical attitudes: Joseph E. Magnet and Eike-Henner W. Kluge, *Withholding Treatment from Defective Newborn Children* (Brown Legal Publications, 1985); and the *Edmonton Journal*, August 25, 1983, p. A9.

Medical students: Martin Shapiro, *Getting Doctored* (Between the Lines, 1978); and Jonathan Lomas, *First and Foremost in Community Health Centres* (University of Toronto Press, 1985), p. 131.

Medical authority: Shapiro (1978); *CMAJ*, vol. 129, p. 278; H. E. Emson, *The Doctor and The Law* (Macmillan, 1979); and Eliot Freidson, *Profession of Medicine* (Dodd, Mead, 1971).

Survey of Canadian doctors: Malcolm Taylor, H. Michael Stevenson and A. Paul Williams, *Medical Perspectives on Canadian Medicare* (York University, 1984); and Laframboise article: *Policy Options*, July 1986.

Chapter 3

Ronald Hamowy, *Canadian Medicine: A Study in Restricted Entry* (Fraser Institute, 1984); Naylor (1986); Robin F. Badgley and Samuel Wolfe, *Doctors' Strike: Medical Care and Conflict in Saskatchewan* (Macmillan, 1967); Malcolm Taylor, *Health Insurance and Canadian Public Policy* (McGill-Queen's University Press, 1978); *International Journal of Health Services*, 1983, pp. 407–32; *Canadian Journal of Public Health*, 1979, pp. 300–6; *Social Science and Medicine*, 1986, pp. 1035–46; S. E. D. Shortt, ed., *Medicine in Canadian Society* (McGill-Queen's University Press, 1981); H. E. MacDermott, *One Hundred Years of Medicine in Canada* (McClelland and Stewart, 1967); *Canadian Historical Review*, vol. 67, no. 2 (1986), pp. 151–80; Heber Jamieson, *Early Medicine in Alberta* (Douglas Printing, 1947); T. F. Rose, *From Shaman to Modern Medicine: A Century of the Healing Arts in British Columbia* (Mitchell Press, 1972); Gordon Fahrni, *Prairie Surgeon* (Queenston House, 1976); Ross Mitchell, *Medicine in Manitoba: The Story of Its Beginnings* (Manitoba Medical Association, 1954); *Canadian Journal of Economics and Political Science*, February 1960, pp. 108–27; and Janice P. Dickin McGinnis, "Whose Responsibility? Public Health in Canada, 1919–1945," in Martin S. Staum and Donald E. Larsen, eds., *Doctors, Patients and Society* (Wilfrid Laurier University Press, 1981).

Female doctors: Donald Jack, *Rogues, Rebels and Geniuses: The Story of Canadian Medicine* (Doubleday, 1981); and Carlotta Hacker, *The Indomitable Lady Doctors* (Clarke, Irwin, 1974).

Chapter 4

General information: Morris Barer, Robert Evans and Roberta Labelle, *The Frozen North: Controlling Physician Costs Through*

Controlling Fees — The Canadian Experience (Office of Technology Assessment, U.S. Congress, 1985).

George Bernard Shaw quotation: Preface to *The Doctor's Dilemma* (1911).

Provincial data on utilization of medical services: See the report of the federal Task Force on the Cost of Health Services in Canada (1970); *Journal of Public Health Policy*, Summer 1986, pp. 224–37; *Edmonton Journal*, May 9, 1985, p. B1; Denis Roch, Robert Evans and David Pascoe, *Manitoba and Medicare* (Manitoba Health Department, 1985); the 1981 and 1982 reports of the chairman of the Ontario Joint Committee on Physicians' Compensation for Professional Services; *Globe and Mail*, March 8, 1986, p. A12; *CMAJ*, vol. 131, p. 1383; and *Calgary Herald*, November 20, 1986.

Survey of Canadian doctors: Taylor, Stevenson and Williams (1984).

Quotations from doctors and medical associations: *CMAJ*, vol. 133, p. 375, and vol. 115, p. 467; Donald Swartz, "The Politics of Reform," in Leo Panitch, ed., *The Canadian State* (University of Toronto Press, 1979); and *Winnipeg Free Press*, February 27, 1971, p. 9.

Patient recruitment: *CMAJ*, vol. 126, pp. 301–9.

Clinical uncertainty: Alain Enthoven, *Health Plan* (Addison-Wesley, 1980); Joseph Califano, *America's Health Care Revolution* (Random House, 1986); and *Vancouver Sun*, October 13, 1984, p. 1.

The doctor surplus: *CMAJ*, vol. 134, p. 162; vol. 130, p. 1588; and vol. 129, p. 863.

Iatrogenesis: *Journal of Community Health*, Spring 1980, pp. 149–57; *Journal of the American Medical Association*, December 12, 1980, pp. 2617–20; *NEJM*, March 12, 1981, pp. 638–42, and April 28, 1983, pp. 1000–1005; *Canadian Forum*, April 1981, pp. 5–9 and 31; W. Gifford-Jones, *The Doctor Game* (McClelland and Stewart, 1975); and Robert Mendelsohn, *Confessions of a Medical Heretic* (Warner Books, 1979).

Iatrogenesis in Canada: *Globe and Mail*, May 14, 1983, p. 3, and October 22, 1983, p. 5; *Regina Leader-Post*, November 8, 1986, p. 5; and Noralou Roos, Marsha Cohen, Rudy Danzinger and Leslie Roos, "The Treatment of Gallstone Disease in Manitoba," Paper presented to the Third Canadian Conference on Health Economics, 1986.

Tonsillectomies: *NEJM*, August 18, 1977, pp. 360–64; *Clinical and Investigative Medicine*, vol. 4, no. 2 (1981), pp. 123–28; and *CMAJ*, vol. 89, p. 1334.

Rates of surgery: *NEJM*, December 6, 1973, pp. 1224–29 and

1249–51; *CMAJ*, vol. 133, p. 50; Ake Blomqvist, *The Health Care Business* (Fraser Institute, 1979); and W. Harding le Riche and Mabel Halliday, "The Toronto Study of Alberta Surgical Rates" (1983), available from the Alberta Legislative Library.

Other medical services: *NEJM*, July 10, 1980, pp. 113–14; and *Winnipeg Free Press*, May 6, 1986.

The case of the Saskatchewan hysterectomies: *NEJM*, June 9, 1977, pp. 1326–28.

Variations in surgical rates: *Manitoba White Paper on Health Policy* (1972); *Medical Care*, 1979, pp. 390–96; *CMAJ*, vol. 131, pp. 111–15; le Riche and Halliday (1983); and Califano (1986).

Caesarian sections: *CMAJ*, vol. 132, pp. 253–55, and vol. 133, p. 266; *Canadian Journal of Public Health*, January-February 1982, pp. 47–49; *Maclean's*, July 28, 1980, pp. 46–47; and *Final Statement of the Panel from the National Consensus Conference on Aspects of Caesarian Birth* (1986).

Billing fraud: Peter Banks in *Interviews with Past Presidents of the CMA* (1980); *CMAJ*, vol. 130, pp. 1352–53; and *Canadian Journal of Criminology*, April 1986, pp. 129–46.

Chapter 5

Midwifery: Hamowy (1984); *CMAJ*, vol. 135, pp. 285–88 and 280–81; *The Canadian Nurse*, January 1985 and April 1986; briefs and reports y the Midwifery Task Force of Ontario, the Association of Ontario Midwives, and the Midwives Coalition; the Medical Reform Group's submission to the Ontario Task Force on the Implementation of Midwifery (October 20, 1986); *Globe and Mail*, columns by William Johnson, July 13–25, 1983; the 1984 annual report of the Alberta Medical Association; and the November 1985 bulletin of the British Columbia Medical Association's MD-MLA committee.

Nurse practitioners: Jonathan Lomas and Greg Stoddart, *Estimates of the Potential Impact of Nurse Practitioners on Future Requirements for General Practitioners* (McMaster University, August 1982); *Socio-Economic Planning Sciences* (1983), pp. 199–209; *NEJM*, January 31, 1974, pp. 251–56, and April 19, 1984; briefs, bulletins and reports by the Canadian Nurses Association — particularly the CNA brief to the Emmett Hall inquiry in 1980; *CMAJ*, vol. 127, pp. 27–28, and vol. 132, pp. 903–5; and *Nurse Practitioner*, June 1983, pp. 45–48, and January 1986, pp. 39–46.

The nursing profession: Naylor (1986); Shapiro (1978); *Saturday Night*, September 1986, pp. 40–46; various publications by the

Canadian Nurses Association and provincial nurses associations; *Canadian Doctor*, October 1985, pp. 54–57; *Canadian Nurse*, April 1984, p. 7, and June 1984, p. 8; *CMAJ*, vol. 129, pp. 1129–32, and vol. 130, p. 1046; and press releases from the World Health Organization (December 1, 1983; May 13, 1983; and April 11, 1986).

Paramedical workers: Blomqvist (1979), pp. 45–47; and the Winter 1986 report of the Alberta College of Physicians and Surgeons.

Chiropractors: *Report of the Committee on the Healing Arts* (Ontario, 1970); *Social Science and Medicine*, 1986, pp. 1035–46; and *Current* (published by the BCMA, November 1985).

Chapter 6

General sources on the Sault Ste. Marie and St. Catharines clinics: Lomas (1985); *Globe and Mail*, January 4, 1978, p. 4, and June 13, 1979, p. 11.

U.S. evidence: Califano (1986); Enthoven (1980); *NEJM*, June 7, 1984, pp. 1505–10; and *CMAJ*, vol. 136, p. 73, vol. 134, pp. 264 and 538, vol. 133, pp. 480–87, and vol. 131, pp. 367–73.

Canadian evidence: Lomas (1985); *Medical Care*, March-April 1973; *Globe and Mail*, July 27, 1985, p. 1; Morris Barer, *Community Health Centres and Hospital Costs in Ontario* (Ontario Economic Council, 1981); *Journal of Public Health Policy*, Summer 1986, pp. 239–47; Ontario Economic Council, *Health Issues and Alternatives* (1976); and the federal Health and Welfare Department, *Inventory of Community Health Centres in Canada* (1985).

Chapter 7

Foreign-trained doctors: *CMAJ*, vol. 135, pp. 375, 679 and 681, vol. 129, p. 1171, and vol. 132, p. 231; *International Journal of Health Services*, 1974, p. 258; and the Lalonde Report (1974), p. 28.

Supply of doctors: Jonathan Lomas, Morris Barer and Greg Stoddart, *Physician Manpower Planning* (Ontario Economic Council, 1985); *NEJM*, December 18, 1986, pp. 1623–28; *CMAJ*, vol. 134, p. 162, vol. 130, p. 1588, and vol. 133, pp. 589–90 and 689–94.

Quality control: Samuel Wolfe and Robin F. Badgley, *The Family Doctor* (Macmillan, 1973); Milton Friedman, *Capitalism and Freedom* (University of Chicago Press, 1962); Robert Evans and W. T. Stanbury, *Occupational Regulation in Canada* (University of Toronto

Law and Economics Workshop Series, 1981); *CMAJ*, vol. 133, pp. 420-22, and vol. 117, pp. 230-32; *NEJM*, April 28, 1983, pp. 1000-1005; and K. E. Klute, *The General Practitioner* (University of Toronto Press, 1963). The comments by Peter Banks are contained in *Interviews with Past Presidents of the CMA* (1980).

Peer review: Annual reports of the Ontario College of Physicians and Surgeons; and *CMAJ*, vol. 132, pp. 1025-29, and vol. 131, pp. 557-60.

Continuing medical education: *CMAJ*, vol. 121, pp. 118 and 127, and vol. 133, p. 913.

Chapter 10

General sources: Newsletters and briefs by the Patients' Rights Association and the Consumers' Association of Canada; annual reports of the Canadian Medical Protective Association and the provincial colleges of physicians and surgeons; Andrew Allentuck, *Who Speaks for the Patient?* (Burns and MacEachern, 1978); Lorne Rozovsky, *The Canadian Patient's Book of Rights* (Doubleday, 1980); and David Coburn's article in *Canadian Forum*, May 1980, pp. 14-18.

Malpractice: *CMAJ*, vol. 135, p. 1400, vol. 134, pp. 414 and 1103, vol. 127, p. 243, and vol. 120, p. 1324; Patricia Danzon, *Medical Malpractice* (Harvard University Press, 1985); *NEJM*, June 8, 1978, pp. 1282-89; Allentuck (1978); and Rozovsky (1980).